TREES

OF BRITAIN & EUROPE

KINGFISHER FIELD GUIDES

TREES
OF BRITAIN & EUROPE

Written by
DAVID SUTTON

KINGFISHER
Kingfisher Publications plc
New Penderel House
283–288 High Holborn
London WC1V 7HZ
www.kingfisherpub.com

First published by Kingfisher Publications plc 1990
This edition printed in 2001

10 9 8 7 6 5 4 3 2 1
1TR/0101/PP/MAR/135MA

Text copyright © David Sutton and Larousse plc 1990
Illustrations copyright © Larousse plc 1990

A CIP CATALOGUE RECORD FOR THIS BOOK IS
AVAILABLE FROM THE BRITISH LIBRARY

ISBN 0-86272-523-2

Editor: Stuart Cooper
Editorial Assistant: Sophie Figgis
Map (p6): King & King
Cover designer: Mike Buckley

Phototypeset by Southern Positives and
Negatives (SPAN), Lingfield, Surrey
Colour separations by Newselle Litho, Milan
Printed in Portugal

CONTENTS

INTRODUCTION

There is something special about trees. They are plants on a grand scale and have long inspired philosophers. An imposing feature of most landscapes, they define the character of an area, telling you where you are – billowing crowns of elms and sturdy oaks at middle latitudes, or slender spires of cypresses and umbrella-shaped pines in the Mediterranean region. Trees also hold many of nature's records: the tallest, most massive and oldest living things are all trees. They can be objects of great beauty and many are grown for this reason. We plant cherries from the Orient and Indian Flame-tree for flowers, and maples and Black-gum for their brilliant autumn colour. Many trees are grown for their imposing form, such as Cedar-of-Lebanon, with its massive flat plates of foliage; Lombardy Poplar, which forms narrow columns; and Golden Weeping-willow, with its hanging curtains of foliage.

Some of the choicest fruits of the earth come from trees. Orchards of apple, plum and pear are planted in the cooler areas, whilst oranges, peaches and nectarines are grown in the warmer south. Even in death, trees contribute to the quality of human life. Softwoods, from conifers, and hardwoods, from broad-leaved trees, provide everything from basic materials for construction to the highly decorative, beautifully figured wood of the walnuts. Timber, converted into paper, holds the world's literature.

Using descriptions, facts panels and illustrations, this book provides the means to identify 430 of the native and most widely planted trees of Britain and Europe.

1 Iceland **2** Atlantic Ocean **3** Ireland **4** Britain **5** France **6** Spain **7** Portugal **8** Balearic Is **9** Mediterranean Sea **10** Sardinia **11** Corsica **12** Sicily **13** Italy **14** Switzerland **15** Austria **16** Germany **17** Belgium **18** Holland **19** Denmark **20** Norway **21** Norwegian Sea **22** Sweden **23** Finland **24** Baltic Sea **25** Poland **26** Czechoslovakia **27** Hungary **28** Yugoslavia **29** Adriatic Sea **30** Albania **31** Greece **32** Crete **33** Turkey **34** Bulgaria **35** Romania **36** Black Sea **37** Russia **38** Caspian Sea

SCOPE OF THIS BOOK

The area covered by this guide extends from the tree limit in Scandinavia and northern Russia to the islands of the Mediterranean; from the Atlantic coast in the west to the Ural Mountains, Black Sea, Caspian Sea, and Aegean Islands in the east. Emphasis has been placed on those species that are most abundant and visible to the majority of people. Most native species are covered, with the exception of the more restricted and obscure trees. A few of the uncommon species have been included where space permits. The book describes most of the commonly planted trees that have been introduced, including timber trees, fruit trees and amenity trees. The last-named category embraces those grown for shelter, shade or ornament in public places, and

Chilean Wine Palm is commonly planted along streets in the Mediterranean region.

street trees, many of which are planted along thousands of miles of roads. The reason for such a broad coverage is that it is often impossible to know whether a tree is native or not without specialist knowledge. Some of the introduced species regularly produce seed and spread, behaving like native trees. Ornamental trees which are also native may be planted far beyond their natural limits of distribution.

What is a tree?

A general working definition of a tree is a plant with a single, woody stem, which grows to 6 metres or more tall. However, many of the trees that are planted for urban use, in streets, parks and gardens, are typically much shorter, for example Dwarf Cherry. Furthermore, the size of a tree can vary according to the habitat in which it is growing. A native species may be tall at low altitudes but just a few metres high in the mountains. A broader definition has been adopted in this book as there is no precise botanical distinction between trees and shrubs, the latter being typically smaller woody plants with multiple stems. Some large trees, which unquestionably belong here, regularly produce multiple trunks by growing sucker shoots, for example English Elm. Trees that grow in hedgerows, and that at some time have been cut to height, will also sprout extra stems. A few shrubs have been included in the book where they reach tree size, particularly when a common, large shrub represents a group which includes some less common trees.

Although it usually occurs as a shrub, Hazel can sometimes attain tree size.

Introduction

THE HISTORY OF TREES

Forests and woodland may appear to have been there forever but they are all in a continual, gradual state of change. In the last Ice Age, much of northern Europe was covered by a continuous sheet of ice. As the climate warmed around 10,000 years ago, the ice began to retreat and the bare ground left behind became available for colonization. Light, wind-borne seeds of trees surviving south of the ice soon arrived, with birches, willows, then pines acting as pioneers, and woodlands were gradually established in the north. Trees with heavier seeds arrived much later but as they grew they overshadowed and eventually replaced the pioneer species.

During the Ice Age and when the ice began its retreat, colossal volumes of sea water were frozen solid and the sea-level was about thirty metres lower than it is today. France, Britain and Ireland were connected by land and early colonizing trees easily spread through the area. As the ice melted the sea rose, and some of the forested area disappeared beneath the sea. It also prevented some of the trees with larger seeds, which were spreading from the south, from colonizing many of the islands of northern Europe. Eventually a pattern of fairly continuous tree cover developed, with the northern forests of Europe dominated by conifers, and middle latitudes by broad-leaved oaks, elms and beeches. In the drier south, species with tough leaves resistant to drought formed extensive forests.

The recent history of trees is dominated by humankind. The most profound effects have been in the south, where the longer history of human habitation has resulted in most of the forests being destroyed. Further north, prehistoric people, using stone implements, found it easier to clear for crops upland areas with more open woodland than the rich valleys with their dense forests. With advances in materials and agricultural tools, more and more of the forest fell. Even if land was subsequently no longer farmed, domesticated grazing animals often prevented the trees from becoming re-established. Timber for construction has long been a highly prized commodity and has accelerated land clearance around the more densely populated areas. Though there has been much planting for timber on a forestry scale in recent years, it has often been done with imported species from other temperate regions of the world.

THE IMPORTANCE OF TREES

The economic importance of trees to humankind is immense. Yet it is nothing compared to the role they play in regulating the world's climate and ecosystems – a role which, because of the scale on which we exploit and destroy trees, is increasingly under threat.

A tree takes up water and mineral salts from the soil, moving them up from the roots to the leaves, where energy-rich sugars are produced using sunlight and carbon dioxide. These simple sugars are the building blocks for materials which are incorporated into the tree as it grows during a life-span of hundreds or perhaps even thousands of years. In an act that takes but a few minutes, it is difficult to see the long-term consequences of cutting down a single tree, but deforestation on the scale that has happened in the past and continues to happen around the globe is another matter.

A single tree can take up 1000–2000 litres of water from the ground a year, releasing most from the leaves as water vapour. Carried by the wind, this water vapour will later fall somewhere else as rain. On a forest scale, this capacity to move massive amounts of water has a profound effect on the local water-table and regional climate. Forested ground acts as a gigantic sponge, holding rainfall and releasing it gradually. Without trees, most of the water immediately runs off the land after rain and results in flooding alternating with drought. If the slope is steep or the rainfall heavy, the soil is eroded away to where it silts up rivers, reservoirs and estuaries. Without returning water to the atmosphere, the winds are drier and less rainfall is received somewhere else.

As well as affecting the local habitat, uncontrolled deforestation could have grave consequences for the world as a whole. As trees are destroyed and much material is burned or left to decompose, the carbon dioxide combined for centuries in the tree is released. This is one of the gases that at excess levels causes the Greenhouse Effect that threatens to change the world climate in a profound manner, raise sea-levels, and possibly cause species extinction on a vast scale.

It is important to conserve remaining natural forest, or manage it very carefully as a renewable resource, and re-establish tree cover in many places where it has been lost. Increased planting of native hardwoods in Europe would take longer to yield financial rewards than exotic softwoods, but would take the pressure off the tropics where massive deforestation must rank as one of the greatest crimes against the environment ever committed by humanity.

Introduction

HOW TO IDENTIFY TREES

When first learning to identify trees, it is important to resolve the general look of a tree into individual characteristics, which can then be checked against the illustrations, key and descriptions. The most useful features for identification are summarized in the following section, with an explanation of the terms used in the book.

Type of tree
A basic distinction to make is between cone-bearing trees (conifers) and flowering trees, which bear typical flowers or specialized flowers, such as catkins. Each type of tree may keep its leaves throughout the year (evergreen), or may lose all its leaves for part of the year (deciduous), either during a cold or a dry season.

Trunk
Unlike most wild flowers, a tree's stem keeps growing from one year to the next. Stiffening materials are laid down and it becomes a woody trunk, almost invariably increasing in size around its periphery each year. By definition, a tree has a single trunk, but some, such as Coast Redwood, can produce multiple trunks from shoots called suckers that grow around the base of the original trunk. The heavy lower branches of Western Red-cedar become bowed down to the ground, rooting and forming extra trunks in many old trees. Trunks of some species have broad flanges (buttresses) near the base, offering additional support to the tree.

buttresses

plates

Bark
The outer protective layer of the trunk is the bark, which accommodates increases in girth of the trunk in various ways. Older layers of bark commonly split, with new bark laid down internally, resulting in the vertical fissures of Sweet Chestnut or the small, square plates of Evergreen Oak. Cork Oak has a bark which proliferates rapidly to form a thick, soft layer; the fibrous bark of Wellingtonia is also thick and soft. Smooth barks, such as that of London Plane, often peel off in layers.

Crown and branching
The branches, twigs and foliage together, termed the crown, may have a distinctive shape which helps identify a tree. The shape is largely formed by the major branches, which may be spreading, angled upwards or weeping. A very regular pattern with rings of radiating, successively older branches in many young conifers results in a conical shape. Another distinctive shape is the very narrow crown of Lombardy Poplar, with almost vertical branching. Usually the shape is characteristic for an individual species but some trees can have very narrow or weeping cultivated forms as well as the typical form with widely spreading branches.

Introduction

Twigs and buds

Twigs offer a number of useful characteristics and are particularly important in deciduous trees, as they provide most of the characters for identifying the tree when it is leafless. On bare twigs, there is often a distinctive pattern of scars left where the leaves have fallen. Some trees have stout and rigid twigs, such as Fig and walnuts; others have slender and pendulous twigs, such as Silver Birch. Spines or thorns narrow identification down to a few species scattered through the book.

leaf
scar

sticky
bud

At the tip of a twig, and usually at the base of each leaf-stalk or leaf-scar, are buds. Most of these buds, with the exception of flower-buds, are juvenile shoots, with the young leaves covered by scales and the growth more or less arrested. The bud at the tip of the twig is generally largest and very noticeable in most deciduous trees. Horse-chestnut has a broad, sticky bud, while that of beeches is slender and smoothly tapered above and below the middle. That of ashes is smooth and blackish while White Willow has buds covered with pale grey hairs. The position of the side buds reflects the arrangement of the leaves and can be a useful feature.

Leaves

Trees are leafy for most of the year, but flowering and fruiting may be restricted to a few months. It can take many years before flowering commences and some mature trees may not develop any mature flowers or fruit in certain years. Consequently, leaves provide the most useful features for general identification. Note the position and whether the leaves are paired or otherwise arranged on the stem. The basic outline of the blade (expanded part) is important. See if the edge is unbroken, toothed or lobed. If the leaf is divided into leaflets, then they may be paired or radiating. Leaves of deciduous trees are commonly thinner than those of evergreen trees and often change colour dramatically in autumn. Leaf surfaces vary from smooth and glossy through varying degrees of hairiness, particularly on the underside. Needle-like leaves occur in many conifers, whilst others have small, scale-like leaves. Junipers can have both sorts on the same plant. A pair of stipules occurs at the base of the leaf-stalk of many flowering trees; they can be large, or small and falling quickly.

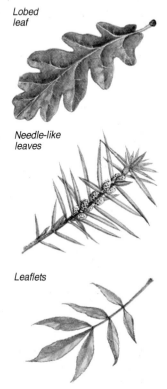

Lobed
leaf

Needle-like
leaves

Leaflets

Introduction

Flowers

Petals are usually the showiest part of a flower in most insect-pollinated trees. Look to see if they are equal or unequal and separate or joined together towards the base. Sepals are positioned beneath the petals and are usually green. If the petals and sepals are not readily distinguishable, then the term perianth applies to both. The male (♂) parts of a flower are the stamens, which produce pollen in anthers; the female (♀) parts are the stigma, usually supported by a stalk-like part (style), attaching it to the ovary. Most flowers have both male and female parts and are called hermaphrodite (☿). There may be separate male and female flowers, either on the same tree or different trees. The flowers of some trees are tiny and massed in elongated heads called catkins; such flowers are usually wind-pollinated. Conifers bear the male and female parts on the scales of male and female cones respectively.

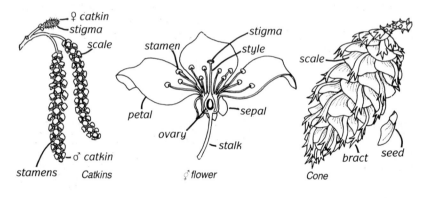

Fruits and seeds

Important things to note about fruits are shape, colour, whether they are fleshy or dry and, in the latter case, if they open to release the seeds. A berry is a fleshy fruit. Berry-like fruits, such as that of Wild Cherry, often have a hard stone inside enclosing the seed. Many fruits have outer layers which become dry as the fruit ripens. Pods are elongated dry fruits that split open to release the seeds when ripe, and are found in species of the Pea family such as Honey Locust. Dry fruits that do not open are commonly nut-like, as in the hazels, and usually contain a single seed. Dry fruits of ashes and maples have a long wing which aids dispersal; the wing of elms and Caucasian Wing-nut encircles the part containing the seed. Conifers mostly have woody cones with seeds carried beneath scales. Individual seeds often have membranous wings. There are sterile bract scales in conifer cones, which may project beyond the seed-bearing scales, as in Douglas-fir, and provide an important identification feature. Cones of pines and spruces usually hang downwards, but those of firs, cedars and larches are upright. Pine cones fall intact, in some species after many years on the tree. Cones of firs and Monkey-puzzle break up on the tree. Yews and junipers are unusual conifers in which the cone scales become fleshy and berry-like as they mature.

HOW TO USE THIS BOOK

If you want to identify a tree and have no idea of what it is, refer to the key starting on page 14 – which should limit your search to a specific group of pages. If, on the other hand, you have a rough idea of the identity, then turn to the relevant section of the book (using the colour code explained on page 16) and you will find similar species grouped on adjacent pages. Match the species against the illustrations, but always check carefully through the descriptions for confirmation. The description of the tree is mostly summarized in a facts panel, which contains comparable elements for every species. This layout differs from the practice in most other field guides and floras, where the descriptions are often very brief and inconsistent.

Each page of the guide features a main species and up to three similar trees. These may be cultivars, subspecies, or similar species, and may sometimes be as common as the main species. The elements illustrated for the main species include the general habit and details such as leaves, flowers and fruit. For the similar trees, only one or two distinguishing details are shown.

This colour shows which group of plants each species belongs to. Use it to help you find the different groups as you flick through the book. The colour code is explained on p. 16.

A text summarizes the general look of the tree or how it looks when part of a forest; it draws attention to important distinguishing features and adds points of interest regarding biology or significance to man.

A fact panel provides a detailed summary of the main features of the main tree; where it grows and when it flowers and fruits; with details on the crown, trunk, leaves, flowers, fruit and seeds.

Accurate illustrations of the whole tree, plus details of the flowers, fruits or other parts of the plant important for identification.

Labels pick out the best clues to identification.

Up to three similar trees are illustrated on the same page, with details of how they differ from the main tree.

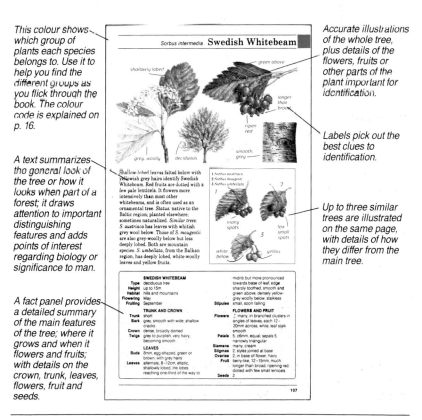

Introduction

KEY TO SPECIES

This key provides an illustrated guide to the groups of species and their page numbers. At each stage, read the first numbered statement and see if it describes your tree. If not, then the second statement with the same number includes all other plants at this stage of the key. Move on to the next statement below and repeat the process until you key out to the correct group.

1 leaves crowded at top of trunk or tips of thick branches
Agaves 180–181; Palms 182–185.

1 leaves spread along branches and twigs
2 leaves all or mostly scale-like, pressed against stem
Monkey-puzzles 19; Redwoods 38–39; Cypresses 42–45, 47–49; She-oaks 89; Tamarisks 154–155.

2 leaves not all scale-like
3 leaves all or mostly needle-like, spreading
4 needles all spirally arranged or forming 2 parallel rows
Pines 20–29; Redwoods 39–40; Yews 41.

4 needles mostly borne in clusters, tufts or whorls of 2 or more
Pines 30–37; Cypresses 46.

3 leaves not needle-like
5 leaves divided into separate leaflets
6 leaflets in 2 rows
Walnuts 90–92; Roses 104; Peas 124–125, 127–129, 131; Quassias 134; Mahoganies 135; Cashews 136–138; Soapberries 139; Maples 144; Olives 170–171; Honeysuckles 178.

6 leaflets radiating from leaf stalk
Peas 130; Citruses 133; Horse-chestnuts 140–141.

5 leaves not divided into separate leaflets
7 leaves in opposite pairs on stem
Maples 142–143, 145–147; Spindles 149; Boxes 150; Buckthorns 153; Dogwoods 161; Pomegranates 167; Olives 172–173; Bignonias 176–177; Honeysuckles 178.

7 leaves alternating or scattered around stem
8 flowers (at least males) in slender catkins
9 leaves lobed, spiny or fan-shaped
Maidenhair-tree 18; Willows 58;
Beeches 70–75.

9 leaves sometimes toothed but neither lobed nor spiny
Willows 50–57, 59–61; Birches 62–64;
Hazels 65–67; Beeches 76; Bog-myrtles 77.

8 flowers single or in clusters but not in slender catkins
10 leaves lobed or spiny
11 flowers white
Roses 105, 107, 112–115; Hollies 148.

11 flowers red, yellow or green
Mulberries 85; Witch-hazels 86;
Planes 88; Magnolias 95.

10 leaves sometimes toothed but neither lobed nor spiny
12 evergreen
13 crushed leaves strong and pleasant-smelling
Laurels 96; Myrtles 162–166.

13 crushed leaves not strong-smelling
Pittosporums 93; Magnolias 94;
Roses 108, 121; Citruses 132;
Heathers 174; Myoporums 175.

12 deciduous
14 leaves heart-shaped
Mulberries 83; Peas 126; Limes
156–158; Davidia 159.

14 leaves not heart-shaped
15 petals white or pink
Roses 98–103, 106, 109–111, 116–
120, 122–123; Storaxes 169.

15 petals yellow, greenish, dull red or absent
16 leaves with edge toothed
Beeches 69; Elms 78–82;
Mulberries 84; Witch-hazels 87;
Buckthorns 152–153.

16 leaves with edge not toothed
Beeches 68; Mulberries 84;
Oleasters 151; Buckthorns 153;
Black-gums 160; Ebonies 168.

Introduction

TREE NAMES

English language names for native trees have been standardised to the list published by the Botanical Society of the British Isles (Dony, Jury and Perring, 1986). Some plants will have no common name if they only grow in other countries of the area.

Botanical names are more stable and international in usage. Most are those given in the standard European flora (Tutin *et al.* (Editors), 1964–1980) but some are updated according to the British Excursion Flora (Clapham, Tutin & Warburg, 1985). Each Latin name is made up of a genus name (starting with a capital letter) and a species name (starting with a small letter). A third, subspecies (abbreviated as subsp.), name is used to distinguish geographical variation within a species. A multiplication symbol between the first and second names indicates that the plant is a hybrid between two species; if the sign is before the first name then it indicates a hybrid between species of two different genera. Particular selections of cultivated trees are often given horticultural names, indicated in single quotation marks.

Order of trees

The trees in this book are arranged more or less in systematic order. Those that have a similar construction of flowers and fruit are placed together in families. Each group of families is given a colour reference marker. Use this coloured square at the corner of the pages to help you find the different groups of plants as you flick through the book.

Maidenhair-tree and Monkey-puzzles	Roses
Pines	Peas
Redwoods and Yews	Citruses, Quassias and Mahoganies
Cypresses	Cashews, Soapberries, Horse-chestnuts and Maples
Willows	Hollies, Spindles, Boxes and Oleasters
Birches and Hazels	Buckthorns, Tamarisks and Limes
Beeches and Bog-myrtles	Davidia, Black-gums and Dogwoods
Elms and Mulberries	Myrtles, Loosestrifes and Pomegranates
Witch-hazels, Planes and She-oaks	Ebonies, Storaxes, Olives and Heathers
Walnuts and Pittosporums	Myoporums, Foxgloves, Bignonias and Honeysuckles
Magnolias, Laurels and Phytolaccas	Agaves and Palms

THE
TREES
OF·BRITAIN·AND·EUROPE

Maidenhair-tree *Ginkgo biloba*

An unmistakable tree, with unique fan-shaped leaves, distinctive irregular crown, and marble-sized, fleshy fruits. This odd species belongs to a group of trees that was important when dinosaurs roamed the earth, but now all but this one species is extinct. Fruits give off a nauseous odour when over-ripe, making the female tree unsuitable for planting in towns of warmer countries. The tree was cultivated for centuries in gardens of Chinese temples and palaces. It is virtually unknown in the wild state. *Status:* introduced from China; planted fairly commonly for ornament, often as a street tree. *Similar trees:* none.

♂ catkins

irregular outline

deciduous

rough

paired ♀ flowers

fan-shaped leaf

stalked fruit

leaves clustered

some paired

MAIDENHAIR-TREE

Type	conifer, deciduous tree
Height	25–30m
Habitat	street tree, parks
Flowering	March–April
Fruiting	September–October

TRUNK AND CROWN

Trunk	slender, straight or forked
Bark	deeply fissured and ridged, brownish grey
Crown	irregularly cylindrical or sometimes broad, branches few, short, irregular
Twigs	of two types: long and straight, with short, stubby side-shoots

LEAVES

Buds	conical, reddish brown
Leaves	spirally arranged, widely spaced on long shoots, clustered on short shoots, 3–12cm, fan-shaped, notched or deeply cleft, irregularly toothed, base wedge-shaped, many veins diverging from base, yellowish green, turning bright yellow in autumn; stalk up to 4.5cm
Stipules	absent

FLOWERS AND FRUIT

Flowers	♂ and ♀ flowers on different plants
♂	cluster of 3–6 yellow catkins, each 60–80mm
♀	1 or 2 on stalk up to 40mm long, pale yellow
Fruit	1–2 on long stalk, 25–30mm, globular or slightly elongated, fleshy, yellowish
Seeds	1 per fruit, large, nut-like

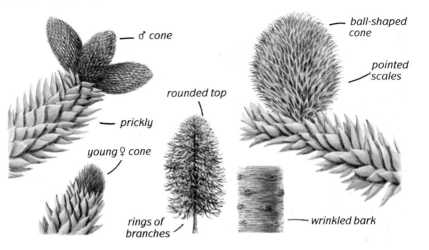

— ♂ cone

ball-shaped cone

pointed scales

rounded top

— prickly

young ♀ cone

rings of branches

wrinkled bark

A most unusual conifer with broad, spine-tipped leaves, thickly set all around the stems. It is the source of a commercially important timber, but rarely produces wood of sufficient quality in Europe. In its native South America, the seeds are eaten as a delicacy but they often fail to set in Europe. *Status:* introduced from Chile and western Argentina; commonly planted in western Europe for ornament. *Similar trees:* Norfolk Island Pine is another ornamental species, but only survives to tree size in the warmer south and west. It has finer foliage, in broad plates, and regular branching.

Norfolk Island Pine (*Araucaria heterophylla*)

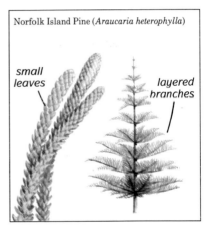

small leaves

layered branches

	MONKEY-PUZZLE		LEAVES	
Type	conifer, evergreen tree	**Buds**	conical, hidden by leaves	
Height	25–30m	**Leaves**	spirally arranged, 3–4cm, triangular or broadly oval, thick, tip spine-tipped, edge unbroken, base broad, dark, glossy green; stalkless	
Habitat	parks, gardens			
Flowering	June–July			
Fruiting	August–September			
	TRUNK AND CROWN	**Stipules**	absent	
Trunk	straight, stout, not forked, sometimes with suckers from roots			
			FLOWERS AND FRUIT	
		Flowers	♂ and ♀ flowers on different plants	
Bark	with horizontal ridges, later becoming vertically ridged, blackish grey	♂	cone, *c*10cm, egg-shaped, brown, clustered at shoot-tip	
Crown	conical, becoming broadly domed; branches in rings at same level, angled upwards or gradually drooping	♀	cone, globular, spiny, on upper side of shoot	
		Fruit	globular, upright cone, up to 15cm, green with yellowish spines, breaks up on tree when ripe in second or third year	
Twigs	concealed by overlapping leaf-bases			
		Seeds	up to 4cm, brown, often sterile	

Common Silver-fir *Abies alba*

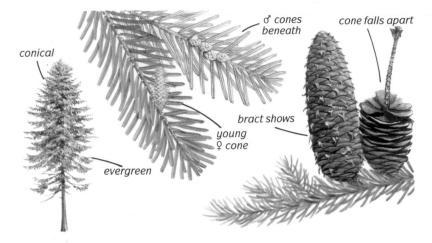

conical

♂ cones beneath

cone falls apart

evergreen

bract shows

young ♀ cone

Once commonly planted in north-western Europe, this species is intolerant of exposure or pollution, and is badly damaged by aphids, so other species are now preferred. Older trees have only a cluster of branches left at the top. *Status:* native to mountains of central and southern Europe; widely planted for timber and ornament in northern Europe. *Similar trees:* Caucasian Fir has a denser and broader crown, crowded leaves, and thicker cones with longer bracts. Heavily branched, with a stout trunk, Grecian Fir differs from the latter in the stiff, spiny leaves, and resinous buds.

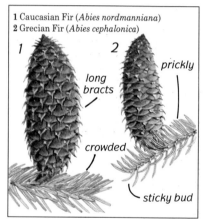

1 Caucasian Fir (*Abies nordmanniana*)
2 Grecian Fir (*Abies cephalonica*)

long bracts

crowded

prickly

sticky bud

	COMMON SILVER-FIR		
Type	conifer, evergreen tree	**Leaves**	arising spirally, twisted to either side, parted above twig, 15–25mm, rarely 35mm, needle-like, flattened but thick, tip shallowly notched, dark green with 2 whitish bands below; stalkless
Height	40–55m		
Habitat	forests, plantations, parks		
Flowering	April		
Fruiting	September		
		Stipules	absent
	TRUNK AND CROWN		
Trunk	stout, more or less straight, not forked below		**FLOWERS AND FRUIT**
		Flowers	♂ and ♀ on same tree
Bark	dark grey, smooth with resin-blisters, gradually becoming cracked into squarish plates	♂	globular, yellow cone, on underside of shoots,
		♀	egg-shaped, greenish cone, on upper side of top branches
Crown	narrowly conical; branches in groups at same level	**Fruit**	cylindrical, upright cone, 10–20cm, brown, with woody cone-scales and slender-tipped, downward-pointing, projecting bracts, disintegrating on tree leaving slender spike
Twigs	greyish brown, shortly hairy, with circular leaf-scars		
	LEAVES		
Buds	egg-shaped, reddish brown, not or scarcely resinous		
		Seeds	2 per scale, winged

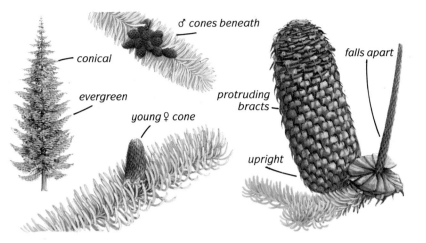

conical

evergreen

♂ *cones beneath*

young ♀ cone

protruding bracts

falls apart

upright

A striking tree, with huge, upright cones that have distinctive, downward-pointing bracts. It is commonly planted for its close-grained timber, and plantations thrive even under harsh conditions. *Status:* introduced from western North America; widely planted in northern and western Europe for timber or ornament. *Similar trees:* two species have very resinous buds and smaller cones, which are bluish until maturity. Native to north-eastern Russia, Siberian Fir has cones with short, hidden bracts. Introduced from Japan, Veitch's Silver-fir has cones with the bracts just projecting.

1 Siberian Fir (*Abies sibirica*)
2 Veitch's Silver-fir (*Abies veitchii*)

1 *bracts hidden*

2 *bracts just show*

bluish young cones

NOBLE FIR

Type	conifer, evergreen tree
Height	40–50m (taller in America)
Habitat	cultivated mainly in plantations
Flowering	May
Fruiting	October

TRUNK AND CROWN

Trunk	stout, straight, not forked
Bark	pale grey, smooth with resin-blisters, becoming fissured
Crown	narrowly conical or columnar, becoming flat-topped; branches level, forming irregular rings
Twigs	reddish brown, finely hairy, with circular leaf-scars

LEAVES

Buds	resinous only at the tips
Leaves	arising spirally but curved up at sides, parted below, crowded above, 1–3.5cm, needle-like, 4-angled, blunt, greyish green, 2 pale grey bands beneath; stalkless
Stipules	absent

FLOWERS AND FRUIT

Flowers	♂ and ♀ flowers on same plant
♂	globular, crimson cone, c6mm, clustered beneath shoots, becoming yellow with pollen
♀	cylindrical greenish cone, 40–50mm, scales orange-tipped
Fruit	barrel-shaped, blunt-tipped, upright cone, 15–25cm, with green, downward-pointing bracts protruding beyond purplish brown cone-scales, disintegrating on tree leaving slender spike
Seeds	2 per scale, winged

Grand Fir *Abies grandis*

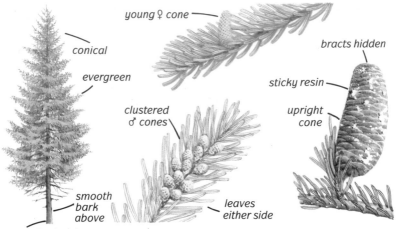

young ♀ cone

conical

evergreen

bracts hidden

sticky resin

upright cone

clustered ♂ cones

smooth bark above

leaves either side

rough bark at base

This large tree is readily distinguished by feather-like shoots with leaves spreading horizontally to either side, and upright, cylindrical cones with hidden bracts. The foliage has a distinct orange-like scent. Remarkably fast growth and tolerance of most soil conditions contribute to the value of this species as a forestry tree. *Status:* introduced from western North America; widely planted in northern and central Europe, mainly for timber. *Similar trees:* Colorado White-fir differs in the dark, rougher bark, longer, upward curving, often bluish leaves, and a larger cone.

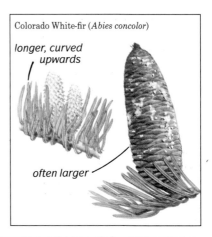

Colorado White-fir (*Abies concolor*)

longer, curved upwards

often larger

	GRAND FIR		
Type	conifer, evergreen tree	**Leaves**	arising spirally but turning to either side leaving parting above and below shoot, 2–6cm, needle-like, notched, glossy green above with 2 whitish bands below; stalkless
Height	40–60m (over 90m in America)		
Habitat	plantations, especially in wetter areas		
Flowering	April		
Fruiting	October	**Stipules**	absent
	TRUNK AND CROWN		**FLOWERS AND FRUIT**
Trunk	straight, not forked, fairly stout	**Flowers**	♂ and ♀ flowers on same plant
Bark	brownish grey, smooth with resin-blisters, eventually cracked into squarish plates	♂	purplish, cone, c2mm, in cluster below shoot, becomes yellow with pollen
Crown	narrowly conical or columnar; branches in rings at same level	♀	solitary cone, above shoot
Twigs	with sparse, short hairs and circular leaf-scars	**Fruit**	woody, upright cone, 5–10cm, cylindrical, reddish brown exuding whitish resin; bracts hidden by cone-scales; cone disintegrates on tree leaving thin spike
	LEAVES		
Buds	c2mm, conical, purplish, becoming covered with resin	**Seeds**	2 per scale, winged

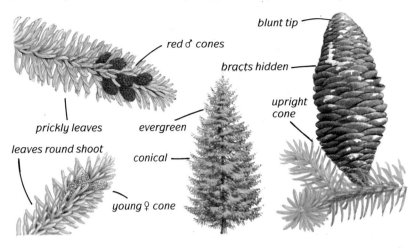

red ♂ cones

blunt tip

bracts hidden

upright cone

prickly leaves

evergreen

leaves round shoot

conical

young ♀ cone

Also known as 'Hedgehog Fir', this species is easily distinguished by stiff, prickly leaves set all around the shoots. Though naturally limited to a few sites in Spain, near Ronda, it is cultivated elsewhere. *Status:* native to mountains of southern Spain; frequently planted for ornament or sometimes timber. *Similar trees:* Algerian Fir has longer, broader, more flexible leaves with whitish bands below, and cones with a raised centre to the otherwise squarish tip. Nikko Fir has very pale, grooved shoots with leaves pointing slightly forwards, and violet-blue young cones.

1 Algerian Fir (*Abies numidica*)
2 Nikko Fir (*Abies homolepis*)

central point

1

bluish cone

longer, flexible

2

paler shoot

SPANISH FIR	
Type	conifer, evergreen tree
Height	20–30m
Habitat	north-facing slopes on limestone mountains; also planted elsewhere
Flowering	May
Fruiting	October
TRUNK AND CROWN	
Trunk	stout, straight, not forked
Bark	smooth, becoming cracked into squarish plates, dark grey or blackish
Crown	conical, becoming irregular; branches in rings at same level
Twigs	orange-brown, smooth except for circular leaf-scars
LEAVES	
Buds	3–5mm, egg-shaped, purplish, sticky with resin
Leaves	spreading outwards all round shoot, 10–18mm, needle-like, stiff, spine-tipped, greyish green with 2 greyish bands above and below; stalkless
Stipules	absent
FLOWERS AND FRUIT	
Flowers	♂ and ♀ flowers on same plant
♂	cluster of cones below shoot, each c5mm, globular, red, becoming yellow with pollen
♀	solitary cone above shoot
Fruit	upright, cylindrical cone, 10–16cm, tip squarish with small point, ripening brown; bracts hidden by cone-scales
Seeds	2 per cone-scale, winged

Douglas-fir *Pseudotsuga menziesii*

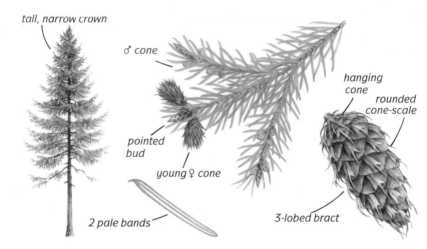

tall, narrow crown

♂ *cone*

pointed bud

young ♀ cone

2 pale bands

hanging cone

rounded cone-scale

3-lobed bract

A magnificent conifer, outgrowing most other trees in Europe and rivalling Coast Redwood and Sierra Redwood in height where these three conifers are native in western North America. A most distinctive characteristic of Douglas-fir is the hanging cone, with protruding, three-pointed bracts. *Status:* introduced from Pacific coast of North America; widely planted in Europe for timber, shelter and ornament. *Similar trees:* Large-coned Douglas-fir has stiff, spiny foliage. Rarely produced in cultivation, the larger cones have bracts which scarcely project beyond the thick cone-scales.

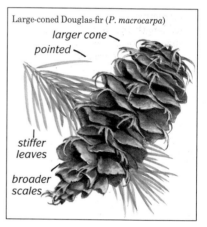

Large-coned Douglas-fir (*P. macrocarpa*)

larger cone

pointed

stiffer leaves

broader scales

Type	conifer, evergreen tree	**Leaves**	arising spirally but turning to either side of shoot, 2–3.5cm, needle-like, dark green, 2 white bands below; stalkless
Height	55m (100m in America)		
Habitat	cultivated in plantations, parks, gardens	**Stipules**	absent
Flowering	May–July		**FLOWERS AND FRUIT**
Fruiting	October	**Flowers**	♂ and ♀ cones on same tree
	TRUNK AND CROWN	♂	at leaf-bases of previous year's shoot, yellow
Trunk	straight, not forked	♀	near tip of previous year's shoot, 5–10mm, red or green
Bark	smooth except for resin-blisters, greyish green, becoming deeply fissured, corky, reddish brown	**Fruit**	hanging, oblong, tapered cone, 5–10cm, ripening in first year; cone-scales rounded; 3-toothed bracts project
Crown	narrowly conical, becoming flat-topped; branches in groups at same level	**Seeds**	winged, 2 per cone-scale
Twigs	with raised, elliptical leaf-scars, softly hairy		
	LEAVES		
Buds	tapered both ends, pointed		

DOUGLAS-FIR

pale bands below

dark green

young ♀ cone

small ♂ cones

conical crown

small cone

bracts hidden

An attractive conifer, recognized by the varied length and rather random arrangement of the leaves, set either side of shoots that arch downwards from spreading branches. Western Hemlock-spruce is highly productive as a timber tree. The foliage has a characteristic odour resembling Hemlock. *Status:* introduced from western North America; widely cultivated in Europe. *Similar trees:* Eastern Hemlock-spruce is smaller, with shorter, tapered leaves, and smaller cones. Mountain Hemlock-spruce has spirally arranged, bluish leaves and larger cones.

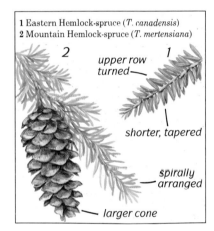

1 Eastern Hemlock-spruce (*T. canadensis*)
2 Mountain Hemlock-spruce (*T. mertensiana*)

upper row turned

shorter, tapered

spirally arranged

larger cone

	WESTERN HEMLOCK-SPRUCE		
Type	conifer, evergreen tree	**Leaves**	arising spirally, turning to either side of twig, 0.5–2cm, of different lengths, needle-like, flattened, blunt, dark green, 2 white bands below; peg-like base remains after leaf falls
Height	45m (up to 70m in America)		
Habitat	cultivated in plantations, parks, gardens		
Flowering	April		
Fruiting	October	**Stipules**	absent
	TRUNK AND BRANCHES		**FLOWERS AND FRUIT**
Trunk	straight, unforked	**Flowers**	♂ and ♀ cones on same plant
Bark	reddish brown, rough, becoming cracked and fluted	♂	clustered at leaf-bases near shoot tip, small, red, turning yellow
Crown	narrowly conical or cylindrical; branches in groups at same level	♀	solitary at shoot tip, *c*6mm, purplish pink
Twigs	slender, tip droops, greyish brown, hairy	**Fruit**	single egg-shaped cone, 2–2.5cm, hanging, brown, ripening in first year; scales rounded, persisting
	LEAVES		
Buds	globular, greyish	**Seeds**	winged, 2 per cone-scale

Norway Spruce *Picea abies*

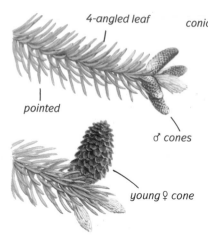

4-angled leaf

pointed

♂ cones

young ♀ cone

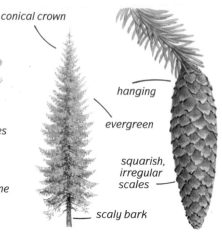

conical crown

hanging

evergreen

squarish, irregular scales

scaly bark

An important timber tree, though perhaps more familiar as a Christmas tree. Spruces are distinctive in the long, hanging cones with thin scales, and needles borne on short, peg-like projections. *Status:* native mainly to northern Europe; planted elsewhere for timber, shelter and ornament. *Similar trees:* forming intermediates where they grow together, Siberian Spruce is sometimes regarded as part of the same species as Norway Spruce. It is smaller with a shorter, more pointed cone and short, dense hairs on the twigs. Oriental Spruce is easily distinguished by its very short leaves.

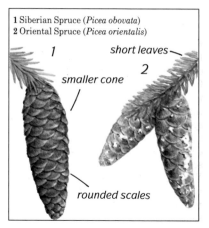

1 Siberian Spruce (*Picea obovata*)
2 Oriental Spruce (*Picea orientalis*)

1

2

short leaves

smaller cone

rounded scales

	NORWAY SPRUCE
Type	conifer, evergreen tree
Height	30–40m (rarely to 60m)
Habitat	forests, plantations, parks
Flowering	May
Fruiting	September

TRUNK AND CROWN

Trunk	straight, not forked
Bark	reddish brown, rough, scaly, darkens, cracks into plates
Crown	conical or columnar; branches in rings at same level
Twigs	orange brown, grooved, rough with peg-like leaf-bases, usually hairless

LEAVES

Buds	4–7mm, egg-shaped, glossy dark brown
Leaves	arising spirally, turning to either side of shoot and leaving gap below, 10–25mm, needle-like, 4-angled, pointed, dark green with greyish band on each side; peg-like base
Stipules	absent

FLOWERS AND FRUIT

Flowers	♂ and ♀ flowers on same plant
♂	globular cones, *c*1cm, near shoot tips, crimson, turning yellow with pollen
♀	solitary cone, dark red, upright, on upper branches
Fruit	cylindrical cone with rounded tip, 12–20cm, hanging, woody, brown; scales thin, diamond-shaped or oval with squarish, irregular tip
Seeds	2 per cone-scale, winged

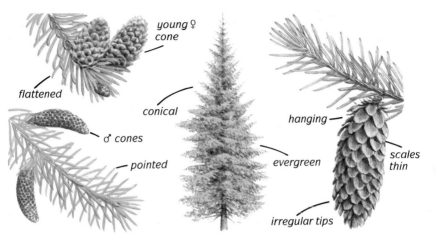

young ♀ cone

flattened

conical

♂ cones

pointed

hanging

scales thin

evergreen

irregular tips

Native to the Pacific coast of North America, this tall, graceful conifer is now an important timber tree in Europe. It has shallow roots and is often blown over in high winds. *Status:* introduced from North America; commonly grown in northern and central Europe for timber or ornament. *Similar trees:* two species differ in the short, blunt leaves and smaller cones. Hondo Spruce, from Japan, has a blunt cone with toothed scales. Serbian Spruce, from Yugoslavia, has hairy twigs and pointed cones with rounded scales. Also with rounded scales, Tiger-tail Spruce has sharp, four-angled leaves.

1 Hondo Spruce (*Picea jezoensis* var. *hondoensis*); 2 Serbian Spruce (*Picea omorika*); 3 Tiger-tail Spruce (*Picea polita*)

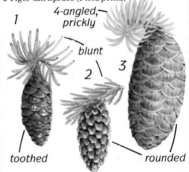

1

4-angled, prickly

blunt

2

3

toothed

rounded

SITKA SPRUCE

Type	conifer, evergreen tree
Height	40–55m (up to 80m in America)
Habitat	plantations, parks; often in areas of high rainfall
Flowering	May
Fruiting	October

TRUNK AND CROWN

Trunk	usually straight, not forked
Bark	dark or purplish grey, cracking into irregular, lifting plates
Crown	narrowly conical; lower branches arch downwards
Twigs	pale brown, grooved, rough

LEAVES

Buds	egg-shaped, pale brown, purplish with resin
Leaves	spirally arranged, mostly turning to either side of shoot, the upper close to shoot, 2–3cm, needle-like, flattened, tip sharply pointed, bright green above with 2 narrow, pale bands, 2 bluish white bands below; stalkless
Stipules	absent

FLOWERS AND FRUIT

Flowers	♂ and ♀ flowers on same plant
♂	blunt, egg-shaped cones, 25–35mm, yellow or purplish
♀	pale red or green cone, 25–50mm, mostly near top of tree
Fruit	solitary, cylindrical, hanging cone, 5–10cm, ripening pale brown; scales thin, papery, crinkled, irregularly toothed
Seeds	2 per scale, winged

Colorado Spruce _Picea pungens_

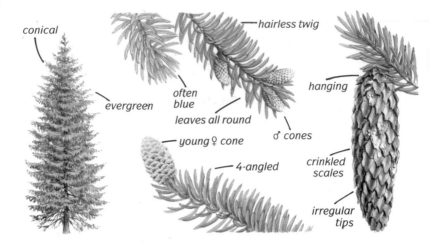

conical

evergreen

often blue

leaves all round

young ♀ cone

hairless twig

hanging

♂ cones

4-angled

crinkled scales

irregular tips

A variable tree with stiff, prickly leaves and hanging cones with thin, crinkled scales. Where native in western North America, forms with both grey-green and bluish leaves are found. Ornamental trees in Europe are almost always blue-leaved. _Status:_ introduced from western North America; grown for ornament and timber in northern and central Europe. _Similar trees:_ two species have unpleasantly scented foliage, leaves parted beneath the shoots and smaller cones. Engelmann Spruce has dense, short hairs on the twigs; White Spruce has shorter leaves, and cones with rounded scales.

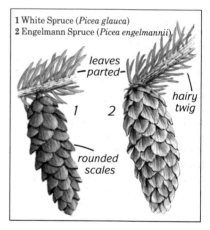

1 White Spruce (_Picea glauca_)
2 Engelmann Spruce (_Picea engelmannii_)

leaves parted

hairy twig

rounded scales

	COLORADO SPRUCE
Type	conifer, evergreen tree
Height	to 30m (rarely 45m in America)
Habitat	plantations, parks
Flowering	May
Fruiting	October

TRUNK AND CROWN

Trunk	straight, not forked
Bark	purplish grey or brown, cracking into flakes or plates
Crown	narrowly conical, dense; branches level or lowest arched downwards
Twigs	whitish or yellowish brown, rough, grooved, hairless

LEAVES

Buds	egg-shaped or conical, pointed, scales curved back

Leaves	spirally arranged all round shoot, 2–3cm, needle-like, stiff, 4-angled, spine-tipped, grey green or bluish with paler band on each side and waxy layer; stalkless
Stipules	absent

FLOWERS AND FRUIT

Flowers	♂ and ♀ cones on same tree
♂	egg-shaped or shortly cylindrical cone, _c_2cm, yellowish
♀	upright cone, _c_4cm, near shoot tip
Fruit	cylindrical, hanging cone, 7–12cm, near top of tree, pale brown; scales diamond-shaped, thin, crinkled with squarish, irregularly toothed tip
Seeds	2 per scale, winged

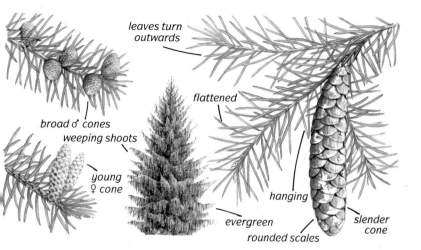

leaves turn outwards

broad ♂ cones
weeping shoots

young ♀ cone

flattened

hanging

evergreen rounded scales

slender cone

A beautiful tree with curtain-like, weeping foliage from upswept branches. An uncommon North American tree of the Siskyou Mountains in California and Oregon, it is not closely related to any other spruce. *Status:* introduced from western North America, frequently planted for ornament. *Similar trees:* Morinda Spruce has a less dramatic weeping habit and hairless shoots. The buds are smaller and rounded, and the leaves, square in cross-section, are very long and green all round. Relatively broader, the cone has rounded scales which become irregular at the tip as they ripen.

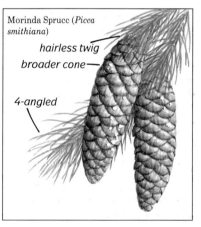

Morinda Spruce (*Picea smithiana*)

hairless twig
broader cone

4-angled

BREWER'S WEEPING-SPRUCE	
Type	conifer, evergreen tree
Height	10–20m (to 35m in America)
Habitat	mainly grown in parks, gardens
Flowering	May
Fruiting	October

TRUNK AND CROWN	
Trunk	straight, not forked
Bark	purplish grey, smooth, eventually with roughly circular flakes
Crown	irregularly conical or columnar; branches level or upswept, lower bent downwards
Twigs	long, slender, weeping, rough, pinkish brown, finely hairy

LEAVES	
Buds	egg-shaped or conical, blunt, with reddish brown hairs
Leaves	arising spirally, curving out all round shoot or sometimes parted below, 2–3.5cm, needle-like, flattened, blunt, dark bluish green below; stalkless
Stipules	absent

FLOWERS AND FRUIT	
Flowers	♂ and ♀ flowers on same tree
♂	egg-shaped cones, 15–30mm, clustered near shoot tip
♀	cylindrical, upright cones, 25–35mm, red or pinkish green, clustered on upper branches
Fruit	narrow, hanging cone, 10–14cm, cylindrical, blunt, purplish, turning brown marked with whitish resin; scales rounded
Seeds	2 per scale, winged

European Larch *Larix decidua*

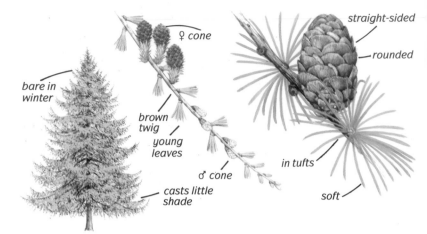

♀ cone

straight-sided

rounded

bare in winter

brown twig

young leaves

♂ cone

casts little shade

in tufts

soft

Leaves of this deciduous conifer turn yellow before falling to reveal knobbly twigs. Soft tufts of emerald-green young leaves in spring accompany pink young female cones and golden male cones. *Status:* native to mountains of central Europe; planted elsewhere for timber and ornament. *Similar trees:* Japanese Larch differs in the orange twigs, bluish leaves with white bands beneath, yellowish young female cones, and ripe cones with scales curved outwards. Its vigorous hybrid with the former species has intermediate cones. Dahurian Larch has cones with fewer, scarcely curved, hairless, broad scales.

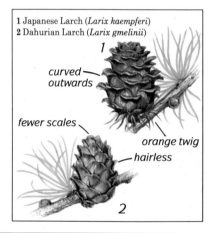

1 Japanese Larch (*Larix kaempferi*)
2 Dahurian Larch (*Larix gmelinii*)

1

curved outwards

fewer scales

orange twig

hairless

2

	EUROPEAN LARCH
Type	conifer, deciduous tree
Height	30–50m
Habitat	forest, woodland, plantations
Flowering	March–April
Fruiting	September; ripens first year

TRUNK AND CROWN

Trunk	straight, not forked below
Bark	greyish brown, smooth, becomes reddish and scaly or fissured
Crown	conical, becoming broader; branches irregularly clustered
Twigs	yellowish, hairless; long shoots and short side shoots

LEAVES

Buds	3mm, oval, yellowish brown

Leaves	tuft of 30–40 on short shoots, or spirally arranged on long shoots, 2–4cm, needle-like, thin, soft, pale green, becoming darker and turning yellow in autumn; stalkless
Stipules	absent

FLOWERS AND FRUIT

Flowers	♂ and ♀ cones on same tree
♂	small, drooping cone, yellow
♀	upright cone, pink or red
Fruit	egg-shaped woody cone, 2–3.5cm, with 40–50 scales; cone-scales more or less flat, round-tipped, softly hairy; bracts slightly protruding
Seeds	2 per cone-scale, winged

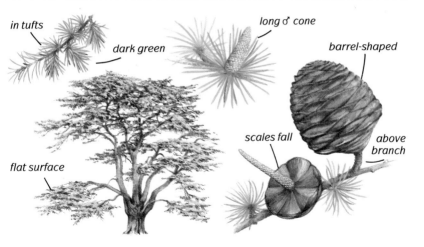

in tufts

dark green

long ♂ cone

barrel-shaped

scales fall

above branch

flat surface

Massive, spreading branches bearing flat plates of needle-like foliage make this tree easily recognizable at a distance. Bunched needles and barrel-shaped cones carried above the foliage are also distinctive. Mature stands of this tree are a rarity in the wild. *Status:* introduced from south-western Asia; frequently planted for ornament. *Similar trees:* Atlas Cedar, from North Africa, is commonly planted, usually as the blue-needled variant. It has branches angled upwards and leaves in clusters of 30–45. Himalayan in origin, Deodar has a pointed crown, longer leaves and drooping young shoots.

1 Atlas Cedar (*Cedrus atlantica*)
2 Deodar (*Cedrus deodara*)

often bluish

1

longer

2

—drooping

	CEDAR-OF-LEBANON
Type	conifer, evergreen tree
Height	15–40m
Habitat	parks, gardens
Flowering	October–November
Fruiting	ripens in second or third year

	TRUNK AND CROWN
Trunk	stout, often forked
Bark	brown or blackish, cracks into fine, scaly ridges
Crown	conical when young, becomes broad, rounded or flat-topped; stout, horizontal branches bear large, flat plates of dense foliage
Twigs	finely hairy, pale brown

	LEAVES
Buds	2–3mm, egg-shaped, brown

	LEAVES (cont.)
Leaves	tuft of 10–20 on short shoots, spirally arranged on long shoots, 2–3cm, needle-like, pointed, stiff, dark green, hairless; stalkless
Stipules	absent

	FLOWERS AND FRUIT
Flowers	♂ and ♀ cones on same tree
♂	cone 4–5cm, greenish yellow
♀	cone 7–12mm, green or purplish
Fruit	woody cone, 8–15cm, barrel-shaped with squarish or dimpled tip, greyish or pinkish brown, resinous, disintegrates on tree
Seeds	winged, 2 per cone-scale

Scots Pine *Pinus sylvestris*

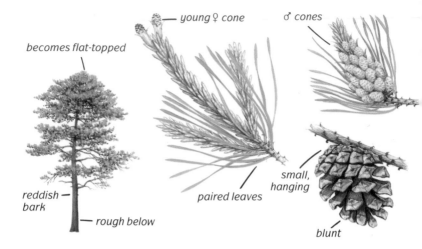

becomes flat-topped

young ♀ cone

♂ cones

reddish bark

rough below

paired leaves

small, hanging

blunt

A widespread conifer from the Atlantic coast of Europe almost to the Pacific coast of Asia. One of several pines with paired needles, it is distinguished by reddish, scaly bark on the upper trunk, relatively short, bluish needles, a small, hanging cone and small buds with scales pressed close together. *Status:* native to northern and central Europe; planted elsewhere for timber. *Similar trees:* Mountain-pine has bright green leaves and a shiny cone projecting at right-angles from the stem. Each scale has a backwardly curved point. Dwarf Mountain-pine is a similar but shorter tree or shrub, with small cones.

Mountain-pine (*Pinus mugo*)

greener leaves

small point

SCOTS PINE			
Type	conifer, evergreen tree		
Height	20–40m		
Habitat	forests, woods, plantations		
Flowering	May–June		
Fruiting	ripens in second year		
TRUNK AND CROWN			
Trunk	straight, not normally forked		
Bark	reddish brown, scaling above, blackish brown, fissured below		
Crown	conical, becomes broader or flat-topped; branches in groups at same level		
Twigs	greenish brown, hairless		
LEAVES			
Buds	small, pointed, resinous		
Leaves	paired on short shoots, 3–7cm, needle-like, twisted, blue-green, hairless; stalkless; small, scale-like on long shoots		
Stipules	absent		
FLOWERS AND FRUIT			
Flowers	♂ and ♀ cones on same tree		
♂	globular cone, yellow or sometimes red before pollen is shed		
♀	1–5 cones at tip of shoot, egg-shaped, pinkish purple cones		
Fruit	woody cone, 3–7cm, egg-shaped, pointed, hanging, dull, grey-brown; scales with broad, flattened end, raised in centre		
Seeds	12–15mm, winged, 2 per scale		

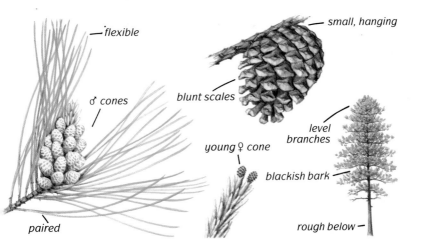

Pinus nigra subsp. *laricio* **Corsican Pine**

— flexible

♂ cones

paired

small, hanging

blunt scales

young ♀ cone

level branches

blackish bark

rough below

From its forests in the Mediterranean region, this pine has been introduced to many parts of northern Europe, where it forms extensive plantations. It resembles Scots Pine but has darker bark and longer, more flexible and darker leaves. In colder regions, it is susceptible to disease. *Status:* native to the central Mediterranean region; planted for timber, shelter or stabilizing sand. *Similar trees:* a dark, heavy-branched tree, Austrian Pine has rigid, straight, spine-tipped leaves, regularly clustered around the stem. Bosnian Pine has similar foliage but purple young cones.

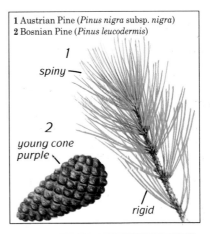

1 Austrian Pine (*Pinus nigra* subsp. *nigra*)
2 Bosnian Pine (*Pinus leucodermis*)

1

spiny —

2

young cone purple

rigid

	CORSICAN PINE
Type	conifer, evergreen tree
Height	30–50m
Habitat	forests, plantations
Flowering	June
Fruiting	ripens in second year

TRUNK AND CROWN

Trunk	straight, rarely forked
Bark	grey, scaling above, blackish grey, deeply fissured below
Crown	conical or columnar, rarely becoming broader; branches in groups at same level
Twigs	hairless, yellowish brown

LEAVES

Buds	conical, pointed, resinous
Leaves	paired on short shoots, 10–18cm, needle-shaped, twisted, flexible, pointed, greyish green, hairless; stalkless
Stipules	absent

FLOWERS AND FRUIT

Flowers	♂ and ♀ cones on same tree
♂	clustered cones, each 8–13mm, yellow, scales purple-tipped
♀	egg-shaped cone, *c*5mm, pink
Fruit	woody cone, 6–8cm, egg-shaped, dull, yellowish or greyish brown; scales with broad, flattened end, with horizontal ridge and small central spine
Seeds	2 per scale, winged

Maritime Pine *Pinus pinaster*

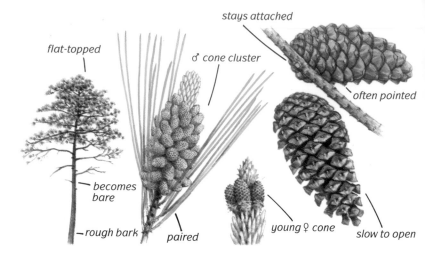

flat-topped

♂ cone cluster

stays attached

often pointed

becomes bare

rough bark

paired

young ♀ cone

slow to open

A distinctive coastal species with a high, open crown and very long needles. Glossy, woody cones can stay closed on the tree for many years before they open and fall. Resin tapped from the trunk is used in the manufacture of turpentine and for flavouring wines. *Status:* native to the western Mediterranean region; planted elsewhere for timber, shelter, sand-binding and resin. *Similar trees:* Aleppo Pine has shorter leaves and smaller cones, with rounded scales and a short stalk, which curves backwards. Calabrian Pine has leaves like the former and a cone like the latter, but with a short, straight stalk.

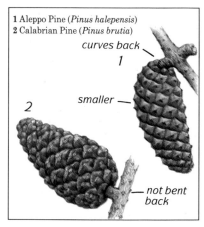

1 Aleppo Pine (*Pinus halepensis*)
2 Calabrian Pine (*Pinus brutia*)

curves back

1

2

smaller

not bent back

	MARITIME PINE		
Type	conifer, evergreen tree	**Leaves**	paired on short shoots, 10–25cm, needle-like, twisted, rigid, pointed, glossy grey-green, becoming deeper green, hairless; stalkless
Height	up to 40m		
Habitat	hot, dry, coastal areas		
Flowering	June		
Fruiting	ripens in second year	**Stipules**	absent
	TRUNK AND CROWN		**FLOWERS AND FRUIT**
Trunk	often twisted, becomes bare of branches below	**Flowers**	♂ and ♀ cones on same tree
Bark	reddish brown, becomes deeply fissured and ridged	♂	clustered cones, 8–10mm, yellow
Crown	conical or domed; branches in irregular wide-spaced groups	♀	groups of 3–5 cones near stem-tip, each 10–12mm, egg-shaped, deep pink
Twigs	grey or red-brown, hairless	**Fruit**	woody cones in small clusters, 8–22cm, conical, pointed, glossy brown; scales with horizontal ridges and often a broad, sharp point
	LEAVES		
Buds	10–20mm, tapered both ends, reddish brown, not resinous; scales bent back	**Seeds**	7–8mm with wing up to 30mm

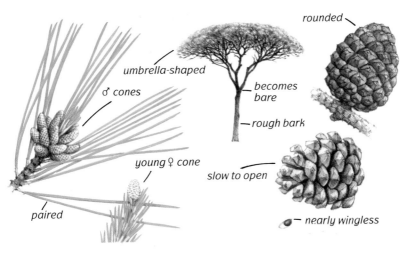

umbrella-shaped

becomes bare

rough bark

♂ cones

rounded

slow to open

young ♀ cone

paired

nearly wingless

This umbrella-shaped tree forms a distinctive element of the Mediterranean landscape and provides much-valued shade during long, hot summers. Huge woody cones contain seeds differing from those of other pines in having scarcely any wing. They are edible and eagerly sought. *Status:* native to Portugal and the Mediterranean region to the Black Sea; often planted as a shade-tree. *Similar trees.* Canary Island Pine is planted in the Mediterranean region for its high-quality timber. It differs in the very long leaves, grouped in threes, and seeds with a much larger wing.

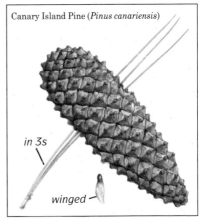

Canary Island Pine (*Pinus canariensis*)

in 3s

winged

	STONE PINE		
Type	conifer, evergreen tree	**Leaves**	paired, 10–20cm, needle-like, rather thick, often twisted, pointed, greyish green, hairless; stalkless
Height	20–30m		
Habitat	woods on light, sandy soils		
Flowering	June	**Stipules**	absent
Fruiting	ripens in third year		
	TRUNK AND CROWN		**FLOWERS AND FRUIT**
Trunk	straight, widely forked above	**Flowers**	♂ and ♀ cones on same tree
Bark	greyish or reddish brown, fissured forming flat plates	♂	cluster of cones, each 10–14mm, egg-shaped, orange-brown
Crown	broad, umbrella-shaped; branches stout, radiating	♀	solitary cone 8–12mm, yellowish green
Twigs	greyish green to orange-brown, often curved, hairless	**Fruit**	woody cone, 8–14cm, globular or slightly elongated, blunt, glossy brown; scale-tips rounded, with radiating folds
	LEAVES	**Seeds**	15–20mm, nut-like with hard coat and narrow, papery wing
Buds	5–12mm, oval, reddish brown, not resinous; white-fringed scales curved backwards		

Shore Pine *Pinus contorta*

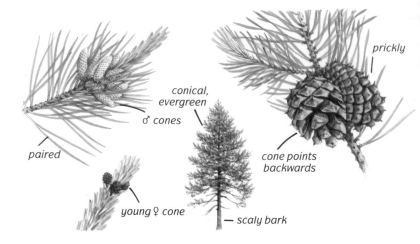

paired

conical, evergreen

♂ *cones*

young ♀ cone

prickly

cone points backwards

scaly bark

Not the most attractive of pines, this tough species survives to produce useful timber even in windswept places with very poor, waterlogged soils. It has short, paired leaves in bunches, and twisted buds. Cones remain on the tree and in nature ripen late, often after a forest fire. *Status:* introduced from the Pacific coast of North America; widely planted in central and northern Europe for timber. *Similar trees:* two other American timber trees differ in having longer leaves in threes and larger cones. Monterey Pine has very asymmetrical cones. Western Yellow-pine has symmetrical cones with strong prickles.

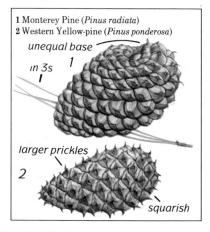

1 Monterey Pine (*Pinus radiata*)
2 Western Yellow-pine (*Pinus ponderosa*)

unequal base

in 3s

1

larger prickles

2

squarish

SHORE PINE			
Type	conifer, evergreen tree	**Leaves**	paired, bunched, pointing towards branch tip, 4–7cm, needle-like, twisted, pointed, dark green, hairless; stalkless
Height	10–30m		
Habitat	plantations, often poor soils		
Flowering	April–May	**Stipules**	absent
Fruiting	ripens in 2 or more years		

TRUNK AND CROWN

Trunk straight, not forked

Bark dark brown, scaly, becoming deeply fissured

Crown slender, conical or columnar, eventually becoming domed; branches short, often twisted

Twigs greenish brown, becoming orange-brown, hairless, shiny

LEAVES

Buds cylindrical, often twisted, brown, resinous

FLOWERS AND FRUIT

Flowers ♂ and ♀ on same tree

♂ tiny cones crowded together at base of new shoot, yellow

♀ 2–4 cones near tip of shoot, *c*6mm, dark red, conical

Fruit woody cone, pointing backwards on shoot, 2.5–7.5cm, conical, elongated, glossy yellowish brown; scale-tips angular with slender, fragile prickle

Seeds 4–5mm, wing *c*8mm

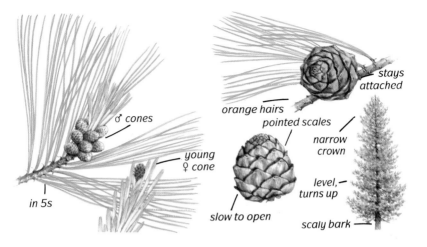

♂ cones

young ♀ cone

in 5s

orange hairs

stays attached

pointed scales

narrow crown

level, turns up

scaly bark

slow to open

Arolla Pine is characterized by needles in groups of five and short cones with thin, pointed, rather than square-ended, scales. Cones ripen and fall after three years, the seeds released only as the cones are broken open by animals or eventually rot. *Status:* native to the mountains of southern and central Europe; planted further north for timber and ornament. *Similar trees:* Weymouth Pine and other five-needled pines have elongated, hanging, sticky cones and winged seeds. Two species differ in the hairless shoots. Bhutan Pine has straight cones; Macedonian Pine has shorter, curved cones.

1 Weymouth Pine (*Pinus strobus*)
2 Bhutan Pine (*Pinus wallichiana*)
3 Macedonian Pine (*Pinus peuce*)

1 *2*

sticky *long*

hairless

shorter *3*

	AROLLA PINE		
Type	conifer, evergreen tree	**Leaves**	in fives, 5–9cm, needle-like, pointed, hairless, dark green with bluish inner face; stalkless
Height	10–30m		
Habitat	dry slopes up to 3000m	**Stipules**	absent
Flowering	May		
Fruiting	ripens in third year		**FLOWERS AND FRUIT**
		Flowers	♂ and ♀ on same tree
	TRUNK AND CROWN	♂	cluster of cones, egg-shaped, yellow or purplish
Trunk	straight, sometimes forked		
Bark	reddish grey, smooth with resin-blisters, becoming shallowly fissured, scaly	♀	cone at stem-tip, *c*10mm, egg-shaped, dark red
		Fruit	woody cone, 5–8cm, broadly egg-shaped, purple-tinged when young, becoming reddish brown; scales thin, broad, pointed
Crown	columnar to broadly conical; branches in groups at same level, tips turn upwards		
Twigs	with brownish orange hairs		
		Seeds	2 per scale, 12–14mm, usually wingless, shed after cones fall
	LEAVES		
Buds	egg-shaped, pointed, pale brown; scales white-edged		

Wellingtonia *Sequoiadendron giganteum*

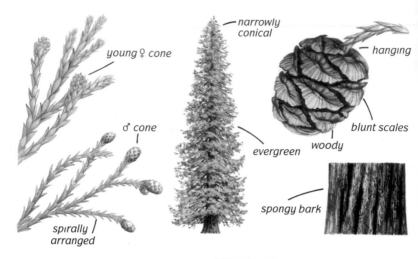

young ♀ cone

narrowly conical

hanging

blunt scales

♂ cone

evergreen woody

spirally arranged

spongy bark

A massive tree, though no plants in Europe come close to the true giants of western North America. They are very long-lived and may survive for around 3400 years, during which time they can reach over 90m with a buttressed trunk 7m or more across. Thick, fibrous, reddish bark acts as an insulating layer against forest fire and contributes to the longevity of the trees. *Status:* introduced from the Sierra Nevada of California; frequently planted for ornament. *Similar trees:* Japanese Red-cedar has more slender leaves but differs markedly in the smaller cones; each scale usually has five spines.

Japanese Red-cedar (*Cryptomeria japonica*)

rounded

longer

spiny scales

WELLINGTONIA	
Type	conifer, evergreen tree
Height	to 50m (85m in North America)
Habitat	parks, ornamental woodland, large gardens
Flowering	March–April
Fruiting	ripens in second year
TRUNK AND CROWN	
Trunk	straight, very broad and fluted at base
Bark	thick, fibrous, soft, reddish brown or darker brown
Crown	narrowly conical; drooping lower branches curve upwards
Twigs	stout, grey-green, covered by bases of scale-leaves
LEAVES	
Buds	small, not scaly

Leaves	spirally arranged, 4–12mm, oval to spear-shaped, rather scale-like, flattened above, pointed, hairless; stalkless, blade joins stem
Stipules	absent
FLOWERS AND FRUIT	
Flowers	♂ and ♀ on same tree
♂	cone at shoot-tip, pale yellow
♀	usually single cone at stem tip, upright, 8–10mm, green with pinkish spines
Fruit	solitary woody cone, 5–8cm, egg-shaped; 25–40 scales, square-ended, wrinkled, centre sunken with small spine
Seeds	3–7 per scale, winged

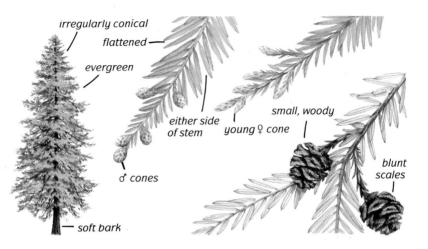

irregularly conical

flattened

evergreen

either side of stem

young ♀ cone

small, woody

blunt scales

♂ cones

soft bark

In its native environment, this species can claim the record for the tallest living thing on earth, at over 110m. Many Coast Redwoods are around 1000 years old and individuals can reach 2600 years. In the event of lightning damage to the trunk, a tree can re-grow from suckers at the base and may form a grove of trees. This ability extends the life of a plant. *Status:* introduced from western North America; widely planted, mainly in western Europe, for ornament or timber. *Similar trees:* Chinese Fir has longer, brighter leaves, clustered male cones, and fruiting cones with thin, pointed scales.

Chinese Fir (*Cunninghamia lanceolata*) all round stem

pointed scales

many ♂ cones

COAST REDWOOD		Leaves	mostly in 2 rows, 6–20mm, narrowly oblong, straight or curved, flattened, pointed, hairless, dark green, 2 white bands below; base of blade joins twig; spirally arranged on leading shoot, scale-like
Type	conifer, evergreen tree		
Height	to 45m (100m in North America)		
Habitat	parks, ornamental woodland		
Flowering	February–March		
Fruiting	ripens in second year		
		Stipules	absent
TRUNK AND CROWN			
Trunk	straight, rarely forked, stout, suckers at base	**FLOWERS AND FRUIT**	
		Flowers	♂ and ♀ on same tree
Bark	reddish brown, thick, spongy, sometimes fissured	♂	cone at tip of side shoot, 1.5–2mm, whitish yellow
Crown	columnar; irregular rings of branches, lower bent downwards	♀	globular, green cone with bristle-tipped scales
Twigs	green, obscured by leaf-bases	**Fruit**	woody cone at branch tip, 2–3cm, egg-shaped, hanging, reddish brown; 15–20 scales, square-ended, centre sunken
LEAVES			
Buds	c3mm, pointed, scaly	**Seeds**	3–5 per scale, winged

Swamp Cypress *Taxodium distichum*

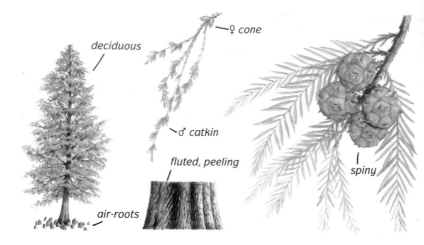

deciduous

♀ cone

♂ catkin

fluted, peeling

spiny

air-roots

An unusual deciduous conifer with pale, feathery foliage, which in autumn sheds not only leaves but entire leafy shoots. Grown by water it produces curious air-roots, which emerge from the ground as a knobbly mound and enable the roots to function when deprived of oxygen in mud. *Status:* introduced from south-eastern North America; grown for ornament in western and central Europe. *Similar trees:* discovered in China during 1941 but previously known from fossils several million years old, Dawn Redwood differs in the paired leaves, paired shoots and blunt cone-scales.

Dawn Redwood (*Metasequoia glyptostroboides*)

paired shoots

blunt scales

	SWAMP CYPRESS		
Type	conifer, deciduous tree		shoots, 1–2cm, thin, flat, pointed, pale green, 2 grey bands below, turning reddish brown in autumn; stalkless
Height	20–30m (50m in America)		
Habitat	usually planted by water		
Flowering	March–April	**Stipules**	absent
Fruiting	ripens in first year		
			FLOWERS AND FRUIT
	TRUNK AND CROWN	**Flowers**	♂ and ♀ flowers on same tree, at shoot tip
Trunk	straight, develops buttresses		
Bark	reddish brown, fibrous, peels, vertical or spiral fissures	♂	3–4 hanging catkins, 6–20cm, branched, slender, purplish, becoming yellow with pollen
Crown	conical with rounded top		
Twigs	reddish brown, slender long shoots, short side-shoots shed with leaves in autumn	♀	tiny cone, green
		Fruit	woody cone, 2–3cm, globular, ripens purplish brown, stalk 2–4mm; scales spine-tipped
	LEAVES		
Buds	rounded, small, scaly	**Seeds**	2 per scale, irregularly 3-angled, narrowly winged
Leaves	spirally placed on long shoots, on alternate sides of short		

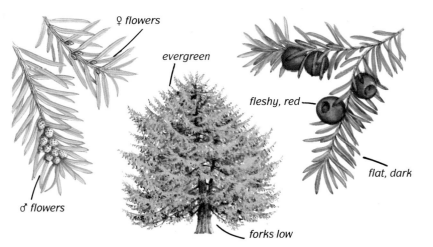

♀ *flowers*

evergreen

fleshy, red

flat, dark

forks low

♂ *flowers*

With distinctive dark foliage and red berries, Yew is a common feature of churchyards, and its strong, supple timber had many uses. Ancient trees occur, more than a thousand years old, with massive, hollow trunks. *Status:* native to most of Europe except for the extreme east and north; commonly planted for ornament. *Similar trees:* two species have longer foliage and larger, greenish fruits. California Nutmeg has branches in rings, large, conical buds, spine-tipped leaves and an egg-shaped fruit. Plum-fruited Yew has softer, brighter blue-green leaves and white-speckled fruit.

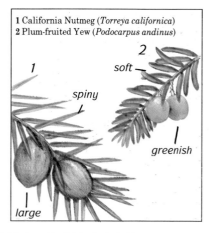

1 California Nutmeg (*Torreya californica*)
2 Plum-fruited Yew (*Podocarpus andinus*)

soft

spiny

greenish

large

		Leaves	on 2 sides of most shoots, spiral
YEW			on upright shoots, 1–3cm,
Type	conifer, evergreen tree or		needle-like, flat, pointed, edge
	sometimes a shrub		curved under, hairless, very
Height	10–25m		dark green above, 2 yellowish
Habitat	woods, scrub, mainly on lime-rich soils, planted elswhere		green bands below; stalk short
Flowering	February–April		**FLOWERS AND FRUIT**
Fruiting	August–September	Flowers	♂ and ♀ flowers on different trees
	TRUNK AND CROWN	♂	cones clustered beneath year-old shoots, 5–6mm, globular,
Trunk	short, forked, sometimes twisted, stout and hollow		turning yellow with pollen
Bark	light brown or reddish, thin, scaly and peeling	♀	cone, 1–2mm, green
Crown	conical or domed; branches angled upwards or spreading	Fruit	berry-like, 8–12mm, solitary, cup-like, red fleshy layer around woody, nut-like centre
Twigs	green, grooved	Seeds	solitary, 5–7mm, elongated
	LEAVES		
Buds	minute, egg-shaped, green		

Lawson Cypress   *Chamaecyparis lawsoniana*

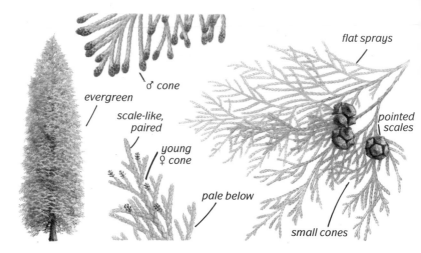

flat sprays

♂ cone

evergreen

scale-like, paired

young ♀ cone

pale below

pointed scales

small cones

Very commonly planted, this North American species is one of the most popular of all ornamental conifers. The foliage has a distinctive, parsley-like smell. Many cultivated variants exist. *Status:* introduced from western North America; planted for ornament, timber and shelter; sometimes naturalized. *Similar trees:* two cultivated species from Japan have brighter leaves, marked with white below and lacking the gland. Hinoki Cypress has blunt, often rounded leaves. Sawara Cypress has pointed leaves spread apart at the tips; the very slender shoots droop in many plants.

1 Hinoki Cypress (*Chamaecyparis obtusa*)
2 Sawara Cypress (*Chamaecyparis pisifera*)

pointed leaves   2

blunt leaves

tips spread apart

1

	LAWSON CYPRESS		
Type	conifer, evergreen tree		
Height	up to 45m		
Habitat	plantations, parks, gardens		
Flowering	March – April		
Fruiting	September – October		

TRUNK AND CROWN

Trunk	straight, sometimes forked
Bark	smooth, greyish brown, becomes cracked into vertical plates
Crown	conical; few large branches, sometimes in irregular rings, leading shoot droops
Twigs	forming flat sprays, often hanging at tips

LEAVES

Buds	tiny, hidden by leaves

Leaves	paired, 0.5–2mm, scale-like, diamond-shaped with central, translucent gland, pointed tip curves inwards, hairless, dark green above, paler below; stalkless; occasionally some needle-like leaves
Stipules	absent

FLOWERS AND FRUIT

Flowers	♂ and ♀ on same tree
♂	cone 2–5mm, at shoot-tip, blackish scales turn red, then yellow with pollen
♀	globular cone, bluish green
Fruit	woody cone, 5–8mm, globular, often bluish, turns yellowish brown; scales in 4 pairs, wrinkled, small central spine
Seeds	usually 2–4 per scale, winged

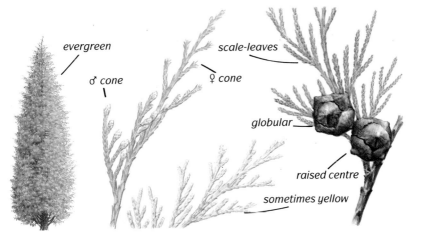

evergreen

♂ cone

scale-leaves

♀ cone

globular

raised centre

sometimes yellow

Renowned for rapid growth, this hybrid conifer is popular for hedging and wherever a screen is required quickly. It is a cross between species of two genera, the form differing slightly depending whether Nootka Cypress or Monterey Cypress was the female parent. *Status:* of garden origin; very commonly planted for ornament. *Similar trees:* both parent species are commonly planted. Nootka Cypress has dull green foliage, which is rough and oily smelling; small cones ripen in two years. Tolerant of salt-laden winds, Monterey Cypress becomes a large tree with flattish plates of foliage and large, lumpy cones.

1 Nootka Cypress (*Chamaecyparis nootkatenis*)
2 Monterey Cypress (*Cupressus macrocarpa*)

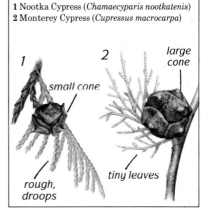

large cone

small cone

1

2

rough, droops

tiny leaves

LEYLAND CYPRESS	**Leaves**	scale-like, paired in 4 ranks, 0.5–2mm, all similar, closely pressed together, pointed, hairless, dark green or grey-green above, yellowish green below; stalkless
Type conifer, evergreen tree		
Height up to 35m		
Habitat parks, gardens, plantations		
Flowering March		
Fruiting October	**Stipules** absent	
TRUNK AND CROWN	**FLOWERS AND FRUIT**	
Trunk straight, sometimes forked	**Flowers** ♂ and ♀ flowers on same plant	
Bark reddish brown, forming shallow, vertical fissures	♂ cone 3–5mm, greenish, turning yellow with pollen	
Crown narrowly columnar to broadly conical; branches crowded, angled upwards, retained to base, leading shoot leans	♀ small, green, globular cone	
	Fruit woody cone, rarely produced by some trees, 2–3cm, globular, brown; few paired scales, each with blunt central spine	
Twigs slender, with old scale-leaves; forms sprays of foliage		
LEAVES	**Seeds** rarely produced, 2–6 per scale	
Buds tiny, hidden by leaves		

Italian Cypress *Cupressus sempervirens*

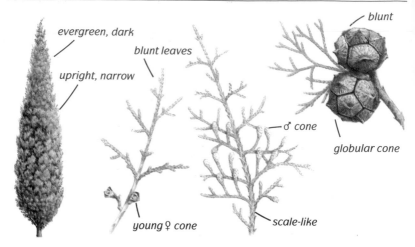

evergreen, dark

upright, narrow

blunt leaves

blunt

♂ cone

globular cone

young ♀ cone

scale-like

An unmistakable feature of many Italian landscapes, this narrowly columnar conifer is widely planted for its distinctive habit. The wild form is rarely planted as its broad, irregularly conical outline is far less striking. *Status:* native to south-eastern Europe; much planted for ornament or timber in southern Europe, often naturalized. *Similar trees:* two species with broad crowns have smaller cones of 6–8 scales. Mexican Cypress has dull green, scarcely scented foliage, spreading leaf-tips and bluish young cones. Smooth Cypress has smooth, scaling bark and blue-grey, scented, resin-flecked leaves.

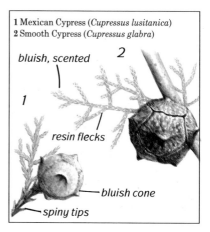

1 Mexican Cypress (*Cupressus lusitanica*)
2 Smooth Cypress (*Cupressus glabra*)

bluish, scented

2

1

resin flecks

bluish cone

spiny tips

	ITALIAN CYPRESS
Type	conifer, evergreen tree
Height	15–30m
Habitat	planted mostly near houses
Flowering	March
Fruiting	ripens in second year
	TRUNK AND CROWN
Trunk	straight, often forked above
Bark	grey-brown, shallow fissures and twisted, scaly ridges
Crown	narrowly columnar with upright branches or sometimes conical
Twigs	slightly 4-angled, curved upwards near tip, reddish brown
	LEAVES
Buds	tiny, hidden by leaves
Leaves	scale-like, paired in 4 ranks,

pressed together, 0.5–1mm, diamond-shaped, blunt, dull, dark green, hairless; stalkless; needle-like leaves rarely on leading shoots

Stipules	absent
	FLOWERS AND FRUIT
Flowers	♂ and ♀ cones on same tree, each at tip of small shoot
♂	elliptical cone, 4–8mm, green, turning yellow with pollen
♀	oblong cone, 3–4mm
Fruit	solitary cone, 2.5–4cm, shortly oblong or globular, reddish brown to yellowish grey; 4–7 pairs of wavy-edged scales, each with broad point
Seeds	8–20 per cone scale, flattened, narrowly winged

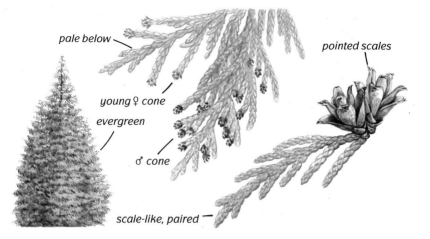

pale below

pointed scales

young ♀ cone

evergreen

♂ cone

scale-like, paired

Old, well-grown trees make magnificent specimens, with huge lower branches curved down to the ground, eventually rooting to become new trunks. Glossy, dark green foliage has a distinctive, fruity scent, and small, elongated cones have spine-tipped scales. *Status:* introduced from western North America; commonly planted for timber, ornament and hedging. *Similar trees:* White-cedar has leaves with a conspicuous gland, lacking whitish marks below, and blunt cone-scales. Chinese White-cedar has uniformly green, scentless leaves, and cones with fewer pairs of scales, each with a strong, curved spine.

1 White-cedar (*Thuja occidentalis*)
2 Chinese White-cedar (*Thuja orientalis*)

1

raised glands

curved spine

2

	WESTERN RED-CEDAR	
Type	conifer, evergreen tree	
Height	up to 40m (50m in America)	
Habitat	plantations, parks, gardens	
Flowering	March	
Fruiting	October of first year	
	TRUNK AND CROWN	
Trunk	straight or forked above, fluted below; lower branches may root forming new trunks	
Bark	reddish brown, soft, thick with lifting strips	
Crown	conical or irregular; lower branches curve down, leading shoot upright	
Twigs	reddish brown shoots form flattened sprays of foliage	
	LEAVES	
Buds	tiny, hidden by leaves	

Leaves	scale-like, paired in 4 ranks, side pair larger, 1.5–3mm, oval, blunt, with tiny gland, glossy deep green above, paler below with whitish streaks, hairless; stalkless
Stipules	absent
	FLOWERS AND FRUIT
Flowers	♂ and ♀ cones on same tree
♂	cone 1–2mm, dark red, becomes pale yellow with pollen
♀	cone 2–5mm, yellowish green
Fruit	woody cone, 1–1.5cm, elliptical, upright, green, turns brown; 5–6 pairs of spine-tipped scales
Seeds	2–3 per scale, winged

Juniper · *Juniperus communis*

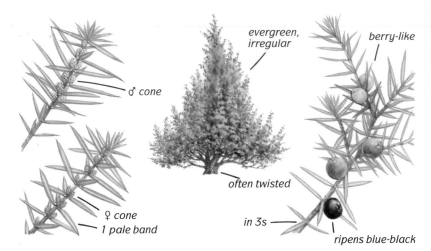

evergreen, irregular

berry-like

♂ *cone*

♀ *cone*
1 pale band

often twisted

in 3s

ripens blue-black

Squat and spiny, Juniper is a common shrub scattered on chalk downland, but also forms an understorey to pine woodland, growing to tree size. Highly variable wild plants include low-growing shrubs on sea cliffs, and narrow columns on hills inland. *Status:* native to north-western Europe, Asia and North America; planted for ornament. *Similar trees:* two Mediterranean species differ in having longer leaves with two pale bands. Syrian Juniper has much larger blue-black fruits. More widespread, Prickly Juniper has fruits ripening through yellow to dull red or purple.

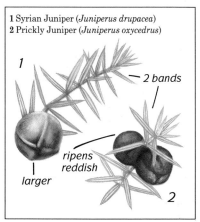

1 Syrian Juniper (*Juniperus drupacea*)
2 Prickly Juniper (*Juniperus oxycedrus*)

1

2 bands

ripens reddish

larger

2

	JUNIPER		**LEAVES**
Type	conifer, evergreen shrub or sometimes a tree	**Buds**	small, hidden by spiny leaves
Height	2–5m, rarely 15m	**Leaves**	clusters of 3 around stem, 5–20mm, needle-like, sharply pointed, hairless, with broad, white band above, grey-green below; base jointed
Habitat	grassland, scrub, woods; lime-rich soils or shallow peat		
Flowering	April–June	**Stipules**	absent
Fruiting	after 2–3 years		
	TRUNK AND CROWN		**FLOWERS AND FRUIT**
Trunk	short, often twisted or bent	**Flowers**	♂ and ♀ on different trees, solitary at leaf-base
Bark	reddish brown, peels in strips	♂	cone 6–8mm, yellow
Crown	very variable, usually irregularly conical, sometimes low-growing or columnar	♀	cone 2–3mm, greenish
		Fruit	berry-like cone, 6–9mm, globular, solitary at leaf-base, turning black with bluish waxy layer
Twigs	greenish or reddish brown, hairless, the lower twigs often retain dead leaves		
		Seeds	3, separate, not winged

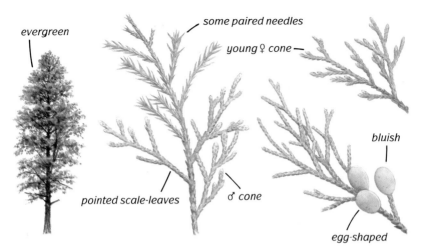

evergreen

some paired needles

young ♀ cone

pointed scale-leaves

♂ cone

bluish

egg-shaped

The tallest of the commonly grown junipers, this slow-growing tree can form a remarkably narrow column. Its foliage has a pleasant aromatic scent. *Status:* introduced from eastern North America; much grown for ornament and for timber in central and southern Europe. *Similar trees:* two species have unpleasant-smelling foliage and globular fruits. Chinese Juniper has pale-edged scale-leaves and larger fruits, showing scale outlines. Apparently forming hybrids with the latter, Savin is a native shrub with blunt leaves, pressed together, and small fruits.

1 Chinese Juniper (*Juniperus chinensis*)
2 Savin (*Juniperus sabina*)

globular, larger

pale edges

1

small, globular

blunt tips

2

	PENCIL CEDAR		
Type	conifer, evergreen tree		
Height	15–30m		
Habitat	parks, gardens, plantations		
Flowering	March–April		
Fruiting	September of first year		

TRUNK AND CROWN

Trunk	straight, becomes buttressed
Bark	reddish brown, peels in long, narrow strips
Crown	conical or columnar; branches diverge narrowly
Twigs	very slender

LEAVES

Buds	tiny, concealed by leaves
Leaves	juvenile leaves needle-like, paired, 5–6mm, pointed, often at shoot-tip; adult leaves scale-like, paired in 4 ranks, 0.5–1.5mm, pointed tips spread apart, dark green or bluish green, hairless; stalkless
Stipules	absent

FLOWERS AND FRUIT

Flowers	♂ and ♀ on different trees
♂	rounded, yellow cone, 4–5mm, at shoot tip
♀	green cone, 2–3mm, at base of leaf
Fruit	solitary, berry-like, 4–6mm, egg-shaped, ripens brownish violet with bluish waxy layer, short-stalked
Seeds	1 or 2, separate

Phoenicean Juniper *Juniperus phoenicea*

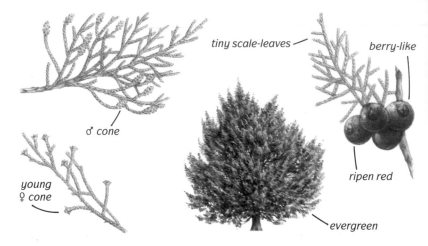

tiny scale-leaves

berry-like

♂ cone

ripen red

young ♀ cone

evergreen

The curious cord-like foliage of this Mediterranean species consists of widely branched shoots, with minute, pale-edged scale-leaves pressed tightly together. A small tree or sometimes a shrub, it also has a mat-like form that is found by the coast. Amongst the Mediterranean species, it is distinctive in having up to nine seeds in the fruit. *Status:* native to southern Europe; rarely cultivated. *Similar trees:* native to mountains of southern France and Spain, Spanish Juniper has paired leaves, which lack the pale, minutely toothed edge. Its slightly smaller fruits ripen to blackish purple.

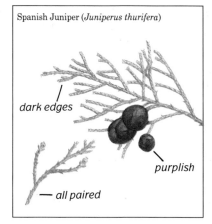

Spanish Juniper (*Juniperus thurifera*)

dark edges

purplish

— all paired

	PHOENICEAN JUNIPER		
Type	conifer, evergreen tree or shrub		
Height	2–8m		
Habitat	dry, rocky places, often coasts		
Flowering	March–April		
Fruiting	ripens in second year		

TRUNK AND CROWN

Trunk	irregular, short
Bark	scaly, reddish brown
Crown	broad, irregular, rarely low-growing; branches spread apart
Twigs	slender, 4-angled, scaly

LEAVES

Buds	tiny, concealed by leaves
Leaves	adult leaves scale-like, paired, in 4 ranks, closely overlapping, 0.7–1mm, oval or diamond-shaped with sunken gland, blunt or slightly pointed, yellowish green with whitish, finely toothed edge; stalkless; juvenile leaves rarely present, needle-like, groups of 3, 5–14mm, pointed, 2 whitish bands on both sides
Stipules	absent

FLOWERS AND FRUIT

Flowers	♂ and ♀ on same tree
♀	cone 4–5mm, at shoot-tip
♂	cone 2–3mm, on small shoot, blackish
Fruit	berry-like, 8–14mm, globular or egg-shaped, green with waxy layer, ripens dark red
Seeds	3–9, separate

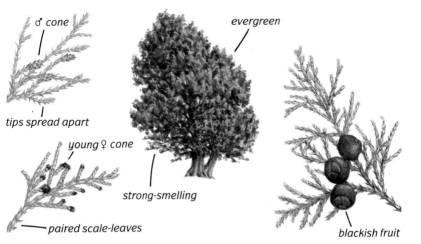

♂ cone

evergreen

tips spread apart

young ♀ cone

strong-smelling

paired scale-leaves

blackish fruit

So-called because of the strong, disagreeable odour given off by the foliage when lightly bruised, Stinking Juniper is largely restricted to mountains of the Balkan Peninsula and Crimea. A scale-leaved species with irregularly branched, four-angled twigs, it is identified by uniformly coloured leaves with pointed tips spread apart. *Status:* native to south-eastern Europe; rarely cultivated elsewhere. *Similar trees:* often confused with Stinking Juniper, Greek Juniper is a taller tree with slender, rounded twigs; smaller, less pointed scale-leaves, pressed together; and fruits with 4 – 6 seeds.

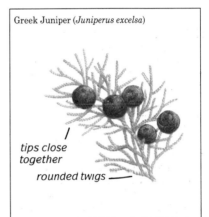

Greek Juniper (*Juniperus excelsa*)

tips close together

rounded twigs

STINKING JUNIPER

Type	conifer, evergreen tree
Height	up to 17m
Habitat	mountains, rocky places
Flowering	March – April
Fruiting	ripens in second year

TRUNK AND CROWN

Trunk	straight or sometimes forked
Bark	reddish brown, becoming grey and bleached, scaly
Crown	narrowly conical, becoming broad and irregular
Twigs	*c*1mm thick, 4-angled, scaly, branching irregularly

LEAVES

Buds	tiny, concealed by leaves
Leaves	adult leaves scale-like, paired, in 4 ranks, overlapping, 1.5–2mm, oval or angular, mostly without gland, pointed, tips spread apart, uniformly dull, grey-green, not pale-edged, hairless; stalkless; juvenile leaves paired, rarely present
Stipules	absent

FLOWERS AND FRUIT

Flowers	♂ and ♀ on same tree or sometimes different trees
♂	cone 4–5mm, at shoot-tip
♀	cone 2–3mm, on small shoot
Fruit	solitary berry-like cone, 7–12mm, globular, waxy when young, ripening dark reddish brown to almost black
Seeds	usually 1 or 2, separate

White Willow *Salix alba*

silvery

deciduous

brown, pliant

fruiting catkin

rough bark

♂ catkin

♀ catkin

sparsely hairy above

leaves with catkins

finely toothed

Tall and graceful, this species is commonly found by water. It is readily identified by its leaves, which are silvery and silky, and slender with a very finely toothed edge. Near habitation many are pollarded; cut at head height they produce a regular supply of small timber. *Status:* native, common to most of Europe, but rarer in the extreme south; widely planted for ornament and stabilizing river banks. *Similar trees:* two subspecies are often cultivated. Cricket-bat Willow has purplish twigs and dull, bluish leaves becoming almost hairless. Golden Willow has orange or yellow twigs.

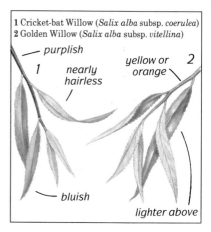

1 Cricket-bat Willow (*Salix alba* subsp. *coerulea*)
2 Golden Willow (*Salix alba* subsp. *vitellina*)

purplish

nearly hairless

1

yellow or orange

2

bluish

lighter above

WHITE WILLOW

Type	deciduous tree
Height	10–25m
Habitat	rivers, damp or wet soils
Flowering	April–May
Fruiting	July

TRUNK AND CROWN

Trunk	mostly upright, often pollarded
Bark	thick ridges, dark grey-brown
Crown	young narrow; old broad; branches angled upwards
Twigs	silkily hairy, becoming smooth, pliant, greenish brown

LEAVES

Buds	egg-shaped, pointed, hairy
Leaves	on alternate side of shoot, 6–10cm, narrowly spear-shaped or elliptical, with pointed tip, small, equal teeth and tapered base, silkily hairy above becoming almost hairless, with greyish, matted hairs below; stalk 5–8mm, hairy
Stipules	very slender, soon falling

FLOWERS AND FRUIT

Flowers	♂ and ♀ catkins on separate trees, opening with leaves
♂	cylindrical catkin, 4–6cm, of tiny flowers, almost upright
Stamens	2 per ♂ flower, separate, yellow
♀	catkin 3–4cm
Stigmas	2, forked, on short style
Ovaries	1 per ♀ flower; stalkless
Fruit	catkin of small capsules, each *c*4mm, releasing seeds
Seeds	with tuft of cottony hairs

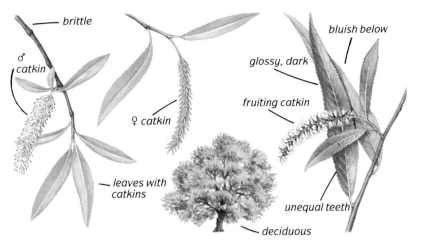

brittle

♂ catkin

♀ catkin

leaves with catkins

bluish below

glossy, dark

fruiting catkin

unequal teeth

deciduous

Similar to White Willow, this large tree is distinguished by glossy, unevenly toothed leaves. If twisted, brittle twigs crack at the base. In water, Crack Willow produces fine, red, coral-like rootlets. *Status:* native or planted, common in much of Europe. *Similar trees:* one of the hybrids between White Willow and Crack Willow, Basford Willow differs from the former by glossy leaves and short catkin scales, and the latter by reddish twigs and slender, fine-toothed leaves. Bay Willow has broad, glossy leaves, which are sticky and fragrant when young, and male flowers with five or more stamens.

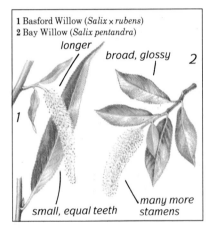

1 Basford Willow (*Salix* x *rubens*)
2 Bay Willow (*Salix pentandra*)

longer

broad, glossy

2

1

small, equal teeth

many more stamens

CRACK WILLOW

Type	deciduous tree
Height	10–18m
Habitat	deep, moist soils, by rivers
Flowering	April–May
Fruiting	June–July

TRUNK AND CROWN

Trunk	stout, often pollarded
Bark	thick ridges, dull grey
Crown	broad, conical or domed; widely branched
Twigs	brittle, becoming smooth, glossy, greenish brown

LEAVES

Buds	conical, yellowish brown
Leaves	9–15cm, narrowly spear-shaped with slender tip, coarse, uneven teeth, wedge-shaped base, sparse hairs that soon fall, glossy, dark green above, bluish below; stalk 5–15mm
Stipules	3–8mm, slender, soon falling

FLOWERS AND FRUIT

Flowers	♂ and ♀ catkins on separate trees, in clusters on leafy shoots
♂	catkin 4–6cm, cylindrical; scales 2–3mm, sparsely hairy
Stamens	2, rarely 3 per ♂ flower, separate, yellow
♀	with larger scales than ♂
Stigmas	2, each 2-lobed; style short
Ovaries	1, hairless
Fruit	catkin of capsules, each 4–5mm, or commonly sterile, some releasing seeds
Seeds	with cottony hairs

Goat Willow *Salix caprea*

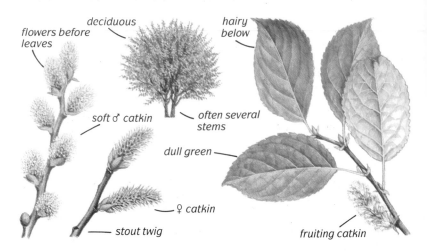

flowers before leaves

deciduous

soft ♂ catkin

often several stems

dull green

♀ catkin

stout twig

hairy below

fruiting catkin

More commonly a shrub than a tree, this broad-leaved plant is most distinctive in spring, when leafless shoots are smothered with short, soft catkins. Stripped twigs have distinct raised lines. *Status:* native and common to much of Europe. *Similar trees:* Grey Willow has dark brown twigs and narrower, more oblong leaves, which are grey-green above and whitish grey with short hairs below. It is common through much of Europe except for the west, where it is replaced by Rusty Willow. This has rougher leaves, which are glossy and dark green above with reddish hairs below.

1 Grey Willow (*Salix cinerea* subsp. *cinerea*)
2 Rusty Willow (*Salix cinerea* subsp. *oleifolia*)

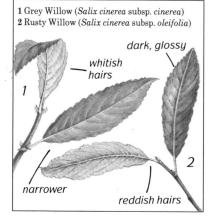

dark, glossy

whitish hairs

narrower

reddish hairs

	GOAT WILLOW
Type	deciduous shrub or tree
Height	rarely more than 10m
Habitat	hedgerows, woods, scrub
Flowering	March–April
Fruiting	May–June

	TRUNK AND CROWN
Trunk	often several
Bark	fissured, greyish brown
Crown	broad, rather open branches mostly angled upwards
Twigs	thick, stiff

	LEAVES
Buds	egg-shaped, blunt, glossy
Leaves	5–12cm, oval, elliptical or oblong, with tip shortly pointed, edge often wavy, toothed, base wedge-shaped or rounded, dull green above with sparse hairs, grey-green below with thick, soft hairs; stalk 1–2.5cm, stiff, hairy
Stipules	8–12mm, ear-shaped, toothed

	FLOWERS AND FRUIT
Flowers	♂ and ♀ catkins on separate trees, near twig tip, before leaves
♂	catkins 15–25mm, egg-shaped or shortly cylindrical; scales broadly oval, blackish with silvery grey hairs
Stamens	2 per ♂ flower, yellow
♀	catkins similar to ♂
Stigmas	2, each often 2-lobed
Ovaries	1, 4–5mm, densely hairy
Fruit	catkins of small capsules, each capsule *c*10mm, splitting to release seeds
Seeds	with cottony hairs

An ornamental species, Violet Willow has dark, reddish twigs overlaid with a bluish, waxy layer, which gradually rubs off. Crimson buds open as large, softly hairy catkins before the narrow leaves appear. It is often grown for winter colour. *Status:* native, scattered across northern and central Europe; widely planted for ornament. *Similar trees: S. acutifolia* has more slender twigs, and narrower leaves with a long point and more veins. Almost invariably a shrub, Purple Willow has mostly paired leaves; each male flower has two red stamens fused as one. The hybrid between Violet and Purple Willows (*S. × calliantha*) makes a small tree.

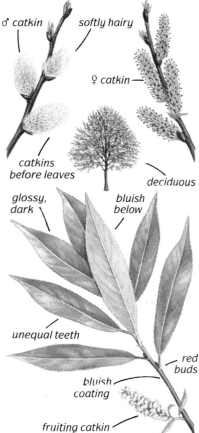

♂ catkin softly hairy

♀ catkin

catkins before leaves

deciduous

glossy, dark

bluish below

unequal teeth

red buds

bluish coating

fruiting catkin

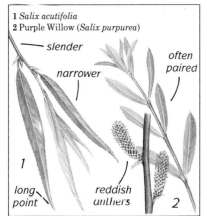

1 *Salix acutifolia*
2 Purple Willow (*Salix purpurea*)

slender

narrower

often paired

1

long point

reddish anthers

2

VIOLET WILLOW

Type	deciduous shrub or tree
Height	6–8m (max 12m)
Habitat	damp places
Flowering	February–March
Fruiting	May–June

TRUNK AND CROWN

Trunk	often several
Bark	rather smooth, greyish brown
Crown	rounded; branches upright or spreading
Twigs	glossy, dark reddish brown with bluish waxy covering

LEAVES

Buds	pointed, flattened, dark red
Leaves	on alternate sides of stem, 7–12cm, oblong or oval, leathery, shortly pointed, edge toothed, base wedge-shaped, slightly woolly but becoming hairless, glossy dark green above, bluish below; stalk 7–20mm, grooved above
Stipules	5–12mm, oval, toothed

FLOWERS AND FRUIT

Flowers	♂ and ♀ catkins on separate trees, before the leaves
♂	catkin 2–4cm, cylindrical, stalkless; scales *c*2mm, oval, blackish, silkily hairy
Stamens	2, separate; anthers yellow
♀	catkin smaller than ♂
Stigmas	2 per ♀ flower
Ovaries	1 per ♀ flower, hairless
Fruit	catkin of small, narrowly egg-shaped capsules, each *c*4mm
Seeds	with tuft of cottony hairs

Osier   *Salix viminalis*

Commonly lining rivers and streams, this willow forms a large shrub or tree. Plants are cut annually to provide slender shoots, which are stripped of bark for basket-weaving. Male plants are attractive in spring when covered with furry, yellow catkins. *Status:* native mainly to central and western Europe; widely planted elsewhere. *Similar trees:* Hoary Willow has even narrower leaves with matt white, felted hairs below, curved catkins and a smooth ovary. Though easily distinguished by broader, toothed leaves, the fragrant Almond Willow is grown like Osier, as is the hybrid (*S. × mollissima*) between these species.

branches turn upwards

not toothed

deciduous

fruiting catkin

dull green

edge turned under

1 Hoary Willow (*Salix elaeagnos*)
2 Almond Willow (*Salix triandra*)

very narrow

broader, toothed

curved

long catkin

♂ catkin

♀ catkin

	OSIER			under and often wavy, base wedge-shaped, dull green with few hairs above, silky, silvery hairs below; stalk rarely more than 1cm
Type	deciduous shrub or tree			
Height	3–6m, rarely 10m			
Habitat	usually near water			
Flowering	February–April			
Fruiting	May–June		**Stipules**	5–10mm, slender, soon falling
	TRUNK AND CROWN			**FLOWERS AND FRUIT**
Trunk	sometimes several		**Flowers**	♂ and ♀ catkins on different plants, before leaves appear
Bark	fissured, greyish brown			
Crown	usually narrow, top rounded; branches mostly upright		♂	catkin 15–30mm, egg-shaped or cylindrical; scales *c*2mm, oval, blunt, reddish brown, hairy
Twigs	long, pliant, hairy, becoming glossy yellowish brown			
			Stamens	2 per ♂ flower, yellow
	LEAVES		♀	catkin similar to ♂
Buds	3–7mm, egg-shaped, often blunt, hairy, becoming smooth		**Stigmas**	2, undivided; style slender
			Ovaries	1, densely hairy
Leaves	on alternate sides of stem, 10–18cm, narrow with long tip, edge not toothed but turned		**Fruit**	catkin of small, egg-shaped capsules, each to 6mm, releasing many seeds
			Seeds	with tuft of cottony hairs

Salix myrsinifolia **Dark-leaved Willow**

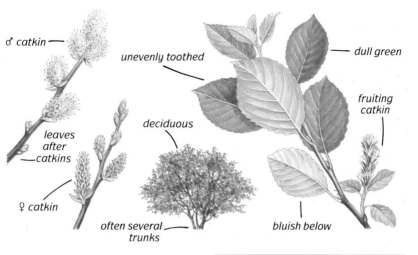

♂ catkin

unevenly toothed

dull green

leaves after catkins

deciduous

fruiting catkin

♀ catkin

often several trunks

bluish below

This very variable willow is more often a low, broad shrub than a small tree. It belongs to a group of species mainly of northern regions and occurs in mountains, though not at the highest altitudes. Like other willows, this species is food for larvae of many butterflies and moths. *Status:* native to northern and central Europe. *Similar trees:* Tea-leaved Willow has glossy brown, usually hairless twigs, tougher leaves, which are glossy green above, smaller stipules, and the ovary is hairy. Catkins are usually produced with the leaves. It forms hybrids (*S. × tetrapla*) with Dark-leaved Willow.

Tea-leaved Willow (*Salix phylicifolia*)

leaves with catkins

tougher, glossy

glossy, hairless

DARK-LEAVED WILLOW

Type	deciduous shrub or small tree
Height	1–4m
Habitat	by streams, pools, in mountains
Flowering	April–May
Fruiting	July–August

TRUNK AND CROWN

Trunk	often several, slender
Bark	slightly fissured, dark grey
Crown	broad; rather widely branched
Twigs	slender, usually with whitish hairs, dull brownish green

LEAVES

Buds	blunt, shortly hairy
Leaves	alternating on stem, 2–6.5cm, oval or elliptical, shortly pointed, unevenly toothed, base wedge-shaped or rounded, sparsely hairy to hairless, dull green above, bluish below; stalk usually less than 1cm
Stipules	rather large, ear-shaped

FLOWERS AND FRUIT

Flowers	♂ and ♀ catkins on separate trees, produced before leaves
♂	catkin 15–40mm, cylindrical; scales 1–2.5mm, dark, thinly hairy
Stamens	2 per ♂ flower, separate, yellow
♀	catkin less compact than ♂
Stigmas	2 mostly forked; style slender
Ovaries	1 per ♀ flower, hairless
Fruit	catkin of small, tapered capsules, each 5–7mm, releasing seeds
Seeds	many, each with long hairs

Golden Weeping-willow

Salix × sepulcralis
nv. *chrysocoma*

A graceful weeping tree, so commonly planted that at times it appears native. It is easily distinguished from other willow species by its pendulous shoots, yellow twigs and bright, yellowish green leaves. For a long time it was treated as a variant of White Willow but it is a hybrid between the golden form of that species and the following Chinese species. Largely sterile, it is propagated by cuttings. *Status:* cultivated origin; widely grown for ornament. *Similar trees:* Chinese Weeping-willow has brown twigs and short, almost stalkless catkins. Relatively tender and short-lived in western Europe, it is much less planted.

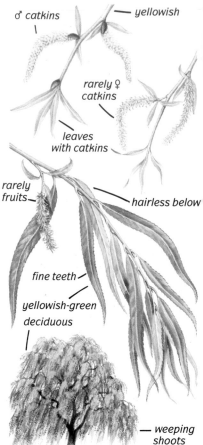

♂ catkins — yellowish
rarely ♀ catkins
leaves with catkins
rarely fruits
hairless below
fine teeth
yellowish-green
deciduous
weeping shoots

Chinese Weeping-willow (*Salix babylonica*)

brown
shorter

	GOLDEN WEEPING-WILLOW
Type	deciduous tree
Height	8–22m
Habitat	mainly wet places
Flowering	April

TRUNK AND CROWN

Trunk	stout, upright
Bark	network of fissures and ridges, pale greyish brown
Crown	broad, domed; branches mostly angled upwards
Twigs	slender, weeping, greenish yellow; sparse hairs soon fall

LEAVES

Buds	slender, pointed, brown, more or less hairless
Leaves	on alternate sides of stem, 7–12cm, narrowly spear-shaped with slender tip, teeth fine and even, base wedge-shaped, sparsely hairy, becoming hairless, bright, yellowish green above, paler below; stalk up to 8mm, rather stout
Stipules	small, toothed, soon falling

FLOWERS AND FRUIT

Flowers	usually ♂ catkins only, with leaves
♂	catkins 3–6cm, slender, cylindrical, pendulous, yellow; scales *c*2mm, oblong or oval, thinly hairy
Stamens	2 per ♂ flower, separate
♀	sometimes a few ♀ catkins
Stigmas	2, each forked; style short
Ovaries	1, stalkless, hairless
Fruit	usually sterile

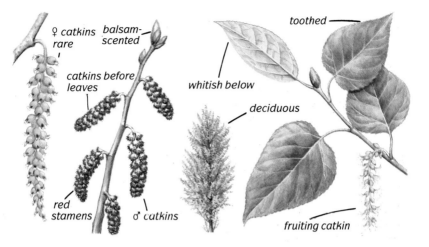

After a spring shower, the balsamic fragrance of Balsam-poplars pervades the air for many metres around; thick resin exuded by opening buds is the source of this scent. Of rapid growth, this handsome tree soon makes a useful screen or shelter. *Status:* introduced from northern North America; widely planted for ornament and timber.
Similar trees: several other poplars have scented buds and are white beneath the leaves. Eastern Balsam-poplar produces many suckers; their oval leaves have a rounded base, and the stalk is up to 7cm long. Balm-of-Gilead has a more slender tip and a heart-shaped base to the leaf.

1 Eastern Balsam-poplar (*Populus balsamifera*)
2 Balm-of-Gilead (*Populus candicans*)

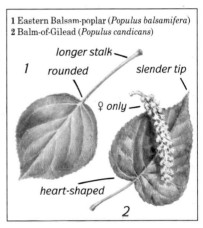

	WESTERN BALSAM-POPLAR
Type	deciduous tree
Height	to 35m (60m in North America)
Habitat	roadsides, plantations
Flowering	March–April
Fruiting	May–June

TRUNK AND CROWN

Trunk	upright or angled upwards
Bark	smooth, greenish grey, dark greyish brown below, fissured
Crown	narrow, conical; many main branches, angled upwards
Twigs	angular or rounded, becoming smooth, yellowish grey

LEAVES

Buds	mostly 10–15mm, egg-shaped, pointed, glossy, reddish brown, very sticky, fragrant
Leaves	on alternate sides of stem, 5–15cm (max. 23cm), oval, thick-textured, shortly pointed with shallow, blunt teeth, base broadly wedge-shaped or squarish, dark, glossy green above, whitish beneath; stalk 1.5–4cm, stout, grooved above

FLOWERS AND FRUIT

Flowers	♂ and ♀ catkins on separate trees, produced before leaves
♂	catkin 5–9cm, red, scales 3–5mm, fringed, sparsely hairy
Stamens	20–60 per ♂ flower
♀	catkin 6–10cm, green, rarely produced in western Europe
Stigmas	2, broad, irregularly lobed
Ovaries	1, egg-shaped, hairy
Fruit	catkin 15–20cm, of small capsules, each splitting open
Seeds	many, each with tuft of hairs

White Poplar *Populus alba*

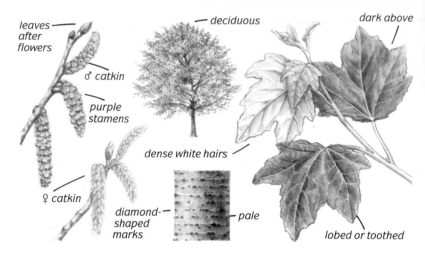

leaves after flowers

♂ catkin

purple stamens

♀ catkin

deciduous

diamond-shaped marks

dense white hairs

pale

dark above

lobed or toothed

Easily recognized by the dark leaves which flash white beneath in the breeze, and the pale grey bark of the upper trunk handsomely marked with blackish diamonds. Leaves of strong, sucker shoots are maple-like and lobed, though other leaves have irregular teeth. *Status:* mainly central and eastern Europe; commonly planted in the west for ornament and shelter. *Similar trees:* Grey Poplar is generally considered to be a hybrid between White Poplar and Aspen, though some regard it as a species. The leaves are grey beneath, becoming hairless, and the edge has blunt, wavy teeth.

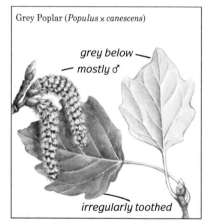

Grey Poplar (*Populus* x *canescens*)

grey below

mostly ♂

irregularly toothed

	WHITE POPLAR		
Type	deciduous tree		
Height	15–25m		
Habitat	mainly wet places, sometimes in sandy coastal areas		
Flowering	February–March		
Fruiting	May–June		

TRUNK AND CROWN

Trunk	often leaning; sucker shoots
Bark	pale greyish brown, marked with blackish diamonds, base blackish and coarsely fissured
Crown	irregular, broadest near top
Twigs	densely hairy, gradually becoming smooth and brown

LEAVES

Buds	c5mm, egg-shaped, pointed, hairy at base becoming smooth
Leaves	on alternate sides of stem, 3– 9cm, broadly oval, blunt with irregular, blunt lobes, those of sucker shoots often deeply lobed, thinly hairy becoming smooth and dark green above, white with thick hairs below; stalk 5–6cm, rounded, hairy

FLOWERS AND FRUIT

Flowers	♂ and ♀ catkins on separate trees, before leaves
♂	catkin 4–7cm; scales oval, toothed, pale brown
Stamens	5–10 per ♂ flower, purple
♀	catkin 3–5cm
Stigmas	2, each divided into 2 lobes
Ovaries	1, egg-shaped, hairless
Fruit	catkin 8–10cm, of small capsules, each c3mm, shortly stalked, releasing seeds
Seeds	many, with cottony hairs

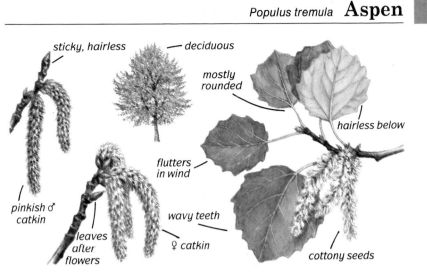

sticky, hairless — deciduous

mostly rounded

hairless below

flutters in wind

pinkish ♂ catkin

wavy teeth

leaves after flowers

♀ catkin

cottony seeds

Fluttering ceaselessly in the breeze, leaves of Aspen make a curious clattering sound. It is a remarkably widespread species, from western Europe to Japan and the tree limit of the tundra to the Mediterranean region. *Status:* native, most of Europe. *Similar trees:* two North American species are cultivated. Big-toothed Aspen has leaves with a squarish or wedge-shaped base and large, sharper teeth and greyish hairs on the buds, young twigs, and beneath the young leaves. American Aspen has finely toothed leaves and yellower bark; its hybrid with Aspen is sometimes grown.

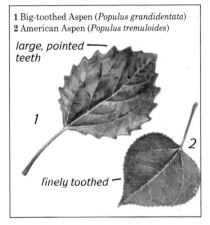

1 Big-toothed Aspen (*Populus grandidentata*)
2 American Aspen (*Populus tremuloides*)

large, pointed teeth

1

2

finely toothed

	ASPEN		
Type	deciduous tree		circular, blunt with irregular, blunt teeth, base squarish to almost heart-shaped, dark green, paler beneath, turning clear yellow in autumn; stalk 4–7cm, flattened
Height	up to 20m		
Habitat	near water, often on mountains		
Flowering	February–March		
Fruiting	May		

	TRUNK AND CROWN		FLOWERS AND FRUIT	
Trunk	slender, often several	**Flowers**	♂ and ♀ catkins on separate trees, before leaves
Bark	smooth, greyish brown above; darker, fissured towards base	♂	catkin 5–8cm cylindrical; scales 5–6mm, broad, fringed, dark brown, with white hairs
Crown	usually broad, much-branched		
Twigs	with raised leaf-scars, grey-brown, becoming hairless	**Stamens**	5–12 per ♂ flower, purplish
		♀	catkin like ♂
	LEAVES	**Stigmas**	2, cut into irregular lobes
		Ovaries	1, egg-shaped, rough
Buds	most c5mm, flower-buds larger, egg-shaped, hairless, glossy brown, slightly sticky	**Fruit**	catkin up to 12cm, of small capsules, each c4mm, short-stalked, releasing seeds
Leaves	alternately arranged, 1.5–8cm, rarely 15cm, oval to nearly	**Seeds**	many, with cottony hairs

Black-poplar *Populus nigra*

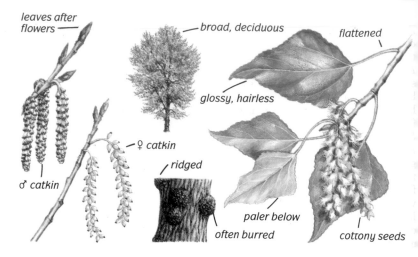

leaves after flowers —

broad, deciduous

flattened

glossy, hairless

♀ catkin

ridged

♂ catkin

paler below

often burred

cottony seeds

Typically broad and rounded, this tree is better known as its narrowly columnar variant, the Lombardy Poplar. Both trees have leaves which are triangular or shaped like an ace-of-spades. *Status:* native to central and southern Europe; widely planted for shelter and timber. *Similar trees:* Lombardy Poplar has a very slender crown; typically male, trees with female catkins or a broader crown are probably crosses with Black Poplar. Berlin Poplar, a hybrid between Lombardy Poplar and *P. laurifolia*, has angular twigs, and leaves with a whiter underside, a wedge-shaped base and a rounded stalk.

1 Lombardy Poplar (*Populus nigra* cv. 'Italica')
2 Berlin Poplar (*Populus × berolinensis*)

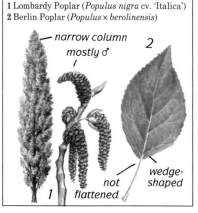

narrow column
mostly ♂

2

wedge-shaped

not flattened

1

	BLACK-POPLAR	
Type	deciduous tree	
Height	20–35m	
Habitat	damp soils of river valleys; grown by roads, in plantations	
Flowering	March–April	
Fruiting	May–June	

TRUNK AND CROWN

Trunk	often with swellings and burrs	
Bark	grey-brown, coarsely fissured	
Crown	broad, irregular; branches often curve downwards	
Twigs	more or less hairless, rounded, yellowish brown	

LEAVES

Buds	to 10mm, egg-shaped, pointed, glossy brown, sticky	
Leaves	on alternate sides of stem, 4–10cm, triangular or broadly oval with slender point, edge with small, rounded teeth, base squarish or broadly wedge-shaped, hairless, dark, glossy green above, paler below; stalk 3–7cm, flattened	

FLOWERS AND FRUIT

Flowers	♂ and ♀ catkins on separate trees, before leaves	
♂	catkin 3–5cm, cylindrical; scales 1–2mm, fringed, green or brownish, soon falling	
Stamens	12–30 per ♂ flower, red	
♀	catkins more slender than ♂	
Stigmas	2 per ♀ flower, each 2-lobed	
Ovaries	1, egg-shaped, hairless	
Fruit	catkin 9–15cm, of capsules, each 5–6mm, releasing seeds	
Seeds	many, each with tuft of cottony hairs	

A large, fast-growing hybrid, so commonly planted that it often replaces the native Black Poplar. That and an American species have produced several such hybrids, one of the most widespread being 'Serotina', a male tree illustrated here. *Status:* of garden origin; planted for ornament, shelter and pulp-wood. *Similar trees:* Cottonwood is the American parent. The leaves have small glands and hairy, sharp teeth; male flowers have up to 60 stamens. Two female hybrids are widely grown. With wider branching and a rounded crown, Maryland Poplar produces masses of cottony seeds. Railway Poplar has mostly sterile fruit.

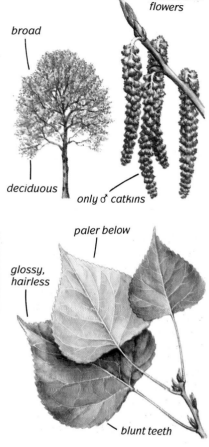

leaves after flowers

broad

deciduous

only ♂ catkins

paler below

glossy, hairless

blunt teeth

1 Cottonwood (*P.deltoides*); **2** Maryland Poplar (*P. × canadensis* cv. 'Marilandica'); **3** Railway Poplar (*P. × canadensis* cv. 'Regenerata')

♀, much seed

♂, more stamens

♀, many sterile

HYBRID BLACK-POPLAR

Type	deciduous tree
Height	often more than 30m
Habitat	roadsides, parks, plantations
Flowering	March – April

TRUNK AND CROWN

Trunk	usually with long, unbranched base
Bark	coarsely fissured, without burrs, greyish brown
Crown	broadest above, flattish topped; lower branches heavy, angled upwards, diverging rather narrowly
Twigs	smooth, glossy greenish grey, often angular

LEAVES

Buds	10–20mm, narrowly egg-shaped, tapered to slender point, glossy greenish brown, sticky
Leaves	on alternate sides of stem, 6–10cm, almost triangular, sharply pointed, with distinct, blunt teeth, base squarish or slightly heart-shaped, sometimes rounded, hairless, bright, glossy green above, paler below, young leaves tinged reddish brown; stalk 4–10cm, flattened sideways

FLOWERS AND FRUIT

Flowers	♂ catkins, before leaves
♂	catkin 3–6cm, cylindrical; scales 4–5mm, broad, fringed, purplish-tipped
Stamens	20–25 per ♂ flower, anthers crimson
Fruit	not produced

Alder *Alnus glutinosa*

A waterside tree, Alder is identified by woody, cone-like, fruiting catkins, which persist for much of the year. Production of new shoots from suckers often results in bushy growth. Alder has the rare ability to turn nitrogen from the air into valuable plant food, thanks to root nodules containing bacteria. *Status:* native to most of Europe; sometimes planted. *Similar trees:* lacking sticky twigs, Grey Alder has grey, smooth bark, pointed leaves that are grey below, and stalkless female catkins. Italian Alder has leaves with shallow, rounded teeth and a solitary female flower or rarely up to 3 in a cluster.

stalked

blunt

small ♀ catkin

old cones

stalked

long ♂ catkin

deciduous

toothed

blunt or notched

clustered

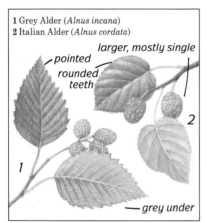

1 Grey Alder (*Alnus incana*)
2 Italian Alder (*Alnus cordata*)

larger, mostly single

pointed

rounded teeth

grey under

	ALDER
Type	deciduous tree
Height	up to 20m (rarely 35m)
Habitat	mainly wet places
Flowering	February–March
Fruiting	October–November

TRUNK AND CROWN

Trunk	often several
Bark	dark brown, fissured
Crown	conical or rounded, open
Twigs	sticky when young, hairless, turning purplish brown

LEAVES

Buds	5–7mm, blunt; stalked
Leaves	on alternate sides of stem, 4–10cm, elliptical to almost circular, blunt or notched, doubly toothed, base wedge-shaped or rounded, 5–8 pairs of veins, hairless where main veins diverge, dark green above and below; stalk 2–3.5cm
Stipules	soon falling

FLOWERS AND FRUIT

Flowers	♂ and ♀, before leaves
♂	3–6 catkins in cluster, each 2–6cm, opening yellow; 3 flowers to each bract
Stamens	4 per ♂ flower
♀	cluster of 3–5 catkins, each 5–7mm, purplish, stalked; 2 tiny flowers to each bract
Stigmas	2 per ♀ flower
Ovaries	1 per ♀ flower
Fruit	cluster of 3–5 woody, cone-like catkins, each 10–30mm, egg-shaped, green, turning brown; stalked; scales 5-lobed
Seeds	nut-like, with narrow wing

A shrub that only occasionally reaches tree proportions, this is usually much smaller than the more widespread European species. Common in the Alps, Green Alder often forms extensive thickets. It is a variable species and several subspecies are sometimes distinguished by leaf characters. *Status:* native in mountains of central and south-eastern Europe; planted elsewhere. *Similar trees:* another small Alder, introduced from North America and often naturalized, Smooth Alder produces catkins before its leaves and has sticky twigs, with up to 10 fruiting catkins in a head, the upper of which are stalkless.

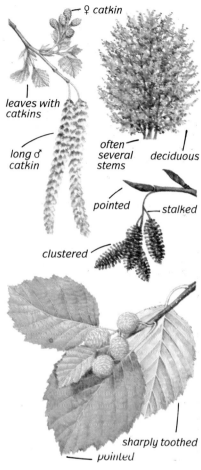

♀ catkin

leaves with catkins

long ♂ catkin

often several stems

deciduous

pointed

stalked

clustered

Smooth Alder (*Alnus rugosa*)

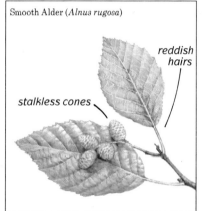

reddish hairs

stalkless cones

sharply toothed

pointed

	GREEN ALDER		
Type	deciduous shrub or tree		variably pointed, sharply, doubly toothed, base wedge-shaped or notched, usually with tufts of hairs below; stalk 8–12mm
Height	1–5m		
Habitat	wet places		
Flowering	March–April	**Stipules**	small, soon falling
Fruiting	September–October		
	TRUNK AND CROWN		**FLOWERS AND FRUIT**
Trunk	often several	**Flowers**	♂ and ♀ together, with leaves
Bark	rough, brown	♂	small cluster of long catkins, each 5–12cm, yellowish
Crown	irregular, rounded		
Twigs	greenish brown or reddish brown, sometimes minutely hairy	**Perianth**	usually 4-lobed
		Stamens	4 per ♂ flower
		♀	cluster of 3–5 catkins, each 6–10mm, reddish, stalked
	LEAVES		
Buds	12–15mm, conical, pointed, glossy reddish brown; stalkless	**Stigmas**	1 per ♀ flower
		Ovaries	2 per ♀ flower
Leaves	on alternate sides of stem, sticky when young, 3–9cm, elliptical to almost circular,	**Fruit**	cluster of 3–5 woody, cone-like catkins, each 8–15mm, egg-shaped, stalked, blackish
		Seeds	nut-like with papery wing

Silver Birch *Betula pendula*

deciduous

♀ catkin

♂ catkin

unequal teeth

smooth, white

fruiting catkin

winged seed

twigs droop

3-lobed bract

Silver Birch's graceful form is best seen in spring, when the slender, silvery trunk and boughs are barely concealed by a filigree of pale green. A colonizer of treeless wastes, it was important in establishing northern Europe's forests after the last Ice Age. *Status:* native to most of Europe; planted for ornament. *Similar trees:* Downy Birch has hairy, stiffer twigs, leaves with more equal teeth, catkin scales with side-lobes angled forwards, and narrowly winged nutlets. Paper-bark Birch has papery, creamy-white or pink bark, larger leaves with unequal teeth, and catkin scales with narrowly diverging lobes.

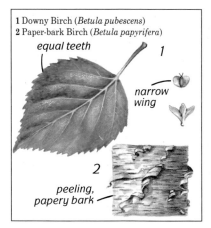

1 Downy Birch (*Betula pubescens*)
2 Paper-bark Birch (*Betula papyrifera*)

equal teeth

1

narrow wing

2

peeling, papery bark

	SILVER BIRCH	
Type	deciduous tree	
Height	up to 30m	
Habitat	light soils, often where forest is cleared or wasteland	
Flowering	April–May	
Fruiting	July–August	
	TRUNK AND CROWN	
Trunk	slender, forked above	
Bark	smooth, silvery-white, black lenticels above, often peeling, blackish and fissured below	
Crown	narrow or broad, light; branches gradually arch down	
Twigs	slender, hanging, brown, with resin-glands	
	LEAVES	
Buds	long, pointed, not sticky	
Leaves	alternating along stem, 2–7cm, triangular, thin, pointed, sharply, doubly toothed, base squarish, yellow in autumn, almost hairless; stalked	
Stipules	small, soon falling	
	FLOWERS AND FRUIT	
Flowers	♂ and ♀ flowers on same plant	
♂	2–4 catkins at tip of twig, 3–6cm, purplish brown, becoming yellow with pollen	
Stamens	2 per ♂ flower	
♀	catkin at leaf-base, brownish	
Stigmas	2 per ♀ flower	
Ovaries	1 per ♀ flower, 2-celled	
Fruit	catkin 15–35mm; scales 3-lobed, middle lobe narrow, side lobes curving backwards and outwards	
Seeds	seed-like nutlet with 2 wings 2–3 times as broad as nutlet	

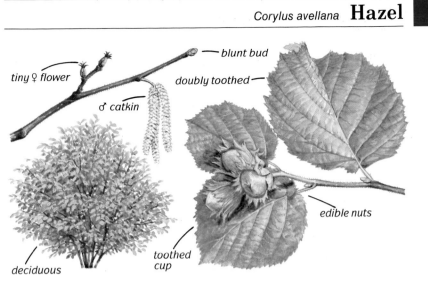

tiny ♀ flower

♂ catkin

blunt bud

doubly toothed

edible nuts

deciduous

toothed cup

At its most striking in late winter when the bright yellow catkins are a welcome sight, Hazel is more often a shrub than a tree. It is frequently coppiced, and the pliant poles and rods were formerly used in building. Large, edible nuts are sought by squirrels, mice, jays and pheasants. *Status:* native to most of Europe except the extreme north; planted for hedging, fruit or ornament. *Similar trees:* usually a tree, Turkish Hazel has more lobed leaves and the cup beneath the nut has narrower, spiky lobes. Filbert is grown for its larger, edible nuts, which are enclosed by a longer cup.

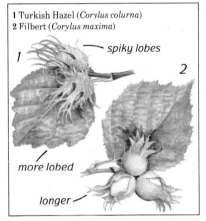

1 Turkish Hazel (*Corylus colurna*)
2 Filbert (*Corylus maxima*)

spiky lobes

1

2

more lobed

longer

HAZEL	
Type	deciduous shrub or sometimes tree
Height	2–6m (rarely 8m)
Habitat	woods, hedgerows, scrub
Flowering	January–March
Fruiting	September–October
TRUNK AND CROWN	
Trunk	often several
Bark	brown, smooth, slightly peeling
Crown	broad, branches slender
Twigs	dull green or brown, with reddish, gland-tipped hairs
LEAVES	
Buds	c4mm, egg-shaped, blunt
Leaves	alternating on stem, 5–12cm, nearly circular, narrowly pointed, doubly toothed, sometimes slightly lobed, base notched, 6–8 pairs of veins, slightly hairy, especially below; stalk 8–15mm, stickily hairy
Stipules	oblong, blunt, soon falling
FLOWERS AND FRUIT	
Flowers	♂ and ♀ flowers, before leaves
♂	slender, hanging catkin, 2–8cm, turning yellow with pollen, 1 flower per bract
Stamens	3–5 per ♂ flower
♀	small cluster, bud-like, 4–5mm
Stigmas	2 per ♀ flower, bright red
Ovaries	1 per ♀ flower, 2-celled
Fruit	1–4 rounded, brown, woody-shelled nuts, each 15–20mm, in greenish cup about equalling nut, cut to middle into irregularly toothed lobes

Hornbeam *Carpinus betulus*

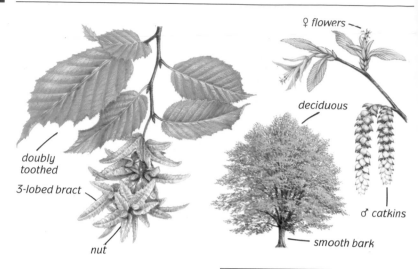

♀ *flowers*

deciduous

doubly toothed

3-lobed bract

nut

♂ catkins

smooth bark

A graceful tree, with smooth, grey bark, upswept branches and dark, toothed foliage; it is easily identified by distinctive three-lobed bracts in the fruiting head. In hedges, it responds well to clipping and keeps leaves in winter, much like Beech. Hornbeam is sometimes pollarded or coppiced, and has a hard, fine-grained timber. *Status:* native; widespread except in much of northern and western Mediterranean region; planted for timber, shelter or ornament. *Similar trees:* Eastern Hornbeam from south-eastern Europe is a smaller tree with the bract around the nut toothed, not lobed.

Eastern Hornbeam (*Carpinus orientalis*)

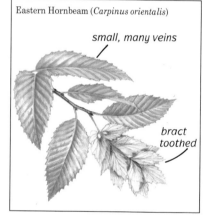

small, many veins

bract toothed

HORNBEAM	
Type	deciduous tree
Height	up to 30m
Habitat	woods, hedges; planted in streets and parks
Flowering	March–May
Fruiting	October–November
TRUNK AND CROWN	
Trunk	often twisted, fluted below
Bark	greyish brown, smooth, becomes deeply fissured below
Crown	broad, tapered above; branches angled upwards, sinuous
Twigs	slender, hairy, greyish brown
LEAVES	
Buds	6–7mm, slender, sharp-pointed, brown, hairy, against twig
Leaves	on alternate sides of stem, 4–10cm, oval, pointed, sharply and doubly toothed, base rounded, hairy beneath on veins, dark green, turning yellow in autumn, c15 pairs of veins; stalk c10mm, reddish
Stipules	small, soon falling
FLOWERS AND FRUIT	
Flowers	♂ and ♀ on same tree
♂	catkin 25–50mm, yellowish, scales red-tipped
♀	drooping catkin, 20–30mm, 2 flowers per 3-lobed bract, green with pink stigmas
Fruit	nut 6–8mm, 1–2 at base of 3-lobed bract, c35mm long, in cluster 5–15cm long
Seeds	1 per fruit, not released

A small, deciduous tree, with glossy, ribbed leaves. It is easily distinguished from all other native trees by the whitish, hop-like fruits. Hop-hornbeam is occasionally planted for ornament and, in southern Europe, it is used for its hard timber. *Status:* native to central and eastern parts of southern Europe; planted elsewhere for ornament.
Similar trees: Eastern Hop-hornbeam is native to eastern North America, but is sometimes cultivated in Europe for ornament. It differs in the larger, less ribbed leaves, which are downy beneath with hairy stalks; the twigs with gland-tipped hairs; and the fruits with longer, hairier stalks.

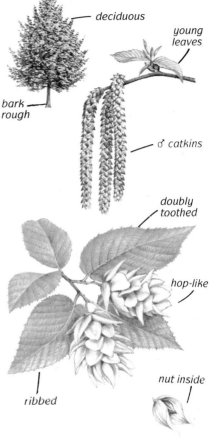

deciduous

young leaves

bark rough

♂ catkins

doubly toothed

hop-like

nut inside

ribbed

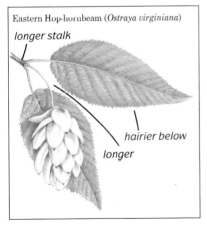

Eastern Hop-hornbeam (*Ostraya virginiana*)

longer stalk

hairier below

longer

HOP-HORNBEAM

Type	deciduous tree
Height	15–18m
Habitat	woods, hedges, parks
Flowering	April
Fruiting	September–October

TRUNK AND CROWN

Trunk	sometimes several
Bark	brown, scales fall leaving lighter patches, smooth, becoming fissured
Crown	conical, becoming rounded; branches angled upwards
Twigs	reddish brown, hairy, with tiny pores

LEAVES

Buds	egg-shaped, pointed, shiny
Leaves	on alternate sides of stem, 5–12cm, oval, pointed, sharply and doubly toothed, base wedge-shaped, hairy, becoming smooth, shiny dark green above, paler below, 12–15 pairs of veins; stalk 3–4mm, softly hairy
Stipules	small, soon falling

FLOWERS AND FRUIT

Flowers	♂ and ♀ on same tree
♂	catkin 3.5–10cm, hanging, yellow; 1 flower per bract
♀	catkin 20–30mm, drooping; 2 greenish flowers at bract base
Fruit	nut *c*5mm, at bract base, in hanging, white or pale brown head, 3–5cm long; elliptical bracts, 15–20mm, hairy, pointed
Seeds	1 per fruit, not released

Beech *Fagus sylvatica*

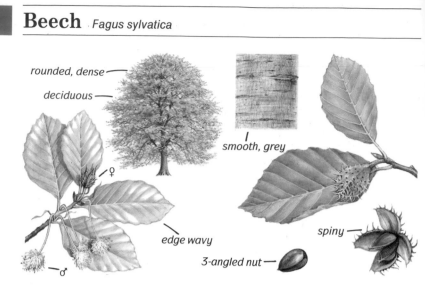

rounded, dense —
deciduous —
smooth, grey
edge wavy
spiny
3-angled nut —
♀
♂

Sunlight streaming through chinks in the sombre canopy, illuminating massive, smooth, grey trunks and arched boughs, brings a cathedral-like atmosphere to a mature stand of Beech. In the deep shade, spring-flowering bulbs grow in the litter of fallen leaves and fruits. *Status:* native mainly to western and central Europe; planted for ornament, shelter and timber. *Similar trees:* Copper Beech is a common variant with deep purplish foliage. Oriental Beech, from eastern Europe, has larger leaves, with up to 12 pairs of veins, and blunt lower spines on the fruit.

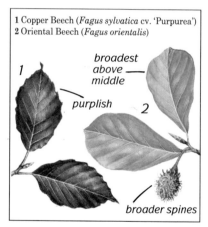

1 Copper Beech (*Fagus sylvatica* cv. 'Purpurea')
2 Oriental Beech (*Fagus orientalis*)

broadest above middle
purplish
broader spines

BEECH

Type	deciduous tree
Height	20–30m (rarely 50m)
Habitat	well-drained soils, especially on chalk hillsides
Flowering	April–May
Fruiting	September–October

TRUNK AND CROWN

Trunk	stout below, forked above
Bark	smooth, grey
Crown	broad, rounded, dense
Twigs	brownish grey

LEAVES

Buds	1–2cm, slender, pointed at both ends, reddish brown
Leaves	on alternate sides of stem, 4–9cm, elliptical or oval, pointed, edge not toothed, often wavy, with fine hairs, base wedge-shaped or rounded, 5–9 pairs of veins, pale green becoming dark, glossy green, turning orange or brown in autumn; stalk 5–15mm; young plants often with dead leaves over winter
Stipules	brown, papery, soon fall

FLOWERS AND FRUIT

Flowers	♂ and ♀ on same plant
♂	tiny, many, in tassel-like head on stalk 5–6cm long
Perianth	bell-shaped, with 4–7 lobes
Stamens	8–16 per ♂ flower
♀	usually 2 enclosed by stalked, cup-like structure of 4 bracts
Stigmas	3 per ♀ flower
Ovaries	1 per ♀ flower
Fruit	3-angled nut, 12–18mm, brown, 1 or 2 in spiny, woody casing, which splits into 4

Introduced from South America, this distant relative of the Beech is becoming popular both for ornament and timber. It is one of the so-called 'Southern Beeches' from the Southern Hemisphere, most of which are evergreen but some are deciduous. *Status:* introduced from Chile and Argentina; planted in western Europe, for ornament and timber. *Similar trees:* Raoul has stouter shoots with longer, pointed buds, finely toothed leaves with 14–18 pairs of veins, and bark with vertical fissures. Antarctic Beech is a shorter tree with smaller leaves usually having 4 pairs of veins.

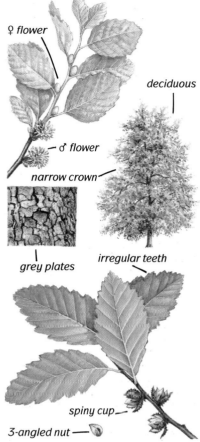

♀ flower

deciduous

♂ flower

narrow crown

grey plates

irregular teeth

1 Raoul (*Nothofagus procera*)
2 Antarctic Beech (*Nothofagus antarctica*)

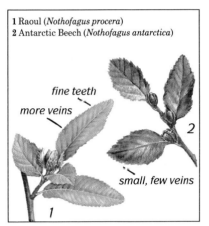

fine teeth

more veins

2

small, few veins

1

spiny cup

3-angled nut

	ROBLE BEECH	
Type	deciduous tree	
Height	20–30m	
Habitat	grown in small plantations, also parks and gardens	
Flowering	May	
Fruiting	September	
	TRUNK AND CROWN	
Trunk	forked above	
Bark	greenish grey, smooth, becoming cracked into small, squarish plates	
Crown	rather narrow, open; branches arch outwards	
Twigs	slender, with sparse, short hairs, regularly branching to either side	
	LEAVES	
Buds	4–6mm, egg-shaped, blunt, light brown, close to twig	
Leaves	on alternate sides of stem, 5–8cm, oval to almost oblong, blunt, sharply and irregularly toothed, base slightly unequal, 7–11 pairs of veins, hairless, dark green above, paler below, turning yellow or red in autumn; stalk 4–7mm	
Stipules	crinkled, soon falling	
	FLOWERS AND FRUIT	
Flowers	♂ and ♀ flowers on same plant	
♂	solitary, stalked	
Stamens	♂ with 30–40	
♀	tiny, pale green, at leaf-base	
Stigmas	3 per ♀ flower	
Ovaries	1 per ♀ flower	
Fruit	nut, 5–10mm, 3 in cup-like, shortly spiny casing which splits into 4	

Evergreen Oak *Quercus ilex*

Characteristic of the Mediterranean region, this tree has been taken to many other countries where it survives frost and keeps its dense foliage in winter. Usually like a small laurel, it has remarkably variable leaves, which are holly-like on sucker shoots. The tannin-rich bark was used by Ancient Greeks and Romans for tanning leather. *Status:* native to the Mediterranean region; much planted elsewhere for ornament and shelter. *Similar trees:* Cork Oak has toothed leaves with a wavy midrib and longer scales on the acorn cup. Rarely reaching tree size, Kermes Oak has spiny, hairless leaves and spiny scales on the acorn cup.

thick

♂ catkin

evergreen

grey below

broad, dense

small plates

greyish-hairy

scales pressed together

some leaves spiny

1 Cork Oak (*Quercus suber*)
2 Kermes Oak (*Quercus coccifera*)

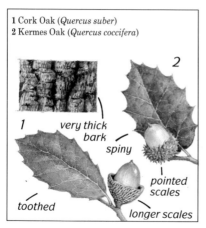

very thick bark

spiny

pointed scales

toothed

longer scales

EVERGREEN OAK		
Type	evergreen tree	
Height	up to 25m	
Habitat	forest, woodland; left in fields for shade; street tree	
Flowering	May–June	
Fruiting	September–October	
TRUNK AND CROWN		
Trunk	stout	
Bark	dark grey, cracking into small, squarish plates	
Crown	broad, domed, dense	
Twigs	grey-hairy, becoming hairless	
LEAVES		
Buds	egg-shaped, hairy	
Leaves	2–9cm, variable, oval to oblong, thick, edge unbroken or spiny-toothed on sucker shoots, base tapered or rounded, straight midrib with 7–11 pairs of veins, glossy, dark green above, greyish-hairy below; stalk 6–15mm	
Stipules	narrow, hairy, soon falling	
FLOWERS AND FRUIT		
Flowers	♂ and ♀ flowers on same plant	
♂	drooping catkins, 3–5cm	
Perianth	tiny, with 4–7 pointed lobes	
Stamens	6–12 per ♂ flower	
♀	spike of 1–4 flowers	
Stigmas	3–4 per ♀ flower	
Ovaries	1 per ♀ flower, 3-celled	
Fruit	nut (acorn) ripening in first year, 2–4cm, egg-shaped; cup greyish-hairy, covering less than half of fruit, scales oval, pressed closely together	

A robust, stately tree with large, lobed leaves, deeply fissured bark, and acorns that are situated on the leafless part of the twig. The timber was once used extensively for panelling walls. *Status:* native to central and southern Europe; planted elsewhere for ornament and shelter. *Similar trees:* Valonia Oak has smooth leaves with bristle-tipped lobes and a larger acorn cup with long, broad scales. Macedonian Oak has glossy, short-stalked leaves and an acorn cup with short, radiating scales. A cultivated hybrid of Turkey Oak and Cork Oak, Lucombe Oak resembles the former but has mostly evergreen leaves and thicker bark.

deciduous

deep fissures

broad crown

♀ flowers

♂ catkin

on leafless part

long scales

long stipules

blunt lobes

1 Valonia Oak (*Quercus macrolepis*)
2 Macedonian Oak (*Quercus trojana*)
3 Lucombe Oak (*Quercus × hispanica*)

1

bristle tip

wide scales

3

2

glossy, evergreen

shorter scales

TURKEY OAK			
Type	deciduous tree		
Height	20–35m		
Habitat	mainly on acid soils		
Flowering	May		
Fruiting	September–October		
TRUNK AND CROWN			
Trunk	stout, forked above		
Bark	dark grey, deeply fissured		
Crown	broad, domed; branches stout		
Twigs	brown, rough, sparsely hairy		
LEAVES			
Buds	oval, blunt, shortly hairy		
Leaves	alternate along stem, variable, 5–10cm, rarely 18cm, oblong or oval, pointed, 7–9 pairs of unequal, oval, blunt lobes, greyish-hairy becoming dull green, almost hairless but rough above, paler below, minutely hairy; stalk 8–25mm		
Stipules	to 25cm, very slender, prominent, remaining attached		
FLOWERS AND FRUIT			
Flowers	♂ and ♀ flowers on same tree		
♂	catkin, 5–8cm		
Perianth	tiny, 4–7 lobes		
Stamens	4 per ♂ flower		
♀	cluster of up to 5 flowers		
Stigmas	4 styles per ♀ flower		
Ovaries	1 per ♀ flower, 3-celled		
Fruit	nut (acorn), ripens in second year, 2–3.5cm, rarely 5cm, oblong, reddish brown, broad cup covers ½ nut, scales to 1cm, slender, spreading or bent back; stalk to 2cm		

Pedunculate Oak _Quercus robur_

usually broad — — deciduous

paired, blunt lobes

♀ flowers

stalked

short scales

♂ catkin

fissured   dark green

Renowned throughout Europe as a symbol of durability and longevity, this tree can survive for a thousand years. Light brown with silvery, close grain, the hard timber is valuable commercially; formerly it was exploited for architecture and ship-building. _Status:_ native to much of Europe except for the extreme north and parts of the Mediterranean region; planted for shelter, timber and ornament. _Similar trees:_ native to south-eastern Europe, _Q. pedunculiflora_ differs in having bluish green leaves with yellowish grey hairs below and warty acorn cups with yellowish hairs.

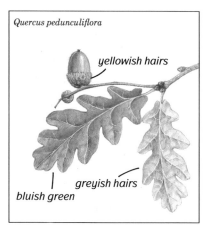

Quercus pedunculiflora

yellowish hairs

greyish hairs

bluish green

	PEDUNCULATE OAK		
Type	deciduous tree		green, hairless above, paler and usually hairless below; stalk 1–5mm
Height	20–35m, rarely 45m		
Habitat	woodland, especially lowland on heavy, fertile soils	**Stipules**	slender, soon falling
Flowering	April–May		**FLOWERS AND FRUIT**
Fruiting	September–October	**Flowers**	♂ and ♀ flowers on same tree
	TRUNK AND CROWN	♂	clustered catkins, 2–4cm
Trunk	stout, often short and burred	**Perianth**	tiny, 4–7 lobes
Bark	fissured, brownish grey	**Stamens**	6–8, rarely 12 per ♂ flower
Crown	usually broad, branches stout, wide-spreading, often sinuous	♀	1–5 flowers in stalked head
		Stigmas	3 per ♀ flower
Twigs	grey-brown, usually hairless	**Ovaries**	1 per ♀ flower, 3-celled
	LEAVES	**Fruit**	nut (acorn) ripens first year, 1.5–4cm, oblong or elliptical, brown; cup 1.5–2cm wide, $\frac{1}{3}$–$\frac{1}{2}$ covers nut; scales small, oval, flat, closely overlapping, shortly hairy; stalk 2–8cm
Buds	2–5mm, oval, blunt, hairless		
Leaves	alternate along stem, 5–12cm, more or less oblong, blunt, 4–7 pairs of blunt, unequal lobes, base with 2 ear-like lobes, dull		

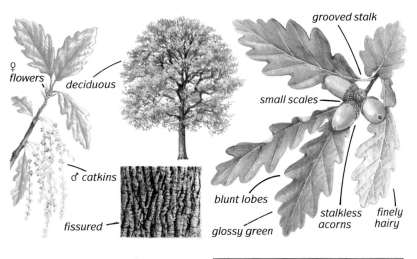

♀ flowers · deciduous · ♂ catkins · fissured · grooved stalk · small scales · blunt lobes · glossy green · stalkless acorns · finely hairy

A majestic tree but one which tends to be overlooked as it is often confused with Pedunculate Oak, from which it differs by the stalkless acorns. As they are less often attacked by insects, the dark, glossy, distinctly stalked leaves are more ornamental. *Status:* native except in the extreme north and the Mediterranean region; planted for timber, shelter and ornament. *Similar trees:* native to south-eastern Europe, *Q. dalechampii* has hairless leaves and acorns with a warty, greyish, practically hairless cup. Hungarian Oak has hairy twigs and leaves with up to ten, deep, wavy-edged lobes.

1 *Quercus dalechampii*
2 Hungarian Oak (*Quercus frainetto*)

many wavy lobes

1

2

warty, hairless · hairless below · short stalk

SESSILE OAK

Type	deciduous tree
Height	20–40m
Habitat	woodland, mainly acid soils
Flowering	April–May
Fruiting	September–October

TRUNK AND CROWN

Trunk	stout, often straight and unbranched below
Bark	brownish grey, fissured
Crown	rather narrowly domed
Twigs	hairless

LEAVES

Buds	5–6mm, many scales, hairy
Leaves	alternate along stem, 7–12.5cm, oval, broadest above, 5–8 pairs of rounded lobes, base tapered, rather glossy, dark green above, finely hairy below with brownish tufts at base of veins; stalk 1.8–2.5cm, grooved
Stipules	soon falling

FLOWERS AND FRUIT

Flowers	♂ and ♀ flowers, with leaves
♂	clustered, hanging catkins
Perianth	tiny, 4–7 lobes, usually 6
Stamens	6–12 per ♂ flower
♀	bud-like, within hairy scales
Stigmas	3 per ♀ flower, stalkless
Ovaries	1 per ♀ flower, 3-celled
Fruit	2–6 nuts (acorns), ripening first year, 1.5–3cm, oblong; cup with oval, closely overlapping scales, finely hairy; almost stalkless

Downy Oak   *Quercus pubescens*

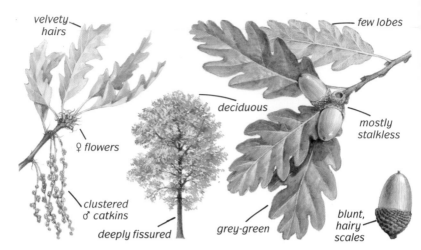

velvety hairs

few lobes

deciduous

mostly stalkless

♀ flowers

clustered ♂ catkins

deeply fissured

grey-green

blunt, hairy scales

A rather small tree or sturdy shrub, distinguished by grey-green, shallowly lobed leaves, covered with velvety hairs when young. Winter buds and acorn cups are also hairy. *Status:* native mainly to southern and western Europe; rarely planted for ornament. *Similar trees:* two species have longer leaf-stalks and looser scales on the acorn cup. Confined mainly to the eastern half of the Mediterranean region, *Q. virgiliana* has leaves with broad, often wavy-edged lobes, and the scales of the acorn cup have a slender, upright tip. Pyrenean Oak from south-western Europe has narrower, blunt scales on the acorn cup.

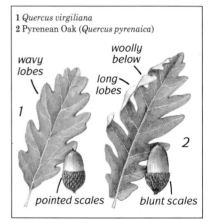

1 *Quercus virgiliana*
2 Pyrenean Oak (*Quercus pyrenaica*)

wavy lobes

woolly below

long lobes

pointed scales

blunt scales

	DOWNY OAK	
Type	deciduous tree or large shrub	
Height	15–25m	
Habitat	dry, usually lime-rich soils	
Flowering	May	
Fruiting	October	

TRUNK AND CROWN

Trunk sometimes very short
Bark dark grey, finely and deeply fissured, forming rough plates
Crown domed, branches swollen at junction with trunk
Twigs brown, densely grey-hairy

LEAVES

Buds 4–7mm, reddish brown, hairy
Leaves alternate along stem, 4–13cm, variable, 4–8 pairs of broad, shallow, forward-pointing lobes, base rounded or broadly tapered, grey-green, densely hairy when young, becoming hairless above; stalk 2–15mm
Stipules soon falling

FLOWERS AND FRUIT

Flowers ♂ and ♀ flowers, with leaves
♂ clustered catkins
Stamens 6–12 per ♂ flower
Perianth tiny, with 4–7 lobes
♀ 1–3, each within cup of scales
Stigmas 3 per ♀ flower, deep red
Ovaries 1 per ♀ flower, 3-celled
Fruit nut (acorn), ripens first year, 2–4cm; cup 1–1.5cm wide, $\frac{1}{4}$–$\frac{1}{3}$ covers nut, scales oval, usually blunt, pressed together, grey-woolly; stalkless or short-stalked

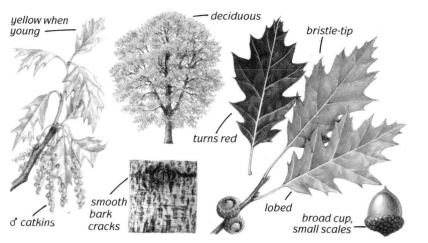

yellow when young —

— deciduous

bristle-tip

turns red

♂ catkins

smooth bark cracks

lobed

broad cup, small scales —

Spectacular when a cold snap in autumn turns its leaves fiery shades of orange and scarlet, Red Oak is widely planted for ornament. Like several other introduced North American species, it has relatively large leaves with pointed lobes and teeth. *Status:* introduced from eastern North America; commonly planted for ornament, timber and shelter. *Similar trees:* two American species have more deeply divided leaves and short, squat acorns. Scarlet Oak's glossy leaves lack hairs below at the base of the veins. Pin Oak has leaves with tufts of hairs beneath, and a narrow acorn cup.

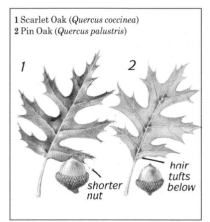

1 Scarlet Oak (*Quercus coccinea*)
2 Pin Oak (*Quercus palustris*)

1

2

shorter nut

hair tufts below

RED OAK

Type	deciduous tree
Height	20–35m
Habitat	planted on most soils
Flowering	April–May
Fruiting	October

TRUNK AND CROWN

Trunk	straight below
Bark	silvery grey, smooth above, with brown fissures below
Crown	broad-domed, branches straight
Twigs	stout, reddish brown, hairless

LEAVES

Buds	5–7mm, oval, reddish brown
Leaves	alternating, 12–25cm, oval or elliptical, variable, cut ½ way into 7–11 pairs of lobes, few bristle-tipped teeth, only few hairs in angles of veins below, yellow, becoming dull green, turning orange, red or brown in autumn; stalk 2.5–3cm
Stipules	soon falling

FLOWERS AND FRUIT

Flowers	♂ and ♀ flowers, with leaves
♂	catkins, 5–8cm, yellow
Perianth	tiny, with 4–7 lobes
Stamens	6–12 per ♂ flower
♀	tiny, at leaf-base, red
Stigmas	3–4 per ♀ flower
Ovaries	1 per ♀ flower, 3-celled
Fruit	nut (acorn), ripens second year, 2–3cm, oblong, reddish brown; cup 2–2.5cm wide, covers ⅓ nut, scales oval, pressed closely together, finely hairy; stalk 8–10mm

Sweet Chestnut *Castanea sativa*

A strikingly attractive tree, with bold, toothed leaves, bunches of long, pale yellow catkins and a stout, deeply fissured trunk, which often has a curious spiral pattern. Long-lived, the trunk may attain a girth of 13m or more, with the crown misshapen from lightning damage or branches shed in high wind. It is grown widely for its edible nuts. *Status:* native to southern Europe; widely planted and naturalized elsewhere. *Similar trees:* an ornamental species from western North America, Golden Chestnut is an evergreen with untoothed, leathery leaves, golden beneath, and fruits which mature in 2 years.

ridges often spiral

often massive

deciduous

♀ flower

♂ catkins

sharp teeth

many veins

large leaf

spiny

large, edible nut

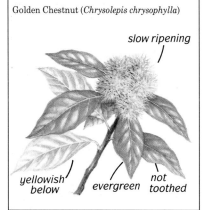

Golden Chestnut (*Chrysolepis chrysophylla*)

slow ripening

yellowish below *evergreen* *not toothed*

	SWEET CHESTNUT	
Type	deciduous tree	
Height	20–30m	
Habitat	well-drained soils, in woods	
Flowering	June–July	
Fruiting	September–October	

TRUNK AND CROWN

Trunk	often massive and gnarled
Bark	brown, vertically or spirally fissured and ridged
Crown	broad, irregular; massive old branches taper abruptly
Twigs	greenish brown, sometimes grooved, with lenticels

LEAVES

Buds	4–5mm, egg-shaped
Leaves	on alternate sides of stem, 10–25cm, narrowly oval to oblong, pointed, regularly toothed, teeth point forwards with slender tip, base tapered or rounded, c20 pairs of veins, glossy, dark green above, paler below, turning yellow or brown in autumn; stalk 0.5–3cm
Stipules	papery, soon falling

FLOWERS AND FRUIT

Flowers	♂ and ♀ flowers on same plant
♂	catkins, 12–30cm, pale yellow
Stamens	10–20 per ♂ flower
♀	2–3 in spiny bracts, in short ♀ catkin or below ♂ catkin
Stigmas	7–9 per ♀ flower
Ovaries	1 per ♀ flower, 6-celled
Fruit	1–3 nuts in husk with branched spines, splits into 2–4; nuts 20–35mm, hemispherical or angular, glossy, reddish brown

♂ catkin

berry-like fruit

scented

hairless

evergreen

reddish fruit

A strongly aromatic shrub or small tree, related to the shrubby Bog-myrtle (*M. gale*) of north-western Europe. Faya is found mainly in broad-leaved evergreen forests of the western Atlantic islands, remnants of a forest type widespread in the Mediterranean region 30 million years ago. *Status:* native to the Azores, Madeira and the Canary Islands; cultivated and naturalized in southern Europe; possibly native to Portugal. *Similar trees:* Bayberry is a deciduous shrub, rarely tree-sized, with leaves covered by glossy, yellow glands, unbranched catkins and small, whitish fruits. It is sometimes naturalized.

Bayberry (*Myrica caroliniensis*)

glossy

waxy

greyish

	FAYA		
Type	evergreen tree or shrub	**Stipules**	absent
Height	2–10m		**FLOWERS AND FRUIT**
Habitat	woodland, scrub	**Flowers**	♂ and ♀ catkins on different plants, among leaves
Flowering	April–May	♂	in branched catkins on growth of current year
Fruiting	September	♀	usually in unbranched catkins, each flower with 2 or more scales at the base
	TRUNK AND CROWN		
Trunk	short, forked		
Bark	smooth, brown	**Perianth**	absent
Crown	rounded, irregular	**Stamens**	2–16 per ♂ flower
Twigs	with small, reddish, tack-shaped hairs	**Stigmas**	2, slender, on short style
		Ovaries	1, 1-chambered
	LEAVES	**Fruit**	berry-like, slightly fleshy, reddish to black, with rough, waxy surface
Buds	egg-shaped, pointed		
Leaves	on alternate sides of stem, 4–12cm, spear-shaped, broadest above middle, edge unbroken, turned under, base wedge-shaped, hairless; stalkless		

English Elm *Ulmus procera*

A prominent tree of the landscape with a billowy crown formed by the domed masses of foliage from each main branch. The roots often produce suckers, so that an old tree is ringed by its younger progeny. In recent years, millions of trees have died from Dutch Elm disease, but young suckers often survive and offer hope for regeneration. *Status:* native to western and southern Europe; planted for shelter and timber. *Similar trees:* from central and south-eastern Europe, European White-elm has long-stalked flowers and fruit, the latter fringed with hairs. The leaves may have long, soft hairs below.

purplish stamens

before leaves

different-sized teeth

unequal base

bristly

broad

encircling wing

irregular crown

deciduous

rarely produced

European White-elm (*Ulmus laevis*)

fringed with hairs

long-stalked

soft hairs below

	ENGLISH ELM
Type	deciduous tree
Height	20–35m
Habitat	woodland, hedgerows
Flowering	February–March
Fruiting	April–June

TRUNK AND CROWN

Trunk	straight, forked above, suckers around base
Bark	brown, rough, fissured
Crown	irregularly domed; often few large, spreading branches
Twigs	rather stout, shortly hairy

LEAVES

Buds	small, pointed, brown, hairy
Leaves	alternate along stem, 4.5–9cm, oval to almost circular, pointed, doubly toothed, base unequal, longer side rounded, not overlapping short stalk, dark green, turning yellow in autumn, rough with stiff hairs to almost hairless above, 10–12 pairs of veins
Stipules	small, soon falling

FLOWERS AND FRUIT

Flowers	♂, before leaves, 5–9mm, clustered, greenish
Perianth	4–5 joined lobes, bell-shaped
Stamens	4–5, purplish red
Stigmas	1, forked
Ovaries	1, flattened
Fruit	rarely produced, nut-like with circular wing notched at tip, 10–17mm, seed above middle
Seeds	1, not released from fruit

A variable species, especially in Britain, where it is often split into several varieties, subspecies or even species. Small-leaved Elm is common in continental Europe, though its numbers have been decimated by Dutch Elm disease. Smooth, glossy leaves and an elliptical fruit with the seed above the middle distinguish it from other common elms. *Status:* native to much of Europe; planted for timber, shelter and ornament. *Similar trees:* Grey-leaved Elm has young shoots densely covered with white hairs, and leaves downy grey below. Chinese Elm is an ornamental species planted for its delicate sprays of much smaller, dark green leaves.

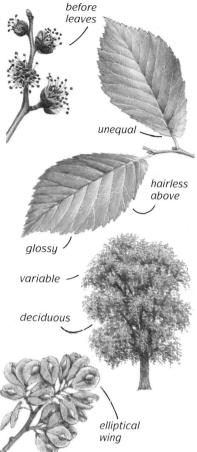

before leaves

unequal

hairless above

glossy

variable

deciduous

elliptical wing

1 Grey-leaved Elm (*Ulmus canescens*)
2 Chinese Elm (*Ulmus parvifolia*)

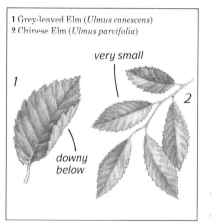

very small

1

2

downy below

	SMALL-LEAVED ELM
Type	deciduous tree
Height	15–30m
Habitat	hedgerows, woodland
Flowering	February–March
Fruiting	May–July

TRUNK AND CROWN

Trunk	straight, suckers around base
Bark	greyish brown, fissured
Crown	variable, domed or conical; few main branches
Twigs	slender, often hanging, pale brown, becoming smooth

LEAVES

Buds	*c*5mm, egg-shaped, red, downy
Leaves	alternate along twig, 6–8cm, oval, broadest towards slender tip, sharply, doubly toothed, base unequal, squarish long side not overlapping stalk, shiny dark green, turning yellow in autumn, hairless above, downy tufts below, 7–12 pairs of veins; stalk *c*5mm, downy
Stipules	small, soon falling

FLOWERS AND FRUIT

Flowers	⚥, before leaves, clustered, each 5–8mm, purplish
Perianth	4–5 joined lobes, bell-shaped
Stamens	4–5, purple anthers
Stigmas	1, forked, white
Ovaries	solitary, flattened
Fruit	nut-like with notched, elliptical wing, 7–18mm, seed above middle
Seeds	1, not released from fruit

Wych Elm *Ulmus glabra*

A handsome, densely-canopied tree, with large, bristly, lop-sided leaves. There is a rounded lobe at the base of each leaf, which usually overlaps the short stalk. Weeping forms are grown, with twisted, pendulous branches. Fruits are enclosed centrally within a broad, oval wing. *Status:* native to much of Europe except parts of the Mediterranean region; often planted by fields, in parks or churchyards. *Similar trees:* also large-leaved are the hybrids with Small-leaved Elm, distinguished from Wych Elm by their smooth leaves. Dutch Elm has corky ridges on the crooked shoots. Huntingdon Elm has straight, scarcely corky shoots.

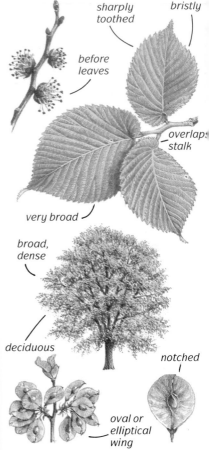

sharply toothed *bristly*

before leaves

overlaps stalk

very broad

broad, dense

deciduous

notched

oval or elliptical wing

1 Dutch Elm (*Ulmus × hollandica* var. *hollandica*); 2 Huntingdon Elm (*Ulmus × hollandica* var. *vegeta*)

1 *corky, smooth*

2

smooth

	WYCH ELM		
Type	deciduous tree		
Height	25–40m		
Habitat	often by water		
Flowering	February–March		
Fruiting	May–June		

TRUNK AND CROWN

Trunk	stout, with burrs and suckers
Bark	grey to brown, smooth becoming cracked and ridged
Crown	rounded, dense; branches angled upwards, twisted, sometimes bent down to ground
Twigs	stout, bristly, become smooth

LEAVES

Buds	stout, with reddish hairs
Leaves	alternate along stem, 8–18cm, broad, almost circular to oval, slender tipped, sharply, doubly toothed, base unequal, longer, rounded side overlaps stalk, bristly, dark green above, paler below, turning deep yellow in autumn, 12–18 pairs of veins; stalk 2–5mm, thick, hairy
Stipules	small, soon falling

FLOWERS AND FRUIT

Flowers	♀, before leaves, clustered, each 7–8mm, purplish red
Perianth	4–5 joined lobes, bell-shaped
Stamens	4–5, anthers purplish red
Stigmas	with 2 styles
Ovaries	1, flattened
Fruit	nut-like, central within oval or elliptical, notched wing, 1.5–2.5cm; stalk 2–3mm
Seeds	1, not released

An attractive tree with dark green leaves edged by large, rounded teeth. The smooth, scaly bark has rounded, orange patches. Some cultivated trees have many stout, almost upright branches arising near the base, forming a dense crown that is oval in outline. *Status:* introduced from the Caucasus; infrequently planted for ornament. *Similar trees:* Keaki is a Japanese ornamental tree with sharply toothed leaves turning yellow, red or orange. *Zelkova abelicea* is an uncommon native species from the mountains of Crete, and is sometimes cultivated. It differs in the small leaves with few, rounded teeth, and white, scented flowers.

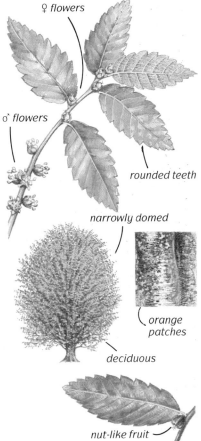

♀ flowers

♂ flowers

rounded teeth

narrowly domed

orange patches

deciduous

nut-like fruit

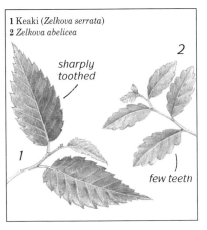

1 Keaki (*Zelkova serrata*)
2 *Zelkova abelicea*

sharply toothed

2

1

few teeth

CAUCASIAN ELM

Type	deciduous tree
Height	20–35m
Habitat	parks, gardens, rarely hedges
Flowering	April–May
Fruiting	August–September

TRUNK AND CROWN

Trunk	often short, becomes buttressed; suckers at base
Bark	yellowish grey, smooth, scaling leaving orange patches
Crown	narrowly domed; branches angled upwards
Twigs	slender, greyish brown, downy

LEAVES

Buds	small, blunt, reddish, downy
Leaves	alternate along stem, 5–10cm, oval or elliptical, pointed, with rounded teeth, base rounded or squarish, slightly unequal, dark green above, turning orange-brown in autumn, dull or shiny, often with scattered, stiff hairs, veins 6–12 pairs; stalk 1–2mm
Stipules	small, soon falling

FLOWERS AND FRUIT

Flowers	♂ and ♀ flowers on different plants, with leaves
♂	on lower part of twig
♀	solitary at leaf-base
Perianth	5 joined lobes
Stamens	5, yellow, upright
Stigmas	2 on slender styles
Fruit	nut-like, solitary, 4–5mm, rounded, ridged
Seeds	1, not released

Southern Nettle-tree *Celtis australis*

This graceful tree differs from the related elms by the narrow, nettle-like leaves drawn out into a long, slender point. Berry-like fruits are sweet-tasting with an edible nut-like centre, and were important in the diet of Stone Age people. *Status:* native to southern Europe; planted elsewhere for ornament and shade. *Similar trees: Celtis tournefortii* is a native shrub or small tree with oval, bluntly toothed leaves. The fruit has a 4-ridged, nut-like centre. Hackberry, a cultivated species from eastern North America, has rough bark and leaves with fewer, long, whiskered teeth. The orange or purple ripe fruit has a shorter stalk.

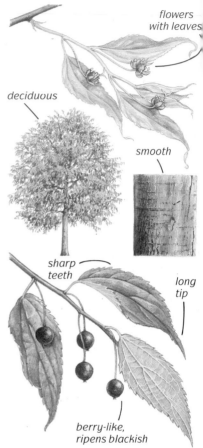

flowers with leaves

deciduous

smooth

sharp teeth

long tip

berry-like, ripens blackish

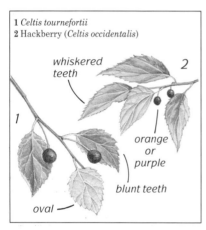

1 *Celtis tournefortii*
2 Hackberry (*Celtis occidentalis*)

whiskered teeth

2

1

orange or purple

blunt teeth

oval

	SOUTHERN NETTLE-TREE	
Type	deciduous tree	
Height	10–25m	
Habitat	woodland, scrub, roadsides	
Flowering	May	
Fruiting	August	

TRUNK AND CROWN

Trunk	straight below, forked above
Bark	grey-brown, smooth with rows of lenticels, some fissured
Crown	domed
Twigs	slender, downy, reddish brown

LEAVES

Buds	small, downy
Leaves	alternate along stem, 4–15cm, narrowly oval, with long, slender, sometimes twisted point, edge often wavy, sharply toothed, base rounded or shallowly notched, dark green, turning yellow in autumn, stiffly hairy above, downy below with white hairs, 3 main veins from base; stalk 1–3.5cm
Stipules	small, soon falling

FLOWERS AND FRUIT

Flowers	♂ and ♀ on same tree, with leaves, 7–10mm, yellowish, long-stalked
Perianth	4–5 separate lobes
Stamens	4–5, yellow
Stigmas	2, on slender styles
Ovaries	1, rounded
Fruit	berry-like, solitary, 9–12mm, globular, smooth, blackish brown, long-stalked
Seeds	pitted, nut-like centre to fruit retains single seed

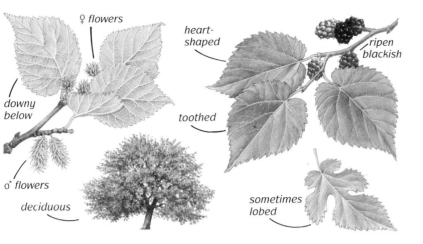

♀ flowers

heart-shaped

ripen blackish

downy below

toothed

♂ flowers

deciduous

sometimes lobed

Commonly a short, broad, gnarled tree, Black Mulberry has been cultivated for its sweet-and-sour fruit in Europe since Greek and Roman times. The exact origin of this species is unknown since all trees are apparently cultivated or naturalized from cultivation. *Status:* introduced, probably from central Asia; widely grown for fruit in southern Europe, often naturalized. *Similar trees:* introduced from China, White Mulberry is the food plant for silk-worms and fuels the silk industry. It differs in the glossy, almost hairless leaves and stalked, white or pale purplish fruit.

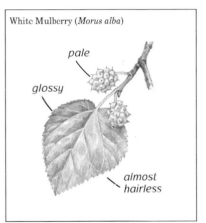

White Mulberry (*Morus alba*)

pale

glossy

almost hairless

	BLACK MULBERRY		
Type	deciduous tree		
Height	3–16m		
Habitat	fields, gardens		
Flowering	April–May		
Fruiting	August–September		

TRUNK AND CROWN

Trunk	short, often leaning
Bark	dark orange-brown, rough, scaling, fissured, with burrs
Crown	low, domed; branches stout, rough, twisted
Twigs	stout, become reddish brown

LEAVES

Buds	stout, conical, glossy brown
Leaves	alternate along stem, 6–20cm, broadly oval or heart-shaped, sharply pointed, toothed, sometimes deeply lobed, base notched, dark green, roughly hairy above, paler, downy below; stalk 1.5–2.5cm, stout, hairy
Stipules	soon falling

FLOWERS AND FRUIT

Flowers	♂ and ♀ flowers on same tree, in short spikes
♂	2–2.5cm, yellowish green
Stamens	4, yellow
♀	1–1.5cm
Perianth	4 lobes, joined at base
Stigmas	2, slender
Ovaries	1 per ♀ flower
Fruit	at leaf-base, 2–2.5cm, many berry-like segments, deep red to blackish purple, almost stalkless, becomes sweet
Seeds	1 per fruit segment

Osage Orange *Maclura pomifera*

This small, thorny tree is most easily distinguished by its orange-sized, yellowish fruit, with milky white, inedible flesh. When trimmed, the plant forms an impenetrable hedge and is used as such in southern Europe. *Status:* introduced from North America; planted for ornament and hedges; naturalized in southern Europe. *Similar trees:* Paper Mulberry has hairy, toothed leaves, which are sometimes deeply lobed. Male flowers are in hanging catkins; female flowers form globular, woolly heads, which turn into spiky, globular fruits. From eastern Asia, it is naturalized in southern Europe.

glossy, hairless

not toothed

globular heads

deciduous

Paper Mulberry (*Broussonetia papyrifera*)

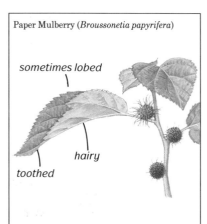

sometimes lobed

hairy

toothed

spiny

globular

yellowish

	OSAGE ORANGE		
Type	deciduous tree		hairless above, paler below; stalk 5–8mm, shortly hairy
Height	up to 14m	**Stipules**	soon falling
Habitat	hedges, street tree, parks		
Flowering	June		**FLOWERS AND FRUIT**
Fruiting	October–November	**Flowers**	♂ and ♀ on different trees
		♂	greenish yellow, in broad, stalked heads, 1.5–2.5cm
	TRUNK AND CROWN	**Stamens**	4, yellowish
Trunk	often forked, slender	♀	many in globular head, 2–2.5cm, green
Bark	rough, orange-brown	**Perianth**	4-lobed
Crown	irregular, domed; branches twisted	**Stigmas**	2, on slender styles
Twigs	spiny, downy becoming hairless	**Ovaries**	1 per ♀ flower
		Fruit	10–14cm, globular, green, turning yellow or orange, with white, stringy flesh
	LEAVES	**Seeds**	not released
Buds	small, brown		
Leaves	alternate along stem, 5–12cm, oval, pointed, edge unbroken, base wedge-shaped or rounded, glossy dark green,		

Much cultivated in the Mediterranean region for its delicious fruit, which is eaten fresh or dried. Though these edible figs are an exception, fruits of most fig species are pollinated by tiny wasps that enter a hole at the fruit tip and lay eggs in specialized flowers. *Status:* native to southern Europe; cultivated for fruit, ornament and shade. *Similar trees:* two evergreens with leathery leaves, grown as street trees in the south, have curious roots sprouting from branches. Indian Rubber-tree, with oblong leaves, is grown as a pot plant in northern Europe. Banyan Tree has broad, wavy-edged leaves.

stout twigs

flowers enclosed

deciduous

1 Indian Rubber-tree (*Ficus elastica*)
2 Banyan Tree (*Ficus benghalensis*)

unbroken edge

thick

1

2

wavy edge

toothed

most lobed

ripens brownish purple

	FIG
Type	deciduous tree or shrub
Height	up to 10m
Habitat	fields, orchards, parks, gardens, naturalized by roads
Flowering	September–November
Fruiting	July–October, following year

	TRUNK AND CROWN
Trunk	usually short, often forked
Bark	pale grey with darker streaks, smooth or uneven
Crown	domed, wide-spreading; branches twisted
Twigs	stout, with large leaf-scars

	LEAVES
Buds	conical, pointed
Leaves	alternate along stem, 7–30cm, most with 3–5 deep, blunt lobes, thick, leathery, irregularly toothed, base notched, glossy dark green, roughly hairy; stalk 5–10cm, stout
Stipules	broad, soon falling leaving circular scar around twig

	FLOWERS AND FRUIT
Flowers	♂ and ♀ tiny, inside hollow structure that becomes fruit
Perianth	2–6 tiny segments
Stamens	♂ flowers with 4
Stigmas	♀ flowers with 2, slender
Ovaries	1 per ♀ flower
Fruit	5–8cm, pear-shaped, green to brownish purple, hollow structure containing individual tiny fruits
Seeds	retained within tiny fruits

Sweet-gum _Liquidambar styraciflua_

A magnificent tree in autumn, when the whole crown can turn bright shades of red, purple or yellow. Similar to maples, it is easily distinguished by the alternate leaves and globular, spiky fruit. Where it is native in North America, it is the source of scented gum, and the fine-grained timber is used for furniture. _Status:_ introduced from North America; frequently planted in northern Europe for ornament, especially for autumn colour. _Similar trees:_ Oriental Sweet-gum, from south-west Asia, has smaller, more deeply lobed, dull green leaves with coarser, irregular teeth.

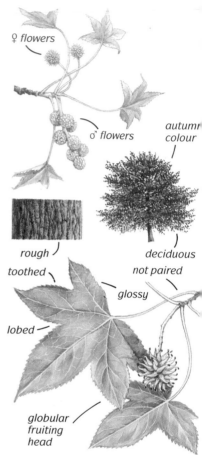

♀ flowers

♂ flowers

autumn colour

rough

deciduous

not paired

toothed

glossy

lobed

globular fruiting head

Oriental Sweet-gum (_Liquidambar orientalis_)

dull green

deeper lobes

irregularly toothed

	SWEET-GUM		
Type	deciduous tree		turning red, purple or orange in autumn, reddish hairs in tufts below; stalk 10–15cm, grooved
Height	5–30m (45m in North America)		
Habitat	parks, gardens, street tree	**Stipules**	small, soon falling
Flowering	May		
Fruiting	October–November		**FLOWERS AND FRUIT**
		Flowers	♂ and ♀ flowers on different plants
	TRUNK AND CROWN		
Trunk	usually short and broad	♂	yellow, globular heads clustered into spike, 5–10cm
Bark	pale grey to brown, rough		
Crown	conical to broadly domed; branches widely spreading	♀	in globular head, 1–1.5cm, solitary or sometimes paired
Twigs	slender, downy becoming hairless	**Stamens**	many in ♂ head
		Stigmas	1 per ♀ flower
	LEAVES	**Ovaries**	1 per ♀ flower
Buds	conical, glossy green	**Fruit**	globular, spiny head, 2–3.5cm, of many slender capsules, each 6–8mm, stalk 4–6cm
Leaves	alternate along stem, 8–15cm, with 3–7 lobes, pointed, finely toothed, glossy green above,		
		Seeds	each capsule with 1 or 2 seeds

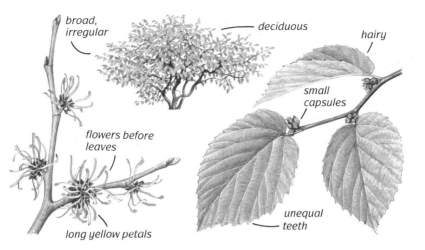

broad, irregular

deciduous

hairy

small capsules

flowers before leaves

long yellow petals

unequal teeth

Flowering in mid-winter, this ornamental species is valued for the colour and scent of its flowers. The commonest of several cultivated species, it is usually a shrub though some species and cultivars form small trees. An extract is used for treating bruises and inflammation. *Status:* introduced from China; commonly planted for ornament. *Similar trees:* Virginian Witch-hazel, from North America, flowers in the autumn. Persian Ironwood is a small tree with scarcely toothed leaves, small, purplish flowers and smooth grey bark flaking to reveal pink or yellow patches.

1 Virginian Witch-hazel (*Hamamelis virginiana*)
2 Persian Ironwood (*Parrotia persica*)

small flowers

scarcely toothed

autumn-flowering

1

2

	WITCH-HAZEL		rounded or wedge-shaped, softly hairy, yellow or orange in autumn; stalk short
Type	deciduous shrub, rarely reaching tree size		
		Stipules	large, soon falling
Height	2.5–4m		
Habitat	parks, roadsides near towns		**FLOWERS AND FRUIT**
Flowering	December–March	**Flowers**	♂, before leaves, few in compact, short-stalked cluster, 3–4cm long, deep yellow
Fruiting	August–September		
	TRUNK AND CROWN	**Petals**	4, long, narrow; sepals 4, rounded, reddish
Trunk	often several, forked		
Bark	smooth, greyish brown	**Stamens**	4, purplish
Crown	broad, irregular; branches angled upwards, twisted	**Ovaries**	single
		Fruit	oblong capsule, splits lengthwise
Twigs	slender, pale grey		
	LEAVES	**Seeds**	2, black, shiny
Buds	conical, pointed		
Leaves	alternate along stem, 7–12cm, broadly oval or rounded, long-pointed, doubly toothed, base		

London Plane *Platanus × hybrida*

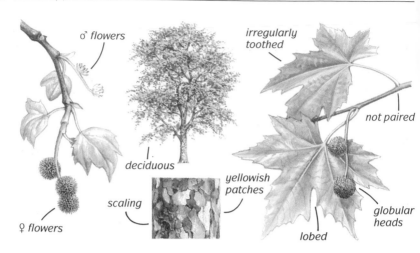

o' flowers

irregularly toothed

deciduous

not paired

yellowish patches

scaling

globular heads

♀ flowers

lobed

Tolerant of pollution, this tree is common in towns of southern and western Europe. Of rapid growth, it makes a huge tree with lobed leaves, globular, spiky fruits and scaly bark revealing large patches of creamy white. Of obscure origin, it is considered to be a hybrid between Oriental Plane and American Plane (*P. occidentalis*). *Status:* of garden origin; widely planted for ornament, shade and timber. *Similar trees:* Oriental Plane has more deeply lobed leaves with a narrower base, and fruiting heads in clusters of 3–6. Native to south-eastern Europe, it is also planted elsewhere.

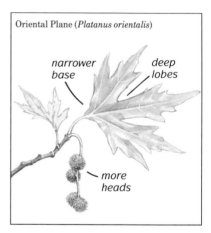

Oriental Plane (*Platanus orientalis*)

narrower base

deep lobes

more heads

	LONDON PLANE		
Type	deciduous tree		bright green above, paler below, veins woolly; stalk long, broad-based
Height	up to 45m		
Habitat	parks, roadsides	**Stipules**	oval, toothed, usually falling
Flowering	April–June		
Fruiting	February–April		**FLOWERS AND FRUIT**
		Flowers	♂ and ♀ on same tree, in globular heads
	TRUNK AND CROWN		
Trunk	long, straight	♂	2–6 yellowish heads in cluster 4–8cm long
Bark	grey-brown, scaling leaving whitish yellow patches, becomes fissured at base		
		Perianth	4–6 lobes
		Stamens	4–6 per ♂ flower
Crown	domed; branches often twisted	♀	2–5 reddish heads on stalk
Twigs	slender, often hanging	**Ovaries**	3–6 per ♀ flower, surrounded by long hairs at base
	LEAVES	**Fruit**	usually 2 globular heads on stalk, breaks into segments, each with tuft of hairs
Buds	6–8mm, reddish brown		
Leaves	alternate along stem, 8–24cm, variably 5-lobed, pointed, irregularly toothed, base squarish or notched, glossy,	**Seeds**	1 per segment, not released

This puzzling tree looks superficially like some sort of cypress from afar, but it has very slender twigs and scale-like leaves resembling a Horsetail *(Equisetum)*. Originally from New South Wales, it is remarkably resistant to drought and tolerant of salt, making it ideal for stabilizing sand dunes. The hard wood is so dense that it sinks in water. *Status:* introduced from Australia; planted in the Mediterranean region for ornament, shelter or stabilizing sand. *Similar trees:* Drooping She-oak has much longer male flower-heads and larger fruiting heads. It is more tolerant of frosts.

slender twigs

flowers in spikes

evergreen

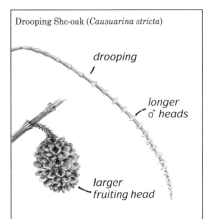

Drooping She-oak (*Casuarina stricta*)

drooping

longer ♂ heads

larger fruiting head

cracks and peels

scale-like leaves

ridged

cone-like fruiting head

HORSETAIL SHE-OAK

Type	evergreen tree
Height	5–20m
Habitat	well-drained, light soils
Flowering	February–March
Fruiting	September–October

TRUNK AND CROWN

Trunk	upright, forked above
Bark	grey-brown, peels in long strips
Crown	conical or columnar; branches slender, angled upwards
Twigs	very slender, wiry, ridged, drooping

LEAVES

Buds	minute
Leaves	in rings of 6–8 around twigs, scale-like, sharply pointed, edge unbroken, base broad, hairless, grey-green; stalkless
Stipules	absent

FLOWERS AND FRUIT

Flowers	♂ and ♀ on same tree, minute, in heads at shoot-tip
♂	in dense spike 1–1.5cm long, brownish, each flower formed by 1 stamen
Stamens	1 per ♂ flower
♀	compact, reddish head, 3–4mm
Stigmas	2, on short style
Ovaries	1 per ♀ flower
Fruit	cone-like head, 1–1.5cm, cylindrical, of tiny, woody scales, fruit nut-like with short wing
Seeds	1 per fruit, not released

Caucasian Wing-nut *Pterocarya fraxinifolia*

An impressive tree with huge leaves composed of paired leaflets. Suckers at the base can grow into new trees, forming a dense, impenetrable clump if left untended. In fruit the tree is easily recognized, as it has long clusters of broadly winged nuts. *Status:* introduced from south-western Asia; grown mainly for ornament in Europe. *Similar trees:* Chinese Wing-nut differs in the hairy shoots and leaves with a flattened wing either side of the central stalk. The hybrid between these two species is also grown, distinguished by its intermediate leaves and great vigour.

thick twigs

♀ flowers

♂ flowers

deciduous

domed

slender stalk

paired leaflets

long cluster

winged fruit

Chinese Wing-nut (*Pterocarya stenoptera*)

winged stalk

CAUCASIAN WING-NUT

Type	deciduous tree
Height	up to 35m
Habitat	woods, parks, often near water
Flowering	April–May
Fruiting	September–October

TRUNK AND CROWN

Trunk	often clumped, with suckers
Bark	grey-brown, fissured, ridged
Crown	domed; branches spreading
Twigs	stout, smooth

LEAVES

Buds	stalked, slender, not scaly
Leaves	alternate along stem, up to 60cm, with 5–15 pairs of oblong, pointed, sharply toothed leaflets, often overlapping, leaflet at tip, glossy green above, paler below, turning bright yellow in autumn; central stalk rounded
Stipules	absent

FLOWERS AND FRUIT

Flowers	♂ and ♀ catkins on same tree, with leaves
♂	on year-old twigs, 5–12cm, thick, hanging, many yellowish green flowers
Stamens	many
♀	on new growth, 10–15cm, hanging, many greenish flowers
Stigmas	2 on single style, pink
Ovaries	1 per ♀ flower
Fruit	nut with rounded or oblong wing *c*2cm wide, in cluster 25–50cm long
Seeds	1 per nut, not released

A magnificent tree with a rugged grey trunk and large, scented leaves bearing paired leaflets. The large fruit is best known as a nut after the spongy outer wall has been removed. Immature fruits are also pickled whole. The timber is hard and beautifully marked, especially when cut from burrs. *Status:* native to south-eastern Europe; often planted for fruit, timber or ornament, and widely naturalized. *Similar trees:* Black Walnut is a North American species grown mainly for timber. It has many sharply toothed leaflets, and shortly hairy fruits containing a ridged, very hard nut.

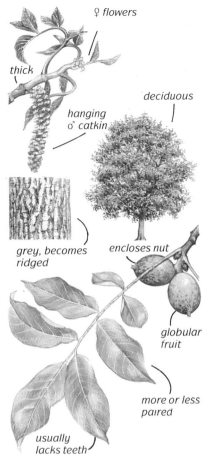

♀ *flowers*

thick

hanging
♂ catkin

deciduous

grey, becomes ridged

encloses nut

globular fruit

more or less paired

usually lacks teeth

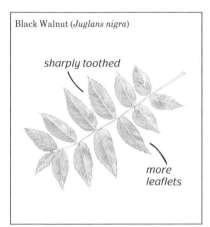

Black Walnut (*Juglans nigra*)

sharply toothed

more leaflets

	WALNUT		
Type	deciduous tree		elliptical leaflets, leaflet at tip, each leaflet 6–15cm, pointed, edge almost unbroken, downy when young, becoming hairless; stalked
Height	up to 30m		
Habitat	woodland, fields, parks		
Flowering	May–June		
Fruiting	September–October	**Stipules**	absent
	TRUNK AND CROWN		**FLOWERS AND FRUIT**
Trunk	stout, often short	**Flowers**	♂ and ♀ on same tree
Bark	grey, young smooth, becomes deeply fissured and ridged	♂	catkins on year-old twigs, 5–15cm, hanging, green
Crown	broad, domed; branches spreading, twisted	**Stamens**	♂ flowers with many
		♀	few flowers, on new growth
Twigs	stout, hairless, pith with separate cavities	**Stigmas**	2 on single style
		Ovaries	1 per ♀ flower
	LEAVES	**Fruit**	solitary or few, 4–5cm, globular, green, hairless, spongy wall around large, wrinkled nut
Buds	*c*6mm, broad, scaly, blackish		
Leaves	alternate along stem, mostly with 3–4 pairs of oval or	**Seeds**	1 per nut, not released

Bitternut *Carya cordiformis*

A tall, narrowly domed tree with leaves similar to the related Walnut, but the fruit differs in having a thin husk, which splits to release a bitter, inedible nut. In winter it has distinctive bright yellow buds. Bitternut and several related species are grown in North America and Europe for the very tough but flexible timber. *Status:* introduced from eastern North America; planted for ornament and timber. *Similar trees:* Pignut-tree has dark buds with more scales, fewer leaflets and a smoothly rounded fruit. Shagbark Hickory has very scaly bark, larger buds and large leaves with the end leaflet stalked.

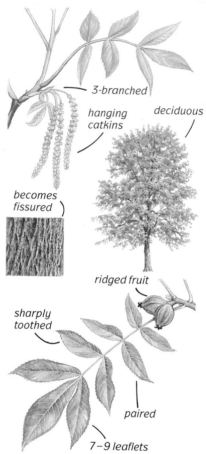

3-branched

hanging catkins

deciduous

becomes fissured

ridged fruit

sharply toothed

paired

7–9 leaflets

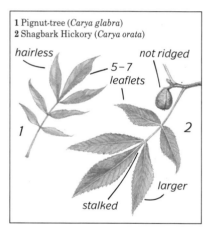

1 Pignut-tree (*Carya glabra*)
2 Shagbark Hickory (*Carya orata*)

hairless

not ridged

5 – 7 leaflets

1

2

stalked

larger

	BITTERNUT	
Type	deciduous tree	
Height	up to 30m	
Habitat	parks, gardens, plantations	
Flowering	May–June	
Fruiting	October	

TRUNK AND CROWN

Trunk	stout, usually straight
Bark	grey-brown, smooth becoming scaly and fissured
Crown	conical to narrowly domed; branches angled upwards
Twigs	rather slender, hairless

LEAVES

Buds	bright yellow, slender, 4–6 scales
Leaves	alternate along stem, 20–30cm, usually with 4 pairs of oval leaflets, each 5–15cm, stalkless leaflet at tip, leaflets pointed, sharply toothed, downy below when young, becoming hairless, golden-yellow in autumn
Stipules	absent

FLOWERS AND FRUIT

Flowers	♂ and ♀ on same tree
♂	3-branched catkins, 5–7.5cm, hanging, green
♀	2–3, tiny, on new growth
Stamens	many
Stigmas	2 on single style
Ovaries	1 per ♀ flower
Fruit	2–4cm, almost globular, 4-ridged, shortly hairy, tough husk enclosing nut
Seeds	1 per nut, not released

Commonly grown as an ornamental tree or for hedging in southern Europe, White Holly's tough leaves resist scorching by the Mediterranean sun, and its fragrant, white flowers scent the evening air. *Status:* introduced from south-eastern Australia; widely planted for ornament in the Mediterranean region and western Europe, sometimes naturalized. *Similar trees:* Karo has thick, blunt leaves and red flowers. Pittosporum has blackish stems, thin, glossy, crinkled leaves and purplish, honey-scented flowers. It is commonly used with cut flowers; variegated cultivars are also grown for ornament.

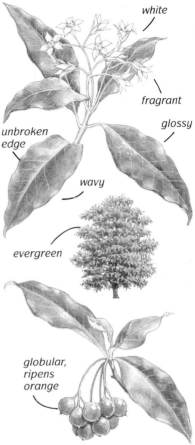

white / fragrant / glossy

unbroken edge

wavy

evergreen

globular, ripens orange

1 Karo (*Pittosporum crassifolium*)
2 Pittosporum (*Pittosporum tenuifolium*)

red

thin

purplish

1

2

thicker

crinkled

	WHITE HOLLY		
Type	evergreen tree or large shrub		
Height	up to 20m		
Habitat	parks, gardens, street tree		
Flowering	May–June		
Fruiting	September		
	TRUNK AND CROWN		
Trunk	usually short, forked		
Bark	grey-brown, smooth, becomes fissured		
Crown	pyramidal or domed; branches spreading		
Twigs	green, rather stout		
	LEAVES		
Buds	small, inconspicuous		
Leaves	alternate along stem, 7–20cm, oval or narrowly oval, sharply pointed, edge unbroken, rather wavy, base wedge-shaped, hairless, dark, glossy green; stalk short		
Stipules	absent		
	FLOWERS AND FRUIT		
Flowers	♀, rather few in broad, branched heads, white, fragrant		
Petals	5, equal, oval, pointed; sepals 5, slender		
Stamens	5, yellow		
Stigmas	1		
Fruit	almost globular capsule, 1–1.2cm, ripens orange, hairless, leathery wall splits into 2, releasing seeds		
Seeds	many, in sticky substance		

Evergreen Magnolia *Magnolia grandiflora*

A spectacular species with large, glossy leaves and huge flowers, the size of dinner plates. White flowers open a few at a time over a long period; later flowers are damaged by frosts and blotched brown. In cooler areas, it is most often grown against a wall. *Status:* introduced from south-eastern North America; commonly grown in western Europe for ornament. *Similar trees:* a taller tree, flowering in the spring before the leaves, Campbell's Magnolia has deep pink flowers that gradually fade. Hybrid Magnolia is shorter, with smaller flowers, which are white inside and tinged purplish outside.

glossy — leathery
white
edge unbroken
huge flowers
hairy
evergreen —
short
fleshy segments

1 Campbell's Magnolia (*Magnolia campbellii*)
2 Hybrid Magnolia (*Magnolia × soulangiana*)

pink
deciduous
1
2
purplish outside

	EVERGREEN MAGNOLIA
Type	evergreen tree or shrub
Height	to 10m (30m in North America)
Habitat	parks, large gardens
Flowering	June–October
Fruiting	September–November

TRUNK AND CROWN

Trunk	usually short, forked
Bark	smooth, dark grey
Crown	narrow; branches spread apart
Twigs	stout, with reddish hairs

LEAVES

Buds	8–15mm, conical
Leaves	alternate along stem, 8–16cm, elliptical or oval, broadest above middle, thick, leathery, edge unbroken, sometimes wavy, hairless, glossy deep green above, thickly covered with reddish brown hairs below; stalk 2–2.5cm, stout
Stipules	large, soon falling

FLOWERS AND FRUIT

Flowers	⚥, single at shoot tip, 20–25cm, bowl-shaped, creamy white, scented
Petals	almost equal, separate to base, thick; no distinct sepals
Stamens	many, arranged spirally
Stigmas	1 per ovary
Ovaries	many, in narrow cone
Fruit	4–6cm, conical, composed of separate fleshy segments,
Seeds	each fruit-segment with large seed on slender thread

A spectacular tree when fully grown, with a massive, straight trunk leading up to a tall, narrow crown. Four-lobed leaves are quite unlike those of other trees, and curious, cup-shaped, green and orange flowers bear a faint resemblance to tulips. Only two species of Tulip-tree are known, one in North America and the other in Asia. *Status:* introduced from eastern North America; widely planted for ornament and timber. *Similar trees:* Chinese Tulip-tree has unfolding, coppery leaves with a more deeply divided, narrowly lobed blade and a reddish stalk.

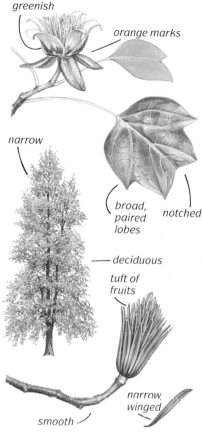

greenish

orange marks

narrow

broad, paired lobes

notched

deciduous

tuft of fruits

narrow, winged

smooth

Chinese Tulip-tree (*Liriodendron chinense*)

narrower lobes

TULIP-TREE	
Type	deciduous tree
Height	to 40m (60m in North America)
Habitat	parks, gardens, plantations
Flowering	June–July
Fruiting	September
TRUNK AND CROWN	
Trunk	straight, oldest buttressed
Bark	grey, smooth, becoming ridged
Crown	narrow; most branches angled upwards, lower bent down
Twigs	smooth, green or reddish brown
LEAVES	
Buds	5–12mm, oblong, flattened
Leaves	alternate along stem, 7–16cm, broad with 2 or 4 oval or triangular lobes, tip squarish or notched, hairless, glossy green above, paler below, turning yellow or orange in autumn; stalk 5–10cm
Stipules	large, oblong or elliptical, blunt, eventually falling
FLOWERS AND FRUIT	
Flowers	♀, at stem-tip, cup-shaped, 6–8cm wide, whitish green, inner marked with orange
Perianth	6 petal-like parts, 4–5cm, equal, separate; 3 smaller, sepal-like parts fold back
Stamens	many, long, spirally arranged
Stigmas	1 per ovary
Ovaries	many in central spike
Fruit	tuft of brown fruits from each flower, each 4–5cm, narrow, flattened with long wing
Seeds	1 per fruit, not released

Sweet Bay *Laurus nobilis*

A small evergreen with tough, leathery leaves emitting a wonderful spicy aroma if lightly crushed. Dried leaves are widely used for flavouring food. Plants in towns are often trimmed to shape. *Status:* native to the Mediterranean region; widely cultivated for ornament, shelter, or as a herb; often naturalized. *Similar trees:* planted in the Mediterranean region, Avocado has larger leaves and elongated clusters of flowers, each of which have 6 lobes to the perianth. The large, edible fruit is pear-shaped and rough-skinned with soft, creamy-textured, yellowish flesh.

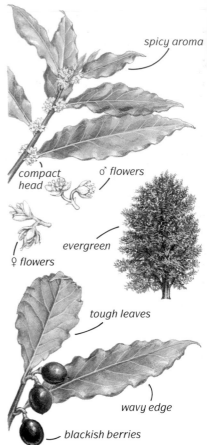

spicy aroma

compact head

♂ flowers

evergreen

♀ flowers

tough leaves

wavy edge

blackish berries

Avocado (*Persea americana*)

elongated head

large, edible fruit

rough skin

	SWEET BAY		
Type	evergreen tree or shrub		with glands, hairless, paler below; stalk 4–6mm, red
Height	2–20m	**Stipules**	absent
Habitat	woodland, scrub, parks		
Flowering	April–June		**FLOWERS AND FRUIT**
Fruiting	September–October	**Flowers**	♂ and ♀ on same tree
		♂	in short-stalked, compact head, each 7–10mm, dull whitish yellow
	TRUNK AND CROWN		
Trunk	usually short, forked	♀	2–6 in head, greenish white, with 2–4 sterile stamens
Bark	grey, smooth or fissured below	**Perianth**	4-lobed, petal-like
Crown	broadly conical; branches angled upwards	**Stamens**	8–12 per ♂ flower
		Stigmas	1 on short style
Twigs	slender, hairless, green or reddish	**Ovaries**	1 per ♀ flower
		Fruit	small cluster of almost globular berries, each 8–15mm, black, stalk 3–4mm
	LEAVES		
Buds	2–3mm, conical, reddish brown	**Seeds**	1 per fruit
Leaves	5–10cm, narrowly oval or oblong, tough, pointed, edge wavy, dark green above, dotted		

A most curious and distinctive feature on older trees of Phytolacca is that the area where the base of the trunk adjoins the roots becomes greatly enlarged at soil level. It is as though the trunk had melted and flowed across the ground. It may spread for a metre or more from the trunk in each direction and is most noticeable on a bank or where the soil has been washed away. Phytolacca's succulent, berry-like fruits hang in long clusters. Related species occurring in Europe are all herbaceous plants, and are sometimes used for their edible young leaves or berries. *Status:* introduced from South America; planted in the Mediterranean region for ornament and shade; naturalized in places. *Similar trees:* none.

edge unbroken

hairless

♀

5 petals

long clusters

evergreen

base often enlarged

many berry-like segments

succulent fruit

PHYTOLACCA		
Type	evergreen tree	
Height	3–8m	
Habitat	towns, street tree	
Flowering	June–August	
Fruiting	September–October	
TRUNK AND CROWN		
Trunk	short, stout, enlarged base	
Bark	smooth, grey-brown	
Crown	broadly domed; branches stout, spreading	
Twigs	stout, rather succulent, hairless	
LEAVES		
Buds	small, green	
Leaves	alternate along stem, 5–12cm, oval or elliptical, pointed, edge unbroken, base wedge-shaped, bright green, hairless; stalked	

Stipules	absent
FLOWERS AND FRUIT	
Flowers	♂ and ♀ on different trees, in hanging clusters, mostly at stem-tip
♂	clusters 8–15cm, greenish white, stalk 1–1.5cm
♀	slightly larger than ♂
Perianth	5 petal-like, oblong lobes
Stamens	many per ♂ flower
Stigmas	1 per ovary
Ovaries	7–10 per ♀ flower
Fruit	long clusters of fruits, each with globular berry-like segments, 5–7.5mm, purplish black
Seeds	each fruit segment with single seed

Quince *Cydonia oblonga*

deciduous

pink

often thorny

smooth above

woolly below

not toothed

fragrant

hard

Introduced in ancient times from Asia, the Quince is nowadays widespread in Europe. In northern and western regions it is most often planted as an ornamental shrub. In southerly areas it is grown for its edible fruits, which have a delightful fragrance and are extremely hard. *Status:* native to south-western and central Asia; cultivated and naturalized in much of Europe. *Similar trees:* two species with similar fruits are widely cultivated shrubs with toothed leaves and red flowers. Flowering Quince has larger flowers and leaves than Dwarf Quince.

1 Flowering Quince (*Chaenomeles speciosa*)
2 Dwarf Quince (*Chaenomeles japonica*)

toothed

small

1

2

red or orange

	QUINCE	**Stipules**	small, usually falling very early
Type	deciduous tree or shrub		**FLOWERS AND FRUIT**
Height	1.5–7.5m	**Flowers**	♂, single in angles of leaves, 3.8–5cm, bowl-shaped, pink, rarely white
Habitat	hedges and copses		
Flowering	April–May		
Fruiting	September	**Petals**	5, broad, blunt or slightly notched at the tip, tapered at base; sepals 5, smaller, very hairy, persistent on fruit, toothed
	TRUNK AND CROWN		
Trunk	slender, usually short		
Bark	grey-brown, smooth		
Crown	often very broad, spreading	**Stamens**	15–25
Twigs	woolly, becoming smooth, spiny	**Stigmas**	5, styles woolly towards base
		Ovaries	1, in base of flower
	LEAVES	**Fruit**	fleshy but extremely hard, 2.5–3.5cm, rarely 12cm, globular or pear-shaped, ripening yellow, very fragrant
Buds	2–3mm, reddish-brown, hairy		
Leaves	alternate, 5–10cm, oval, blunt, green and smooth above, greyish and woolly below; stalkless		
		Seeds	many, brown to blackish

deciduous

often thorny

white

narrow above

cracks into plates

becomes hairless

sepals remain

This widespread tree is a hybrid of complex and obscure origin. Wild trees have small, sour fruit; orchard trees, which produce the familiar large, sweet-tasting fruit, belong to var. *culta*. The trees often seen in hedgerows or on field margins may be escapes from cultivation, but sometimes represent the remains of old orchards. *Status:* cultivated throughout Europe, except for the far north and far south, often on a large scale. *Similar trees:* Plymouth Pear is native to Atlantic Europe. It has broad leaves and small, speckled fruits, which ripen red and lack sepals.

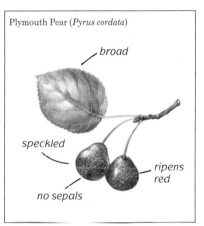

Plymouth Pear (*Pyrus cordata*)

broad

speckled

ripens red

no sepals

	COMMON PEAR	**Leaves**	alternate, 5–8cm, oval to elliptical, pointed, base rounded, finely short-toothed, hairy, becoming smooth; stalkless
Type	deciduous tree		
Height	up to 20m		
Habitat	orchards, hedges, often as isolated trees	**Stipules**	soon falling
			FLOWERS AND FRUIT
Flowering	April–May	**Flowers**	♂, 5–9 in clusters with leaves, white, stalks up to 1cm
Fruiting	September–October		
	TRUNK AND CROWN	**Petals**	5, 12–14mm, broadly oval, tapering abruptly at base; sepals 5, 6–8mm, narrow, persistent on fruit
Trunk	straight, often suckering		
Bark	blackish, cracking into small plates		
Crown	broadly pyramidal; branches angled upwards on young trees, spreading on old trees	**Stamens**	20–30, red
		Stigmas	5, free, often hairy at base
		Ovaries	1, in base of flower
Twigs	stout, reddish brown, soon smooth and shiny, often spiny	**Fruit**	fleshy, firm, gritty-textured, 6–16cm, pear-shaped, oblong or almost globular, ripening green or yellowish
	LEAVES		
Buds	5mm, yellowish brown, smooth, egg-shaped, pointed	**Seeds**	several, black

Wild Pear *Pyrus pyraster*

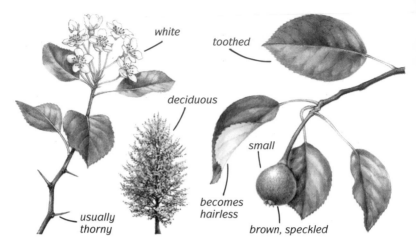

white

toothed

deciduous

small

becomes hairless

usually thorny

brown, speckled

Often confused with Common Pear, Wild Pear can be distinguished by its more bushy and spiny growth, and by the much smaller, hard and tart fruit. *Status:* native throughout much of Europe, absent from some Mediterranean islands and parts of the far north. *Similar trees:* two species with narrower leaves are Sage-leaved Pear, from central Europe; and Almond-leaved Pear, from France and Spain eastwards. The former has leaves with unbroken edges, and larger fruits. The latter usually has a few teeth towards the leaf-tip.

1 Sage-leaved Pear (*Pyrus salvifolia*)
2 Almond-leaved Pear (*Pyrus amygdaliformis*)

no teeth

grey-woolly

larger

few teeth

narrower

WILD PEAR	
Type	deciduous tree
Height	8–20m
Habitat	thickets, open woodland
Flowering	April–May
Fruiting	September–October
TRUNK AND CROWN	
Trunk	straight, short
Bark	rough, cracked
Crown	round-headed; branches spreading or angled upwards
Twigs	grey to brown, usually spiny
LEAVES	
Buds	small, brown, scales 5–8
Leaves	alternate, 2.5–7cm, elliptical, oval or circular, pointed, base wedge-shaped, rounded or heart-shaped, finely toothed, hairy but soon smooth; stalkless

Stipules	soon falling
FLOWERS AND FRUIT	
Flowers	♀, in clusters, white
Petals	5, 10–17mm, elliptical to circular, slightly crinkled, tapered at base; sepals 5, 3–8mm, persistent on fruit
Stamens	20–30, red
Stigmas	5, styles often hairy at base
Ovaries	1, 5-chambered, in base of flower
Fruit	1–3.5cm, fleshy, firm, gritty-textured, globular or top-shaped, ripening yellow, brown or black, with conspicuous lenticels
Seeds	several, black

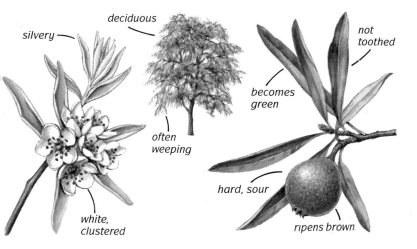

silvery

deciduous

not toothed

becomes green

often weeping

hard, sour

white, clustered

ripens brown

A slender, elegant shape and silvery leaves make Willow-leaved Pear an attractive tree of parks and gardens; the weeping cultivar 'Pendula' is common. The small fruits do not always develop fully, and are unsuitable for eating.
Status: native to Asia from the Caucasus mountains and Iran to Siberia; widely cultivated in Europe.
Similar trees: two species have broader leaves, toothed towards the tip.
P. elaeagrifolia, from south-eastern Europe, has woolly leaves and styles that are hairy up to the middle.
P. nivalis has leaves that become hairless above, and larger fruits.

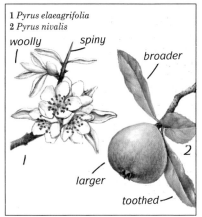

1 *Pyrus elaeagrifolia*
2 *Pyrus nivalis*

woolly

spiny

broader

larger

toothed

	WILLOW-LEAVED PEAR	
Type	deciduous tree	
Height	up to 10m	
Habitat	deciduous woods	
Flowering	April	
Fruiting	October	
	TRUNK AND CROWN	
Trunk	slender, straight	
Bark	dark silver-grey, smooth	
Crown	domed; main branches horizontal	
Twigs	drooping, densely white-woolly	
	LEAVES	
Buds	4–6mm, pyramidal, brown, downy	
Leaves	alternate, 3.5–9cm, narrow, pointed, grey-green and silvery downy on both sides, becoming smooth and glossy green above; stalkless	
Stipules	soon falling	
	FLOWERS AND FRUIT	
Flowers	☿, in tight clusters, white, opening with the emerging leaves, stalks downy	
Petals	5, c10mm, rounded or notched at tip, tapering at base; sepals 5, woolly, persistent on fruit	
Stamens	15–30, red	
Stigmas	2–5, styles woolly at base	
Ovaries	1, in base of flower	
Fruit	2.5cm, fleshy, firm, gritty-textured, sour, pear-shaped, top-shaped or cylindrical, ripening brown, stalk white, woolly	
Seeds	several	

Crab-apple _Malus sylvestris_

becomes hairless

white tinged pink

deciduous

small, sour

often thorny

The sour-fruited Crab-apple was once cultivated for fruit. Truly wild trees are spiny and have white flowers. Descendants of domesticated trees which have escaped back into the wild are unarmed and have pink-tinged flowers. _Status:_ native to most of Europe and western Asia. _Similar trees: Malus dasyphylla_ has woolly young twigs and occurs in the Balkan Peninsula and Danube basin. Cultivated Apple is a hybrid with leaves that are hairy below, and large, sweet fruit. It is the most widely grown orchard fruit, with more than one thousand cultivars recorded.

1 _Malus dasyphylla_
2 Cultivated Apple (_Malus domestica_)
woolly when young

large fruit

hairy below

	CRAB-APPLE	
Type	deciduous tree	
Height	2–10m	
Habitat	woods, hedges, in hilly, chalky areas	
Flowering	April–June	
Fruiting	September–October	

TRUNK AND CROWN

Trunk	short, often branching low down	
Bark	brown, cracking	
Crown	spreading, often dense; branches large and twisted	
Twigs	reddish brown, numerous short shoots, sometimes thorny	

LEAVES

Buds	4mm, reddish, hairy	
Leaves	alternate, 3–11cm, oval, elliptical or nearly circular, pointed, wedge-shaped or rounded at base, finely toothed, hairy but soon becoming smooth; stalkless	
Stipules	soon falling	

FLOWERS AND FRUIT

Flowers	♂, in few-flowered clusters, 3–4cm, white tinged pale pink	
Petals	5, oval, widest above middle, tapered at base; sepals 5, 3–7mm, hairy on inside, persistent on fruit	
Stamens	15–50, yellow	
Stigmas	2–5, styles joined and sometimes hairy at base	
Ovaries	1, in base of flower	
Fruit	fleshy, firm, 2.5–3cm, globular, ripening yellowish green tinged with red, sour	
Seeds	several, brown to blackish	

pink

deciduous

long stalk

downy below

ripens yellowish

Wreathing the branches in spring, the pink and white flowers of this small tree are produced in great profusion. One of the most popular ornamental species of all time, it probably arose as a garden hybrid in Japan, from where it was introduced to many countries. *Status:* exact origin unknown but probably Japan; widely planted in Europe for ornament. *Similar trees:* two widely grown ornamentals from China are Siberian Crab-apple, with white flowers and red fruits; and Purple Crab-apple, a garden hybrid with purplish flowers and fruits.

1 Siberian Crab-apple (*Malus baccata*)
2 Purple Crab-apple (*Malus × purpurea*)

white

purplish

1

red

purplish

2

	JAPANESE CRAB-APPLE		
Type	deciduous tree		
Height	6–9m		
Habitat	parks and gardens		
Flowering	April–May		
Fruiting	October		

TRUNK AND CROWN

Trunk	short, straight, tapering
Bark	grey-brown
Crown	rounded, dense; branches numerous
Twigs	reddish when young, drooping, hairy

LEAVES

Buds	2–4mm, dark red-brown, pointed
Leaves	alternate, 4–8cm, oblong to oval, pointed, sharply toothed, sometimes lobed, downy beneath but becoming smooth; stalkless
Stipules	small, soon falling

FLOWERS AND FRUIT

Flowers	☿, 4–7 in clusters, 2.5–3cm across, deep pink in bud, opening pale pink, fading white, fragrant
Petals	5, 13–15mm, oblong, blunt, base abruptly tapered; sepals 5, short, triangular, hairy within, soon falling
Stamens	15–50, yellow, pink at base
Stigmas	2–5, styles joined at base
Ovaries	1, in base of flower
Fruit	fleshy, firm, 2.5cm, globular, ripening bright yellow
Seeds	several, brown

Rowan   *Sorbus aucuparia*

A small, attractive tree, with paired leaflets, broad heads of white flowers followed by red berries and, in colder areas, autumn colour. Berries are eagerly sought by fruit-eating birds and, rich in Vitamin C, the fruit can be made into a jelly. Cv. 'Beissneri' is planted for its orange-pink bark and more intense autumn colour. *Status:* native; common in much of Europe; planted for ornament in streets and parks. *Similar trees:* Hupeh Rowan is a Chinese ornamental species differing in the white or purplish fruits. Native in southern Europe and planted elsewhere, Service-tree is a larger tree with much larger, brownish green fruits.

white

broad heads

paired leaflets

smooth bark

deciduous

autumn colour

red

1 Hupeh Rowan (*Sorbus hupehensis*)
2 Service-tree (*Sorbus domestica*)

1

white or purplish

2

large

greenish

	ROWAN		Leaves	on alternate sides of stem, up to 25 × 12cm; 5–9 pairs of oblong leaflets 3–6cm long, pointed, sharp-toothed, hairy, becoming smooth, dark green above, paler below, turning yellow or red in autumn; stalk 2–4mm
Type	deciduous tree			
Height	up to 20m			
Habitat	mountainous areas, lowland on light soils			
Flowering	May – June		**Stipules**	small, soon falling
Fruiting	August–September			
	TRUNK AND CROWN			**FLOWERS AND FRUIT**
Trunk	slender, sometimes forked		**Flowers**	☿, many, in branched heads, 8–10mm, creamy white
Bark	smooth, rarely slightly ridged, greyish brown		**Petals**	5, c3.5mm, equal; sepals 5, triangular, hairy
Crown	irregularly rounded, open		**Stamens**	many
Branches	angled upwards		**Stigmas**	3–4
Twigs	hairy becoming smooth, purplish brown		**Ovaries**	3–4, in base of flower
			Fruit	many, in broad head, berry-like, almost globular, each 6–9mm, ripening bright red
	LEAVES		**Seeds**	several, not released
Buds	10–17mm long, narrow, egg-shaped, tip curved, purplish, hairy			

An unusual relative of the Rowan and Whitebeam, with distinctive, maple-like leaves and brown, speckled fruits resembling those of the Service-tree. Also like some maples, the foliage turns deep red in the autumn. Acid until late in ripening, the fruit eventually becomes sweet enough to eat. *Status:* native to most of Europe except parts of the north; occasionally planted for ornament. *Similar trees:* two related plants are often regarded as hybrids. Broad-leaved Whitebeam has slightly lobed leaves with grey hairs beneath. Bastard Service-tree, from Scandinavia, has a few pairs of leaflets at the leaf-base and red fruit.

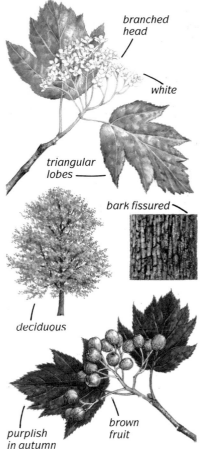

branched head

white

triangular lobes

bark fissured

deciduous

brown fruit

purplish in autumn

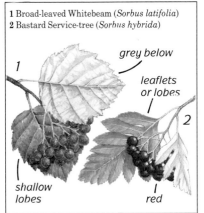

1 Broad-leaved Whitebeam (*Sorbus latifolia*)
2 Bastard Service-tree (*Sorbus hybrida*)

grey below

leaflets or lobes

1

2

shallow lobes

red

WILD SERVICE-TREE

Type	deciduous tree
Height	up to 25m
Habitat	woods, often lime-rich soils
Flowering	May–June
Fruiting	September

TRUNK AND CROWN

Trunk	slender, sometimes forked
Bark	shallowly fissured, forming squarish scales, dark, greyish brown
Crown	conical to broadly rounded
Branches	spreading
Twigs	woolly, soon becoming smooth, dark brown

LEAVES

Buds	4–5mm, globular, green, smooth
Leaves	on alternate sides of stem, 5–9cm, oval with 3–5 pairs of triangular lobes, pointed, sharply toothed, base rounded or heart-shaped, green above and below, turning purplish red in autumn, hairy below, becoming smooth, 4–6 pairs of veins; stalk 15–40mm
Stipules	small, soon falling

FLOWERS AND FRUIT

Flowers	⚥, in loose, branched heads, 10–15mm, white; stalk hairy
Petals	5, equal, rounded; sepals 5, triangular, hairy
Stamens	many
Stigmas	2
Ovaries	2, in base of flower
Fruit	berry-like, egg-shaped to globular, each 12–18mm, brown, speckled
Seeds	several, not released

Common Whitebeam *Sorbus aria*

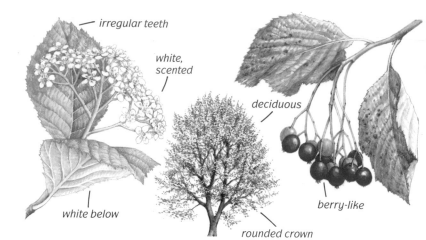

irregular teeth

white, scented

deciduous

white below

rounded crown

berry-like

Silvery white as they unfold in spring, the leaves of this tree gradually turn green on the upper surface as their pale hairs are shed; the lower leaf surface remains densely hairy. It is a characteristic tree of chalk downland. *Status:* native to most of Europe; several cultivars are commonly planted street trees. *Similar trees:* two rather shrubby species have more or less globular fruits. Greek Whitebeam has leathery leaves, which are greenish-woolly below and have rounded teeth; fruits have white spots. Rock Whitebeam has leaves with symmetrical teeth and fruits with many spots.

1 Greek Whitebeam (*Sorbus graeca*)
2 Rock Whitebeam (*Sorbus rupicola*)

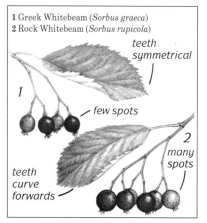

teeth symmetrical

few spots

teeth curve forwards

many spots

COMMON WHITEBEAM

Type	deciduous tree
Height	up to 15m
Habitat	chalky soils
Flowering	May–June
Fruiting	September

TRUNK AND CROWN

Trunk	well-defined
Bark	grey, smooth, becoming flaky and fissured
Crown	conical in young trees, later broadly domed; branches angled upwards
Twigs	olive brown, hairy, becoming smooth

LEAVES

Buds	green, egg-shaped, often hairy
Leaves	alternate, 8cm, variable in shape but usually broadly oval, edges sharply toothed and sometimes shallowly lobed, densely silvery-hairy, the upper surface eventually becoming smooth and green; stalkless
Stipules	small, soon falling

FLOWERS AND FRUIT

Flowers	☿, many in loose, branched clusters at tips of shoots, each 1.5cm across, white
Petals	5, *c*6mm, equal; sepals 5, triangular, hairy
Stamens	many, cream or pink
Stigmas	2
Ovaries	2, in base of flower, hairy
Fruit	berry-like, 8mm, usually longer than broad, ripening scarlet with many small lenticels
Seeds	2

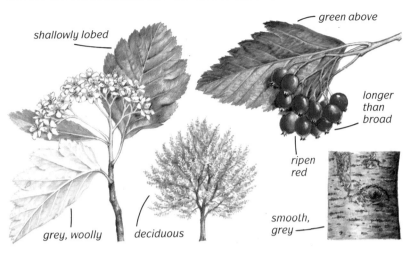

green above

shallowly lobed

longer than broad

ripen red

grey, woolly   deciduous

smooth, grey

Shallow-lobed leaves felted below with yellowish grey hairs identify Swedish Whitebeam. Red fruits are dotted with a few pale lenticels. It flowers more intensively than most other whitebeams, and is often used as an ornamental tree. *Status:* native to the Baltic region; planted elsewhere; sometimes naturalized. *Similar trees:* S. *austriaca* has leaves with whitish grey wool below. Those of S. *mougeolii* are also grey-woolly below but less deeply lobed. Both are mountain species. S. *umbellata*, from the Balkan region, has deeply lobed, white-woolly leaves and yellow fruits.

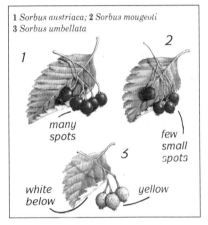

1 *Sorbus austriaca;* **2** *Sorbus mougeoli*
3 *Sorbus umbellata*

1

2

many spots

few small spots

3

white below

yellow

SWEDISH WHITEBEAM

Type	deciduous tree
Height	up to 15m
Habitat	hills and mountains
Flowering	May
Fruiting	September

TRUNK AND CROWN

Trunk	short
Bark	grey, smooth with wide, shallow cracks
Crown	dense, broadly domed
Twigs	grey to purplish, very hairy, becoming smooth

LEAVES

Buds	8mm, egg-shaped, green or brown, with grey hairs
Leaves	alternate, 8–12cm, elliptic, shallowly lobed, the lobes reaching one-third of the way to midrib but more pronounced towards base of leaf, edge sharply toothed, smooth and green above, densely yellow-grey woolly below; stalkless
Stipules	small, soon falling

FLOWERS AND FRUIT

Flowers	☿, many, in branched clusters in angles of leaves, each 12–20mm across, white, leaf stalk smooth
Petals	5, c6mm, equal; sepals 5, narrowly triangular
Stamens	many, cream
Stigmas	2, styles joined at base
Ovaries	2, in base of flower, hairy
Fruit	berry-like, 12–15mm, much longer than broad, ripening red, dotted with few small lenticels
Seeds	2

Loquat *Eriobotrya japonica*

white, fragrant

brown hairs

woolly below

evergreen

glossy green

branched clusters

branching low

toothed

clustered

ripen yellow

Easily recognized by its leathery, evergreen leaves and the copious reddish, velvety hairs on twigs, leaves and flowers, this small tree is a common sight in Mediterranean areas. It is widely grown for its golden-yellow, sweet fruits, which resemble apricots and are often sold in markets. It may be grown in orchards but is more common as a single tree. The tree sometimes escapes and has established itself in the wild in many areas. Farther north, Loquat is grown mainly as an ornamental. *Status:* introduced from China and widely cultivated; often naturalized. *Similar trees:* none.

	LOQUAT
Type	evergreen tree
Height	up to 10m
Habitat	dry, light soils
Flowering	October–February
Fruiting	April–June

	TRUNK AND CROWN
Trunk	very slender, often branching near base
Bark	grey, slightly rough
Crown	irregular but usually narrow
Twigs	velvety-hairy

	LEAVES
Buds	c4mm, pointed, very hairy
Leaves	alternate, 12–25cm, elliptical or oval and widest above middle, sharply toothed, leathery, conspicuously veined, dark glossy green above, densely woolly with reddish brown hairs below; stalkless
Stipules	very narrow

	FLOWERS AND FRUIT
Flowers	♀, in branched, pyramidal clusters, c1cm, creamy-white, almost hidden by dense brown hair, fragrant
Petals	5, oval or nearly circular, tip notched, base tapered; sepals 5, persisting on fruit
Stamens	20
Stigmas	2–5, styles joined at base
Ovaries	1, in base of flower
Fruit	fleshy, sweet, 3–6cm, elliptical to pear-shaped, ripening deep yellow
Seeds	1–several, each 1–1.5cm

long sepals

white, solitary

few teeth

centre sunken

sepals persist

deciduous

often short

cracks into plates

Dull and rather dowdy for much of the year, the Medlar is often a shrub, at best making only a small tree. The large, solitary flowers have sepals that are longer than the white petals and are followed by distinctive fruits, most nearly resembling huge, brown rosehips, with the narrow persistent sepals forming a crown. The fruits are edible, but only after they are 'bletted' – softened by overripening or being frosted. *Status:* native to south-eastern Europe but often cultivated as a fruit tree and naturalized in many central and western parts as far north as southern Britain. *Similar trees:* none.

	MEDLAR		
Type	deciduous tree or shrub		edges with tiny teeth near tip, dull yellowish-green above, dense white hairs below; stalk *c*2mm
Height	up to 6m		
Habitat	hedgerows, woods		
Flowering	May–June		
Fruiting	October–November	**Stipules**	falling early
	TRUNK AND CROWN		**FLOWERS AND FRUIT**
Trunk	slender, often short	**Flowers**	♀, single, in angle of leaf stalks, 3–6cm, white
Bark	grey-brown, cracking into oblong plates	**Petals**	5, 12mm; sepals 5, 1–1.6cm, narrowly triangular, persistent on fruit
Crown	spreading, dense and tangled		
Twigs	densely white-hairy, becoming smooth and black	**Stamens**	30–40, red
		Stigmas	5, each on a long style
	LEAVES	**Ovaries**	1, in base of flower
Buds	1–2mm, brown, hairy	**Fruit**	fleshy but hard, roughly globular, ripening brown and remaining on tree
Leaves	alternate, 5–15cm, crinkled, narrowly oval, widest above or below the middle, tip broadly pointed, base wedge-shaped,		
		Seeds	10

Juneberry   *Amelanchier lamackii*

deciduous

white

small teeth

narrow petals

often shrubby

purplish when young

purple, juicy

red in autumn

The contrast of white blossom against coppery young leaves makes this tree a striking sight in spring; leaves also produce rich autumn colours. Of uncertain origin and perhaps a hybrid, it has been established in the wild in Britain for over one hundred years. *Status:* possibly native to eastern North America; introduced and naturalized in northern Europe; often planted for ornament. *Similar trees:* the only European native is the less showy Snowy Mespil. It has more coarsely toothed leaves, whitish woolly below, and blackish fruit.

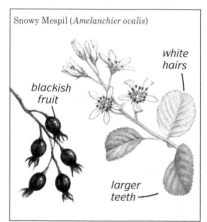

Snowy Mespil (*Amelanchier ovalis*)

white hairs

blackish fruit

larger teeth

	JUNEBERRY		
Type	deciduous tree or shrub		
Height	up to 10m		
Habitat	woods and scrub on acid soil		
Flowering	April–May		
Fruiting	September–October		

TRUNK AND CROWN

Trunk slender, short, often several
Bark pale grey-brown
Crown open and spreading
Twigs shaggy white-hairy, becoming smooth

LEAVES

Buds 7–11mm, reddish, narrow, pointed
Leaves alternate, oval-oblong to elliptical, shortly pointed, base rounded to heart-shaped, edges curled upwards, young leaves coppery red, silky beneath, turning green, rich yellow and red in autumn; stalk hairy, becoming smooth
Stipules small, soon falling

FLOWERS AND FRUIT

Flowers ♂, 6–12 in loose, often drooping clusters with the leaves, white, flower-tube bell-shaped, stalks 1.5–2.5cm, hairy
Petals 5, 9–14mm, narrow, widest above middle, blunt; sepals 5, 3–5mm, hairy within, persistent on fruit
Stamens about 20
Stigmas 5, on a single style
Ovaries 1, in base of flower
Fruit berry-like, ripening purple-black, sweet-tasting
Seeds 4–10

Cotoneaster frigidus **Himalayan Tree-cotoneaster**

dull green

branched
flower-head

white hairs
below

berry-like

deciduous

One of the few cotoneasters to form a tree, this species is deciduous. The berries remain on the tree through the winter, showing conspicuously against the bare boughs. It is widely planted as an ornamental and has become naturalized in hedgerows and woods. *Status:* native to the Himalayas; widely cultivated; occasionally naturalized in various parts of Europe. *Similar trees:* Waterer's Cotoneaster forms a large, evergreen shrub or small tree with narrow leaves. It produces larger clusters of red or orange fruits. *C. bullatus* reaches tree size and has broader, corrugated leaves.

1 Waterer's Cotoneaster (*Cotoneaster* × *watereri*); **2** *Cotoneaster bullatus*

semi-
evergreen

long,
narrow

corrugated

	HIMALAYAN TREE-COTONEASTER
Type	deciduous tree
Height	20m
Habitat	parks, gardens, hedges, woods
Flowering	June
Fruiting	September – October

	TRUNK AND CROWN
Trunk	short, slender, often several
Bark	grey-brown, smooth
Crown	broad, domed; branches arching
Twigs	greenish, ridged

	LEAVES
Buds	small, lacking scales, hairy
Leaves	alternate, 6–16cm, elliptical to oval and widest above the middle, bluntly pointed, base wedge-shaped, dark green above, densely white hairy below; stalkless
Stipules	falling early

	FLOWERS AND FRUIT
Flowers	☿, 20–40 in flat, branched clusters, white, fragrant
Petals	5, broadly oval, widest above middle, blunt, tapering at base; sepals 5, persistent on fruit
Stamens	20
Stigmas	2, on free styles
Ovaries	1, 2-chambered, in base of flower
Fruit	berry-like, 5mm, globular, ripening bright red, remaining on tree through winter
Seeds	2, stony

Common Hawthorn *Crataegus monogyna*

small, deciduous

dark red

scented

thorny

white

rough, scaly

deep lobes

When left to grow undisturbed, Common Hawthorn forms a densely-crowned tree. However, if cut or trimmed regularly, it soon makes a dense thorny barrier ideal for enclosing fields and fencing in animals. It is very variable in leaf shape and lobing, and in fruit colour. *Status:* native throughout Europe and much of Asia, widely used for hedging. *Similar trees:* Midland Hawthorn and *C. calycina*, both native to woodlands in northwestern and central Europe, have finely toothed leaf-lobes and stipules. Midland Hawthorn also has two stigmas and two seeds per fruit.

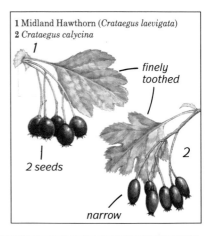

1 Midland Hawthorn (*Crataegus laevigata*)
2 *Crataegus calycina*

1

finely toothed

2 seeds

2

narrow

	COMMON HAWTHORN	
Type	deciduous tree or shrub	
Height	18m but often less	
Habitat	woods, hedges, especially on chalky soils	
Flowering	May–June	
Fruiting	September–October	
	TRUNK AND CROWN	
Trunk	fluted, often branching near base	
Bark	silvery grey, cracking to show orange or pink beneath	
Crown	variable, usually dense	
Twigs	brown, thorns up to 15mm	
	LEAVES	
Buds	2mm, rounded	
Leaves	alternate, 1.5–4.5cm, oval to diamond-shaped in outline, 3–5 deep lobes, toothed near tips, leathery, dark, shiny green above, paler and dull below; stalk dark pink, grooved	
Stipules	small, curved, sometimes toothed	
	FLOWERS AND FRUIT	
Flowers	♂, 9–18, in loose, branched clusters, 8–15mm, white, rarely pink, sickly sweet-scented, stalks woolly	
Petals	5, 4–6mm, oval, widest above the middle; sepals 5, triangular, persistent on fruit	
Stamens	typically 20, pink or purple	
Stigmas	1, on a short style	
Ovaries	1, sunk into base of fruit	
Fruit	berry-like, 7–14mm, globose or egg-shaped, ripening scarlet to maroon	
Seeds	1, rarely 2, stony	

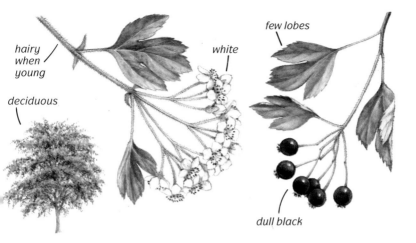

The most common of several eastern hawthorns with black fruits, this species is distinguished by the cobwebby hairs on the undersides of the young leaves and by the flowers, which have four or five stigmas. As the name suggests, the fruits commonly have five seeds. *Status:* native to east-central Europe, south to the northern Balkan Peninsula and east to Russia. *Similar trees:* Hungarian Hawthorn occurs in woodlands in the Danube basin. It has leaves that are woolly on both sides, with up to 11 lobes, few flowers and shiny fruits.

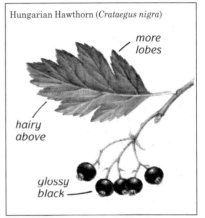

Hungarian Hawthorn (*Crataegus nigra*)

FIVE-SEEDED HAWTHORN	
Type	deciduous tree or shrub
Height	up to 8m
Habitat	woodland margins
Flowering	May–June
Fruiting	August

TRUNK AND CROWN	
Trunk	short, straight
Bark	pale brown
Crown	irregularly domed; upper branches arching
Twigs	with sparse, long hairs, soon smooth, grey-brown, occasional stout spines 10mm

LEAVES	
Buds	2mm, brown, globular
Leaves	alternating, 2–5cm, oval in outline, leathery, dark olive-green and smooth above, paler below with cobweb-like hairs which eventually disappear, 3–7 deep lobes, the lowest spreading, toothed; stalk 1.5–3cm, hairy
Stipules	narrow, curved, toothed

FLOWERS AND FRUIT	
Flowers	♂, many in loose clusters, 12–15mm, white, stalks downy
Petals	5, oval, widest above middle; sepals 5, tiny, triangular, soon falling
Stamens	20
Stigmas	4–5, styles free
Ovaries	1, in base of flower, downy
Fruit	berry-like, 10–15mm, elliptical to globular, ripening dull black or dark purplish black
Seeds	4–5, stony

Azarole *Crataegus azarolus*

Azarole owes its present fairly widespread distribution to its edible fruits, which taste somewhat of apple. They are sufficiently large and fleshy to be worth gathering, and the tree was taken from its eastern Mediterranean home to other areas, notably France and Italy, as a fruit tree. *Status:* native to Crete; cultivated and naturalized in southern Europe. *Similar trees:* Oriental Hawthorn, from the Balkan Peninsula and parts of eastern Europe, has leaf-lobes with few teeth, compact flower clusters, four or five stigmas and globular fruits.

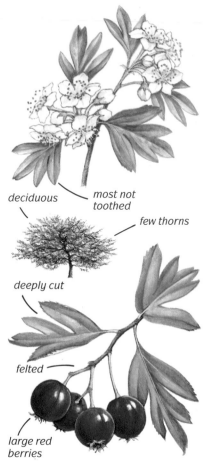

deciduous — most not toothed

few thorns

deeply cut

felted

large red berries

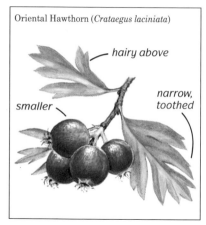

Oriental Hawthorn (*Crataegus laciniata*)

hairy above

narrow, toothed

smaller

AZAROLE			sometimes with a few teeth, downy on both sides; stalk 3–8mm
Type	deciduous tree or shrub		
Height	up to 8m	**Stipules**	curved, coarsely toothed
Habitat	humid scrubland		**FLOWERS AND FRUIT**
Flowering	March–April	**Flowers**	♂, 3–18 in compact clusters, 12–18mm, white, stalks woolly
Fruiting	June–September		
	TRUNK AND CROWN	**Petals**	5, oval, widest above middle; sepals 5, short-pointed, persistent on fruit
Trunk	short, slender		
Bark	pale grey-brown	**Stamens**	15–20
Crown	rounded, bushy; branches spreading	**Stigmas**	1–2, rarely 3, styles thick
		Ovaries	1, in base of fruit
Twigs	downy, becoming smooth; few, stout spines up to 10mm	**Fruit**	berry-like, 20–25mm, roughly globular with longitudinal, rounded ridges, ripening yellow or orange-red
	LEAVES		
Buds	3–4mm, rounded, red-brown	**Seeds**	1–3, stony
Leaves	alternate, 3–5cm, oval to triangular in outline, base wedge-shaped and extending onto stalk, 3–5 deep lobes,		

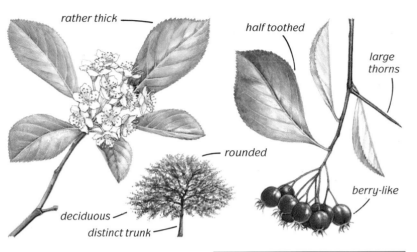

rather thick

half toothed

large thorns

rounded

berry-like

deciduous

distinct trunk

Ferociously armed with numerous long thorns, Cockspur Hawthorn is found wild in North America. In Europe, its popularity as an ornamental tree derives from the unusual rich, bright orange of the autumn foliage. *Status:* native to north eastern North America; planted in Europe for ornament and as a street tree. *Similar trees:* two hybrids between Cockspur Hawthorn and other American species are grown. Broad-leaved Cockspur Hawthorn has shorter spines, hairy flower clusters and broad leaves. Hybrid Cockspur Hawthorn has downy twigs and flower clusters, and narrow leaves.

1 Hybrid Cockspur Hawthorn (*Crataegus × lavallei*); **2** Broad-leaved Cockspur Hawthorn (*Crataegus × prunifolia*)

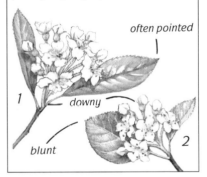

often pointed

downy

blunt

	COCKSPUR HAWTHORN		
Type	deciduous tree		finely sharp-toothed, smooth, dark, shiny green, turning bright orange in autumn; stalk 5–15mm
Height	10m		
Habitat	meadows, woodland margins		
Flowering	May	**Stipules**	toothed
Fruiting	October		
			FLOWERS AND FRUIT
	TRUNK AND CROWN	**Flowers**	♂, in small, loose clusters, 1.5cm, white, stalks smooth
Trunk	slender, unbranched		
Bark	grey to brown, smooth, becoming finely fissured	**Petals**	5, oval, widest above middle; sepals 5, persistent on fruit
Crown	flat-topped, spreading	**Stamens**	10, pink
Twigs	purplish brown, smooth; numerous spines 7–10mm	**Stigmas**	2, rarely 1 or 3, styles free
		Ovaries	1, in base of flower
	LEAVES	**Fruit**	berry-like, 10–12mm, globose, ripening red, remaining on tree through winter
Buds	small, rounded		
Leaves	alternate, 5–8cm, oval, widest above the middle, blunt at tip, base wedge-shaped, edges	**Seeds**	2, stony

Peach *Prunus persica*

Prized for its succulent, downy fruits,
the Peach was brought from China and
is now widely grown in southern
Europe. In harsher northern climes,
fruit production is less reliable. This
tree is also planted for ornament and in
places has established itself in the wild.
Nectarine is a smooth-fruited variety of
Peach, cultivated on a commercial
scale. *Status:* native to China;
cultivated in fields and gardens;
naturalized in some parts of southern
Europe. *Similar trees:* Apricot has pale
pink flowers and smaller fruits.

deciduous

most deep pink

large, furry

finely toothed

nectarine is smooth

Apricot (*Prunus armeniaca*)

most paler

broad

smaller

	PEACH		
Type	deciduous tree		glandular
Height	6m	**Stipules**	narrow, papery, falling early
Habitat	gardens, orchards, parks, woods, thickets		**FLOWERS AND FRUIT**
Flowering	March–May	**Flowers**	♂, single or paired, appearing before the leaves, deep pink, rarely pale pink or white, flower-tube bell-shaped; stalk short
Fruiting	June–July		
	TRUNK AND CROWN	**Petals**	5, 10–20mm, equal, broadly oval, widest above middle, tapered at base; sepals 5, 6–8mm
Trunk	straight, slender		
Bark	grey-brown, finely cracked		
Crown	rounded, bushy	**Stamens**	20–30, red when young
Twigs	smooth, reddish, angular	**Stigmas**	1, 2-lobed, style long and slender
	LEAVES	**Ovaries**	1, downy
Buds	6mm, oval, greenish brown with white hairs	**Fruit**	berry-like, 4–8cm, globular, ripening greenish or yellow tinged with red, sweet-tasting
Leaves	alternate, 5–15cm, narrowly oval-oblong to elliptical, long-pointed, edges with small, sharp teeth, smooth; stalk 1.5cm,	**Seeds**	1, in a grooved stone

flowers before leaves

long, toothed

green, furry

deciduous

One of the first trees to flower in spring, Almond can turn hillsides white with blossom. The fruits have only a thin fleshy layer covering the large, pitted stone containing the familiar edible seed. *Status:* probably native to south-western and central Asia; anciently cultivated in southern Europe as a fruit tree and sometimes naturalized. *Similar trees:* Cherry Plum has white flowers and smooth, fleshy fruits, for which it is widely grown. A variety with pink flowers and red leaves (cv. 'Pissardii') is a common street tree.

Cherry Plum (*Prunus cerasifera*)

most white

some dark-leaved

juicy fruit

ALMOND

Type	deciduous tree
Height	8m
Habitat	orchards, parks, hillsides
Flowering	February–April
Fruiting	May–June

TRUNK AND CROWN

Trunk	straight, slender
Bark	black, cracking into small squares
Crown	rounded; branches angled upwards, later spreading, tangled in wild trees, straight in cultivated trees
Twigs	smooth, spiny in wild trees

LEAVES

Buds	brown, scales fringed with hairs
Leaves	alternate, 4–13cm, narrowly oval-oblong, long-pointed, edges with small, blunt teeth, smooth; stalk 2cm, glandular
Stipules	narrow, papery, falling early

FLOWERS AND FRUIT

Flowers	♀, paired, appearing before the leaves, pink fading to white, flower-tube bell-shaped
Petals	5, 15–25mm, broadly oval and widest above middle, tapered at base; sepals 5, 7–8mm, woolly, reddish
Stamens	15–25, yellow
Stigmas	1, slender, long
Ovaries	1, hairy
Fruit	leathery, 3.5–6cm, egg-shaped, flattened, velvety, ripening grey-green
Seeds	1, in a large, pitted stone, which is ridged around the edge

Blackthorn *Prunus spinosa*

White flowers of Blackthorn contrast
starkly with its blackish, thorny shoots,
brightening the hedgerows before its
leaves appear. Typically a shrub
spreading by suckers to form dense
thickets, it can reach tree size. Small
blue-black fruits (sloes) have a whitish,
waxy covering and are very sour.
Status: native; widespread in Europe
except the extreme north. *Similar trees:*
Wild Plum, part of a variable species
which includes cultivated plums,
damsons and greengages, has a brown
bark and larger fruit. Native mainly to
southern Italy and the Balkans, *P.
cocomilia* differs in the non-spiny twigs,
hairless leaves and yellow fruit.

flowers before leaves

spiny

deciduous

whitish coating

dark twig

round, fleshy

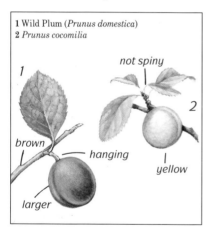

1 Wild Plum (*Prunus domestica*)
2 *Prunus cocomilia*

not spiny

1

2

brown

hanging

yellow

larger

BLACKTHORN		
Type	deciduous shrub or tree	
Height	usually up to 4m	
Habitat	scrub, light woodland, hedgerows; most soils	
Flowering	March – April	
Fruiting	September – October	

TRUNK AND CROWN

Trunk	often several, suckering
Bark	blackish, rough
Crown	irregular, dense; branching frequently and widely
Twigs	spiny, initially shortly hairy, dull blackish or dark brown

LEAVES

Buds	egg-shaped, hairy
Leaves	on alternate sides of stem, 2–4.5cm, narrowly to broadly oval, broadest above middle, tip blunt or pointed, edge with fine rounded or pointed teeth, base wedge-shaped, hairless above, shortly hairy on veins below, dull green; stalk 2–10mm
Stipules	present

FLOWERS AND FRUIT

Flowers	♂, before leaves, 10–15mm, single or some paired; stalk c5mm, hairless
Petals	5, 5–8mm, broadest towards tip, white; sepals 5
Stamens	c20
Stigmas	single; anthers reddish
Ovaries	1
Fruit	1, berry-like, 10–15mm, globular, bluish black with whitish waxy covering, sour
Seeds	single, in globular, smooth or slightly rough, 'stone', 7.5–10mm

Long branches of this attractive tree are smothered with white flowers just before the toothed leaves appear, and later weighed down with fruit. Edible sweet cherries are derived from this species. The double white cv. 'Plena' is one of the last ornamental cherries to flower. *Status:* native except in the extreme north and east; planted for ornament and fruit. *Similar trees:* usually shrubs, two other cherries reach tree size. Dwarf Cherry has spreading, glossy leaves and a broader, bell-shaped base to the flower. Saint Lucie Cherry has smaller, very glossy, minutely toothed leaves and branched heads of small, bitter, black fruits.

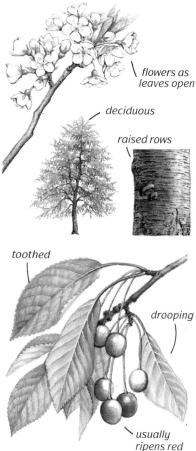

flowers as leaves open

deciduous

raised rows

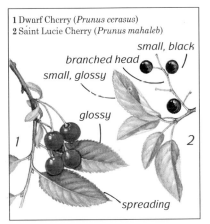

1 Dwarf Cherry (*Prunus cerasus*)
2 Saint Lucie Cherry (*Prunus mahaleb*)

small, black

branched head

small, glossy

glossy

spreading

toothed

drooping

usually ripens red

	WILD CHERRY	
Type	deciduous tree	
Height	10–30m	
Habitat	woods, hedges, especially on lime-rich, clay soils	
Flowering	April–May	
Fruiting	July	

TRUNK AND CROWN

Trunk	single, well-defined
Bark	reddish brown with horizontal peeling strips, bands of lenticels and blackish fissures
Crown	conical, becoming rounded with almost horizontal branches
Twigs	pale reddish brown, hairless

LEAVES

Buds	pointed, glossy reddish brown
Leaves	on alternate sides of stem, drooping, 8–15cm, oval, broader above, tip slender, with rounded, forward-pointing, blunt teeth and tapered base, dull green, smooth above, paler, slightly hairy below, turning yellow or red in autumn; stalk 2–5cm, glands near top

FLOWERS AND FRUIT

Flowers	♂, before leaves; in stalkless clusters of 2–6; each flower 25–35mm, white, base swollen, narrowed above; stalk 2–5cm,
Petals	5, 9–15mm; sepals 5
Stamens	c20
Stigma	1
Ovaries	1
Fruit	berry-like, in bunches, 9–12mm, globular, glossy dark red, yellow or blackish
Seeds	1, in globular, smooth, 'stone'

Bird Cherry *Prunus padus*

An attractive tree, easily recognized amongst native deciduous cherries by its long spikes of fragrant white flowers in late spring. The small, glossy black fruit has a bittersweet or astringent taste, but is edible to birds. *Status:* native to much of Europe; planted for ornament in parks, gardens and streets. *Similar trees:* two introduced North American species have smaller flowers. Rum Cherry has glossy, dark green leaves with wavy, toothed edges, the teeth curving forwards. Choke Cherry has dull leaves with fewer veins and very sharp, spreading teeth, and bears dark red fruits.

deciduous

finely toothed

flowers with leaves

hanging, elongated heads

berry-like

ripens black

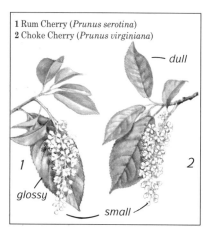

1 Rum Cherry (*Prunus serotina*)
2 Choke Cherry (*Prunus virginiana*)

dull

glossy

small

	BIRD CHERRY		
Type	deciduous tree or shrub		
Height	3–17m		
Habitat	common on lime-rich soils, often in woods or by water		
Flowering	May		
Fruiting	July–August		

TRUNK AND CROWN

Trunk	distinct, upright
Bark	dark greyish brown, smooth, peeling in horizontal strips
Crown	conical, becoming rounded; branches angled upwards, or lower branches level
Twigs	brown or grey, becoming hairless

LEAVES

Buds	egg-shaped, glossy brown
Leaves	5–10cm, oval or oblong with slender tip, edge finely toothed, base rounded, dull green above, paler and sometimes hairy below, turning yellow or red in autumn; stalk 1–2cm, grooved, red-brown

FLOWERS AND FRUIT

Flowers	♀, strongly scented, 15–40 in drooping cluster 7–15cm long on leafy shoot, each flower 14–20mm, white
Petals	5, 6–9mm, irregularly toothed; sepals 5, short, blunt
Stamens	numerous
Stigmas	1
Ovaries	1
Fruit	berry-like in long heads, each 6–8mm, almost globular, glossy black, bitter
Seeds	1, in globular, grooved 'stone'

evergreen

often several stems

upright spikes

thick, glossy

few teeth

berry-like

ripens black

A glossy evergreen tree or shrub that was originally confined to the Balkans but is now widespread elsewhere. It produces long, upright clusters of flowers but its main use is as a foliage plant. *Status:* native to eastern parts of the Balkan Peninsula; introduced to southern and western regions as an ornamental and widely naturalized. *Similar trees:* Portugal Laurel has dark red leaf-stalks, which are much longer than the leaves, and flower-heads that contain up to 100 flowers. It is native to Spain, Portugal and southern France and also planted for ornament.

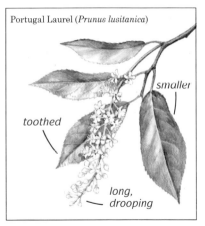

Portugal Laurel (*Prunus lusitanica*)

toothed

smaller

long, drooping

	CHERRY LAUREL	
Type	evergreen tree or shrub	
Height	up to 8m	
Habitat	woodlands	
Flowering	April	
Fruiting	September	

TRUNK AND CROWN

Trunk	slender
Bark	dark grey-brown, roughened by many lenticels
Crown	irregularly domed, spreading
Twigs	pale green, smooth

LEAVES

Buds	4–7mm, bright green, egg-shaped, pointed
Leaves	alternate, 10–20cm, oblong to narrowly oval, shortly pointed, base rounded or wedge-shaped, edges sometimes with a few tiny teeth, rather rigid and leathery, dark glossy green above, yellowish green below; stalk green, 1.2cm, with 1–several glands near blade
Stipules	narrow, papery

FLOWERS AND FRUIT

Flowers	♀, *c*30 in long, upright spikes, as long as leaves, creamy-white, flower-tube funnel- to bell-shaped
Petals	5, 4mm, oval to circular, widely separated; sepals 5, short
Stamens	15–20, yellow
Stigmas	1, style protrudes well beyond flower
Ovaries	1
Fruit	berry-like, *c*1–2cm, globular, ripening purplish black
Seeds	1, in a smooth, globular 'stone'

Japanese Cherry *Prunus serrulata*

Horizontal or wide-spreading branches give this tree a characteristically low-domed shape. It is widely planted, especially in streets and avenues, which it brightens in spring with prolific displays of blossom. There are many hybrids and cultivars, with a range of leaf and petal colours, and single or double flowers. *Status:* origin obscure but probably native to China; widespread throughout Europe as an ornamental tree. *Similar trees:* two common ornamental Japanese species are Sargent's Cherry, which has deep pink flowers, and Yoshino Cherry, a hybrid with glossy leaves.

deciduous

often broad

often double

many grafted

white or pink

long tip

bristle-tipped

fine teeth

1 Sargent's Cherry (*Prunus sargentii*)
2 Yoshino Cherry (*Prunus × yedoensis*)

pointed teeth

notched

pale   2

1

	JAPANESE CHERRY
Type	deciduous tree
Height	up to 15m
Habitat	streets, parks and gardens
Flowering	April–May
Fruiting	June

TRUNK AND CROWN

Trunk	short, abruptly branching to form crown
Bark	purplish-brown, with bands of lenticels
Crown	spreading; branches horizontal or angled upwards
Twigs	smooth

LEAVES

Buds	large, dark brown
Leaves	alternate, 8–20cm, broadly oval and widest above middle, tip tapering abruptly, teeth sharp with spreading, hair-like points; stalk 2–4cm, with 1–4 reddish glands near blade
Stipules	narrow, papery

FLOWERS AND FRUIT

Flowers	♂, 2–4, in clusters appearing before leaves, white or pink, flower-tube narrowly bell-shaped
Petals	5, 15–40mm, oval, notched at tip; sepals 5, long, narrow
Stamens	c25–30
Stigmas	1, style long and slender
Ovaries	1
Fruit	berry-like, 7mm, globular, ripening purplish red, seldom produced
Seeds	1, in globular stone

Spring Cherry normally flowers in the early months of the year, but the cultivar 'Autumnalis', the Autumn Cherry, flowers from October to April. Various other cultivars, including weeping and double-flowered forms, are also planted as ornamentals, but it is the Autumn Cherry which is most often seen. *Status:* native to Japan; widespread as a street tree and garden ornamental. *Similar trees:* Tibetan Cherry has glossy red-brown, peeling bark, white flowers and bright red fruits. It is a common tree in parks.

deciduous

pink

most before leaves

toothed

pointed teeth

some autumn-flowering

semi-double

Tibetan Cherry (*Prunus serrula*)

flowers with leaves

glossy

peeling

narrow

	SPRING CHERRY		
Type	deciduous tree		
Height	up to 20m		
Habitat	parks, gardens, streets		
Flowering	March – April		
Fruiting	June		
	TRUNK AND CROWN		
Trunk	thick, straight		
Bark	grey-brown		
Crown	dense, rounded; branches slender		
Twigs	crimson, downy		
	LEAVES		
Buds	3–5mm, egg-shaped, dark		
Leaves	alternate, c6cm, oval to oblong, drawn out to a long point, base wedge-shaped, sharply toothed, smooth above, downy on veins		

beneath; stalk 7–12mm, downy, crimson

Stipules narrow, papery

FLOWERS AND FRUIT

Flowers ♀, 2–5 on short stalks, in clusters appearing before leaves, very pale or rose pink, flower-tube urn-shaped

Petals 5, 8–12mm, oval, widest above middle, notched at tips; sepals 5, 3mm, triangular

Stamens c20

Stigmas 1, style slender, longer than stamens, hairy towards base

Ovaries 1

Fruit berry-like, 7–9mm, globose or ellipsoid, ripening purplish black

Seeds 1, in globular stone

Carob *Ceratonia siliqua*

Leathery-leaved and surviving well in dry conditions, Carob is a characteristic tree of the Mediterranean landscape. The flowers are unusual among members of the pea family, completely lacking petals. A native tree, Carob is also widely cultivated for its pods. Found on the tree at most times of year, these are large and contain seeds and a sugary pulp. They are a rich source of food, used mainly for animal feeds. *Status* native to the Mediterranean region; naturalized in some countries; widely grown as a fodder crop. *Similar trees:* none.

no petals

long cluster

♂

leathery

paired leaflets

evergreen

dense crown

stout

drooping pods

	CAROB	**Stipules**	tiny, soon falling
Type	evergreen tree		**FLOWERS AND FRUIT**
Height	up to 10m	**Flowers**	♂ and ♀ on same tree or on
Habitat	dry soils		different trees, many, in short
Flowering	August–October		spikes in angles of leaves, green
Fruiting	September onwards	**Petals**	0; sepals 5, tiny, soon falling
	TRUNK AND CROWN	**Stamens**	5, radiating from a central disc
Trunk	short, often branched from base	**Stigmas**	1, very shortly lobed, style thick, green
Bark	grey, rough		
Crown	dense, low dome	**Ovaries**	1, flask-shaped
Twigs	stout, minutely downy	**Fruit**	pod, 10–20cm, drooping, flattened, ripening violet-brown
	LEAVES	**Seeds**	many, not released
Buds	small, golden-hairy		
Leaves	alternate, 2–5 pairs of leaflets, each 3–5cm, narrowly oval to almost circular, tips notched, smooth, leathery, dark and shiny above, paler below; stalk brown or green		

A tall tree formidably armed with clusters of spines on the trunk and main branches. On smaller branches and twigs, the spines are usually grouped in threes. There are spineless varieties, generally preferred for planting as street trees. *Status:* native to the Mississippi basin; introduced to southern and central Europe and sometimes naturalized. *Similar trees:* Siberian Pea-tree is a native of Northern Asia often planted for ornament, and naturalized in France. It has leaves with 8–12 leaflets and clusters of yellow flowers.

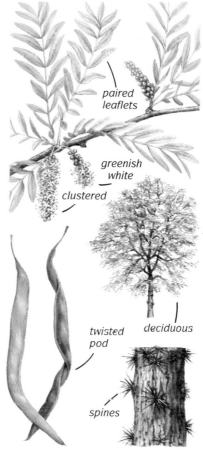

paired leaflets

greenish white

clustered

twisted pod

deciduous

spines

Siberian Pea-tree (*Caragana arborescens*)

unequal petals

yellow

small pod

	HONEY LOCUST	
Type	deciduous tree	
Height	up to 45m	
Habitat	mainly parks and streets, also rivers and woods	
Flowering	June	
Fruiting	July–September	

TRUNK AND CROWN

Trunk	long, with large clusters of spines
Bark	brown, vertically fissured
Crown	tall and spreading
Twigs	smooth, ribbed

LEAVES

Buds	1–2mm, pyramidal, reddish
Leaves	alternate, 10–20cm, either once divided, when leaves have 7–18 pairs of leaflets, each 20–35mm, or twice divided, when leaflets are themselves divided into 8–14 segments, each 8–20mm, leaf tip ending with a spine; stalk short
Stipules	minute

FLOWERS AND FRUIT

Flowers	♂, ♀ or ⚥, many, in clusters in angles of leaves, each c3mm, greenish white
Petals	3–5, oval, equal; sepals 3–5, joined below
Stamens	6–10
Stigmas	1, lobed, style short and thick
Ovaries	1, narrow, upright
Fruit	pod, 30–45cm long, 2–3cm wide, flattened, curved and often twisted
Seeds	numerous, not released

Judas Tree *Cercis siliquastrum*

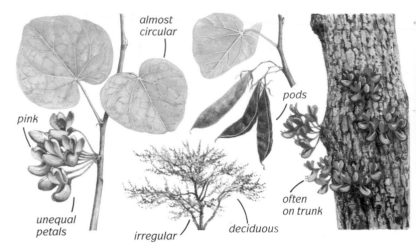

almost circular

pink

unequal petals

irregular

pods

deciduous

often on trunk

An unusual tree that bears its bright pink flowers directly on the trunk and main branches as well as on the twigs. Almost circular leaves with characteristic radiating veins follow the flowers. Attractive reddish purple pods are formed later in the year. *Status:* native throughout Mediterranean regions; often planted and sometimes naturalized in other areas. *Similar trees:* Coral Tree is a Brazilian species forming a small, thick-trunked tree or shrub and grown in mild areas for its scarlet flowers.

Coral Tree (*Erythrina crista-galli*)

large petals

scarlet

spikes or flowers

JUDAS TREE

Type	deciduous tree or shrub
Height	up to 10m
Habitat	mainly on dry, rocky soils
Flowering	April–May
Fruiting	July

TRUNK AND CROWN

Trunk	slender, often several
Bark	dark, blackish, cracked
Crown	rounded, branches angled upwards, spreading
Twigs	reddish brown, warty

LEAVES

Buds	5–8mm, reddish brown or crimson, egg-shaped, pointed
Leaves	alternate, 7–12cm, almost circular, rounded or notched at tips, base heart-shaped, smooth, bluish green when young, becoming dark green above, veins radiating; stalk shorter than blade
Stipules	small, soon falling

FLOWERS AND FRUIT

Flowers	♀, in loose clusters, before or with leaves, on twigs, trunk and branches, pink, 1.5–2cm
Petals	5, unequal, lower pair joined, side pair overlapping, upper erect; sepals 5, equal, joined below to form a tube
Stamens	10, free
Stigmas	1, style curved
Ovaries	1, narrow
Fruit	pod, 6–10cm, flattened, with a very narrow wing on one side, smooth, ripening reddish purple, eventually brown
Seeds	many, released when pod splits

A densely foliaged tree with pink, brush-like flowers borne on the upper branches. Individual flowers are small, but have very long, showy stamens and are crowded into dense heads. *Status:* native to Asia; widely planted as an ornamental and street tree in southern Europe, and as an annual in northern Europe. *Similar trees:* Plume Albizia, from south-western Australia, is also planted in Mediterranean regions. It has densely hairy twigs and cylindrical heads of yellow flowers.

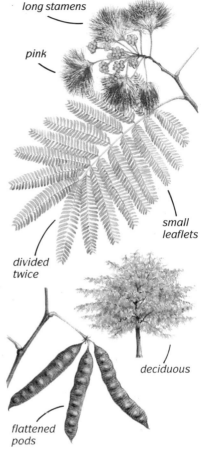

long stamens

pink

small leaflets

divided twice

deciduous

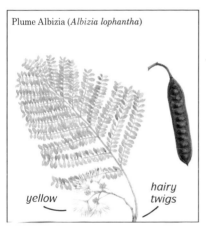

Plume Albizia (*Albizia lophantha*)

yellow

hairy twigs

flattened pods

	PINK SIRIS	
Type	deciduous tree	
Height	up to 13m	
Habitat	woods, stream sides	
Flowering	July–August	
Fruiting	October	

	TRUNK AND CROWN
Trunk	slender
Bark	smooth
Crown	dense, slightly flattened dome; branches spreading
Twigs	brown with many pale, warty lenticels

	LEAVES
Buds	short, black, hairy
Leaves	alternate, 20–30cm, divided into 10–25 paired segments, each segment with 35–50 paired leaflets, each 1–1.5cm, narrowly oval, curved, green above, edges and underside shortly hairy; stalk with cup-shaped gland on upper side
Stipules	absent

	FLOWERS AND FRUIT
Flowers	♂, ♀ and sometimes ⚥, in branched clusters, each branch with 20 flowers in a dense tuft
Petals	5, joined into a narrow tube, 7–9mm, pink; sepals forming a 5-lobed tube, 3mm
Stamens	many, 3.5–4cm, pink, extending well beyond petals
Stigmas	1
Ovaries	1
Fruit	pod, 8–15cm, flat with tapering tip, slightly pinched in between seeds, ripening brown
Seeds	10–15, orbicular

Silver Wattle *Acacia dealbata*

A pale, silvery green tree, with finely divided, feathery leaves. It is the mimosa of floristry. The pretty, globular flower-heads are very numerous and can turn the whole crown yellow. *Status:* native to south-eastern Australia and Tasmania; planted on a large scale in southern Europe as a timber tree and soil stabilizer; now widely naturalized and spreading. *Similar trees:* Green Wattle has bright green deciduous leaves with spiny stipules. Native to the Caribbean, it is grown in south-western Europe for ornament and for the perfume industry.

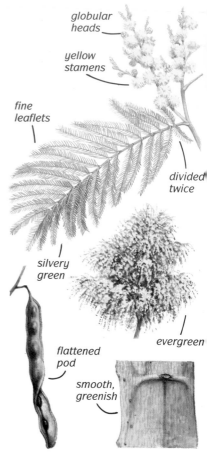

globular heads

yellow stamens

fine leaflets

divided twice

silvery green

evergreen

flattened pod

smooth, greenish

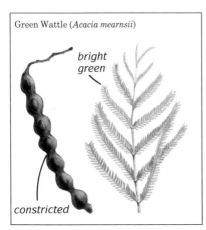

Green Wattle (*Acacia mearnsii*)

bright green

constricted

	SILVER WATTLE		
Type	evergreen tree		narrow, densely white-hairy when young; stalk with cup-shaped glands wherever segments branch off
Height	up to 30m		
Habitat	hillsides, forests and plantations		
Flowering	January–March	**Stipules**	absent
Fruiting	May		
			FLOWERS AND FRUIT
	TRUNK AND CROWN	**Flowers**	♂, in branched, spreading clusters of globular heads, each head 5–6mm, containing 30–40 bright yellow flowers, stalks of flower-heads with dense hairs
Trunk	slender		
Bark	smooth, greyish green, becoming black		
Crown	irregular, rather open		
Twigs	densely hairy, hairs short, silvery white	**Petals**	5, equal, short; sepals 5, hairy
		Stamens	many, protruding well beyond petals, yellow
	LEAVES	**Stigmas**	1, style very long, slender
Buds	minute	**Ovaries**	1
Leaves	alternate, divided into 8–20 pairs of segments, each segment with 30–50 pairs of leaflets, each 3–5mm, very	**Fruit**	pod, 4–10cm, flattened, of equal width for most of its length, ripening waxy brown
		Seeds	many, released when pod splits

A slender tree with drooping foliage and distinctly blue-green leaves. The bright yellow flower-heads are relatively large among *Acacia* species found in Europe. *Status:* native to western Australia; widely planted in many Mediterranean countries as a soil stabilizer and ornamental. *Similar trees:* Swamp Wattle and Blackwood, both native to southern Australia, are also planted and naturalized in southern Europe. Swamp Wattle has seeds with scarlet stalks. Blackwood has leaves with two to six veins, and twisted pods.

globular
heads

yellow
stamens

1 vein

not divided

1 Blackwood (*Acacia melanoxylon*)
2 Swamp Wattle (*Acacia retinodes*)

several veins

often twisted

narrower

2

constricted

long pod

evergreen

	GOLDEN WREATH			
Type	evergreen tree or shrub			bluish green, with a single pale and conspicuous vein; stalkless
Height	up to 10m		**Stipules**	absent
Habitat	mainly in dry, coastal areas			
Flowering	March–May			**FLOWERS AND FRUIT**
Fruiting	July		**Flowers**	♀, in drooping clusters of 2–8 globular heads, each head 1–1.5cm in diameter and containing 25–70 bright yellow flowers
	TRUNK AND CROWN			
Trunk	often forked from base and suckering			
Bark	smooth, grey, becoming grey-brown and cracked		**Petals**	5, 1.5mm, equal; sepals 5
			Stamens	many, yellow
Crown	broad, irregular		**Stigmas**	1; style long, slender
Twigs	smooth, ribbed, drooping, bluish green		**Ovaries**	1
			Fruit	pod, 6–12cm, narrow, flattened, pinched in between each seed, ripening brown
	LEAVES			
Buds	tiny, egg-shaped to rounded		**Seeds**	many, attached by short, whitish stalk encircling seed, released when pod splits
Leaves	alternate, variable, usually 6–20cm, spear-shaped, straight or curved, drooping, dull or shiny,			

Common Laburnum

Laburnum anagyroides

An erect tree with arching branches and cascades of flowers hanging from the twigs. Split pods hang on the tree for some time after the seeds are shed. All parts are poisonous, especially the seeds. *Status:* native to mountainous areas of southern and central Europe; widely planted for ornament; naturalized elsewhere. *Similar trees:* Scotch Laburnum, native to the same areas as Common Laburnum, is a shrub or small tree with glossy leaves and longer flower clusters. Voss's Laburnum is a hybrid between the above two species, which has largely replaced Common Laburnum as an ornamental in many areas.

3 leaflets

large upper petal

yellow

deciduous

smooth

silkily hairy

1 Scotch Laburnum (*Laburnum alpinum*)
2 Voss's Laburnum (*Laburnum × watereri*)

long clusters

glossy, hairless

COMMON LABURNUM	
Type	deciduous tree or shrub
Height	up to 7m
Habitat	mountain woods and scrub
Flowering	May–June
Fruiting	July–September
	TRUNK AND CROWN
Trunk	slender
Bark	smooth, greenish to brown
Crown	irregular, open; branches angled upwards or arching
Twigs	grey-green, downy with long, silky, close-pressed hairs
	LEAVES
Buds	5–6mm, egg-shaped, with white, silky hairs
Leaves	alternate, 3 leaflets, each 3–8cm, elliptical or widest above middle, blunt but with a tiny, sharp tip, grey-green, young leaves hairy below; stalk 2–6cm
Stipules	absent
	FLOWERS AND FRUIT
Flowers	♀, many, in long, drooping clusters from angles of leaves and tips of shoots, each 2cm, golden yellow
Petals	5, unequal, lower pair joined, side pair overlapping, upper erect; sepals joined into a 2-lipped tube, with short teeth
Stamens	10, fused together into a tube
Stigmas	1, style curved upwards
Ovaries	1, narrow, curved, silky-hairy
Fruit	pod, 4–6cm, hairy, ripening smooth, dull brown, persisting on tree after splitting
Seeds	numerous, black, round, released after pod splits

Suckering readily, False-acacia may produce many young stems. Mature trees develop ridged and furrowed bark. It has attractive yellowish green leaves and fragrant white flowers, which are sometimes confined to the upper branches. *Status:* a woodland species native to eastern and central North America; widespread as an ornamental; naturalized in southern and western Europe. *Similar trees:* pink flowered and stickily hairy Clammy Locust is also planted for ornament. Pagoda-tree is a mountain species from Asia. It is tall, with twisted branches; the white flowers appear only on old trees.

paired leaflets

unequal petals

deciduous

white

1 Clammy Locust (*Robinia viscosa*)
2 Pagoda-tree (*Sophora japonica*)

hairy

2

1

pink

constricted

ridged or deeply furrowed

smooth

	FALSE-ACACIA		
Type	deciduous tree		hairy below; leaves and leaflets stalked
Height	up to 25m	**Stipules**	woody and spiny; tiny stipules at base of each leaflet
Habitat	streets, parks, woods		
Flowering	June		**FLOWERS AND FRUIT**
Fruiting	September–October	**Flowers**	☿, many, in long, drooping clusters of 10–20cm, white with yellow spot, fragrant
	TRUNK AND CROWN		
Trunk	short, often suckering	**Petals**	5, unequal, lower pair joined, side pair overlapping, upper erect; sepals joined into a tube with 2 shallow lips
Bark	smooth, dark brown, becoming grey with spiralled ridges		
Crown	broad, open; branches twisted		
Twigs	green with dark reddish lines	**Stamens**	10, 9 joined in a tube, 1 free
	LEAVES	**Stigmas**	1, style curved, hairy at tip
		Ovaries	1, long, narrow, hairy
Buds	sunk in base of leaf-stalk, flanked by 2 spines	**Fruit**	pod, 5–10cm, smooth, ripening dull brown, often slow to release seeds
Leaves	alternate, 15–20cm, 7–21 leaflets, mostly paired leaflet at tip, each 2.5–4.5cm, oval or elliptic, yellowish green, sparsely	**Seeds**	4–8, brown with black streaks, kidney-shaped

Sweet Orange *Citrus sinensis*

A small evergreen tree bearing delightfully scented flowers and familiar, juicy fruits. Oranges take up to a year or more to ripen; there may be one or even two crops of fruit still on the tree when it flowers. Various cultivars with different ripening times ensure oranges are available more or less all year round. *Status:* native to China and eastern Asia; a common orchard tree in Mediterranean regions. *Similar trees:* several relatives, each with distinctive fruits, are commonly cultivated. Lemon has leaves with a spine at the base of the stalk. Grapefruit has large, broadly winged leaves as well as large fruits.

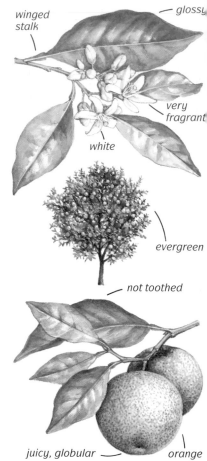

winged stalk

glossy

very fragrant

white

evergreen

not toothed

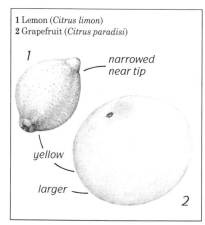

1 Lemon (*Citrus limon*)
2 Grapefruit (*Citrus paradisi*)

1

narrowed near tip

yellow

larger

2

juicy, globular

orange

	SWEET ORANGE
Type	evergreen tree
Height	up to 10m
Habitat	orchard tree, often near sea
Flowering	mainly May, also other times of year
Fruiting	up to 1 year or more after flowering

TRUNK AND CROWN

Trunk	short, slender
Bark	blackish brown
Crown	rounded, bushy
Twigs	angled, spiny when young, becoming cylindrical, unarmed

LEAVES

Buds	very small, domed, green
Leaves	alternate, 5–8cm oval, pointed, base rounded, glossy, smooth and leathery but thin, dotted with shiny oil glands; stalk with a narrow, leafy wing
Stipules	absent

FLOWERS AND FRUIT

Flowers	☿, single or few in short, loose spikes in leaf angles, pure white, fragrant
Petals	5, narrowly oval; sepals 4–5, short, pointed, joined below
Stamens	20–60, grouped in bundles
Stigmas	1, club-shaped on thick style
Ovaries	1, green, 10–13-chambered
Fruit	berry-like, with nearly smooth, leathery rind enclosing sweet juicy pulp, ripening orange
Seeds	6–many, creamy, pointed, not released

Strong- and unpleasant-smelling when crushed, the leaves of this tree are divided into three spreading leaflets. The bark and young fruits are similarly aromatic. The ripe, straw-coloured fruit has a broad, papery wing. *Status:* native to eastern North America; planted for ornament and naturalized in central Europe. *Similar trees:* Amur Cork-tree, from China, has leaves with 5–11 leaflets and black, berry-like fruits. It is grown in parks and gardens.

broad clusters

white

3 leaflets

deciduous

short

encircling wing

Amur Cork tree (*Phellodendron amurense*)

ripens blackish

berry-like   5–11 leaflets

	HOP-TREE
Type	deciduous tree or shrub
Height	up to 8m
Habitat	mainly in parks
Flowering	June–July
Fruiting	July–October
	TRUNK AND CROWN
Trunk	short, often branching
Bark	brown, strong-smelling
Crown	rounded
Twigs	smooth, dark, shiny brown
	LEAVES
Buds	small, very hairy, hidden by base of leaf stalk
Leaves	alternate, 3 leaflets, each 6–12cm, oval, tapered at both ends, edge unbroken or with faint teeth, smooth, shiny; stalkless

Stipules	absent
	FLOWERS AND FRUIT
Flowers	♂, ♀ and ☿, mixed in clusters at tips of shoots, greenish white
Petals	4–5, 4mm, narrowly oval, blunt, hairy on inner surface; sepals 4–5, *c*1.5mm, pointed, hairy
Stamens	4, woolly below, rudimentary in ♀ flowers
Stigmas	1, 2-lobed on short, thick style
Ovaries	1, 2-chambered, rudimentary in ♂ flowers
Fruit	nut-like, with a circular, notched, straw-coloured wing 1.5–2.5cm across and net-veined
Seeds	1, not released

Tree-of-Heaven *Ailanthus altissima*

A stately tree with young leaves emerging bright red before turning green. Unfortunately, the foliage is rank-smelling. The fruits hang in large bunches, each fruit with a twisted, propeller-like wing. In Europe, the tree reproduces most easily by means of suckers. *Status:* native to China; very common as a street and park tree, and naturalized in much of Europe except for the far north. *Similar trees:* a second Chinese species, Downy Tree-of-Heaven, is more rarely grown. The leaves have a bright red stalk, and darker leaflets that are hairy below, with unbroken edges.

greenish

paired leaflets

strong-smelling

deciduous

reddish

smooth

whitish lines

elongated wing

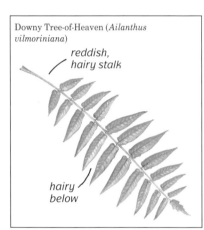

Downy Tree-of-Heaven (*Ailanthus vilmoriniana*)

reddish, hairy stalk

hairy below

	TREE-OF-HEAVEN		
Type	deciduous tree		25 paired leaflets, each 7–12cm, narrowly oval, pointed, smooth but for fringe of hairs, with 2–4 teeth towards base; stalked
Height	20–30m		
Habitat	light, dry and unstable soils		
Flowering	May–July		
Fruiting	August–September	**Stipules**	absent

TRUNK AND CROWN

Trunk	straight, often suckering
Bark	grey, often with silvery lines smooth, becoming scaly
Crown	irregular; branches stout, angled upwards
Twigs	thick, smooth, brown, with large leaf-scars and lenticels

LEAVES

Buds	2mm, scarlet, egg-shaped
Leaves	alternate, 45–60cm, deep red when emerging, later glossy green, unpleasant-smelling; 13–

FLOWERS AND FRUIT

Flowers	usually ♂ and ♀, on different trees, sometimes ♂, many in branched clusters 10–20cm long, each 7–8mm, greenish white, strong-smelling
Petals	5, pointed; sepals 5, green
Stamens	10 in ♂ flowers, 2–3 in ♀ flowers
Stigmas	2–5, joined
Ovaries	1, 5–6-chambered
Fruit	nut-like, with narrow, twisted, papery wing 3–4cm long, reddish, ripening straw-coloured
Seeds	1, not released

A slender, open tree with delicately coloured and scented flowers. United stamens form an upright tube that is darker than the spreading petals. Bead-like fruits remain on the tree for a long time after the leaves have fallen. *Status:* a mountain species native to eastern Asia; naturalized in the Balkan Peninsula; widely planted in southern Europe for ornament and shade. *Similar trees:* Chinese Cedar has shaggy bark and drooping white flowers. Native to eastern Asia, it is grown for its fragrant timber.

purplish

branched heads

doubly divided

many leaflets

deciduous

furrowed

globular

yellow

Chinese Cedar (*Cedrela sinensis*)

paired leaflets

drooping, white

	PERSIAN LILAC		
Type	deciduous tree or shrub		5cm, narrowly oval, pointed, base wedge-shaped, sharply-toothed, glossy green; stalked
Height	up to 15m		
Habitat	dry mountain areas, planted elsewhere	**Stipules**	absent
Flowering	June		**FLOWERS AND FRUIT**
Fruiting	July–October	**Flowers**	♀, many, in branched, open clusters 10–20cm long, in leaf angles, lilac, fragrant
	TRUNK AND CROWN		
Trunk	short, often slender	**Petals**	5, 18mm, narrow, spreading or curved back; sepals 5, green, short, joined below
Bark	greyish brown, furrowed		
Crown	open and spreading		
Twigs	sparsely hairy with star-shaped hairs, becoming smooth	**Stamens**	10, joined into an erect tube
		Stigmas	1, club-shaped with a thick style, hidden in stamen tube
	LEAVES	**Ovaries**	1, 5–8-chambered
Buds	small, globular, densely white-hairy	**Fruit**	6–18mm, globular, ripening creamy-yellow
Leaves	alternate, up to 90cm, divided into segments, each segment divided into leaflets, each 2.5–	**Seeds**	1, not released

Stag's-horn Sumach *Rhus typhina*

Velvet-hairy twigs, and leaves with drooping leaflets immediately distinguish this small, suckering tree. It produces bright autumn colours and female plants have dark crimson fruiting heads. *Status:* native to eastern North America; widespread as an ornamental and naturalized in parts of northern and central Europe. *Similar trees:* Sumach is a semi-evergreen shrub or small tree with narrowly winged, hairy leaflets and purplish fruits. It occurs in rocky places in southern Europe. Varnish-tree, from China, is sometimes planted. It has loose, branched fruiting heads.

1 Sumach (*Rhus coriaria*)
2 Varnish-tree (*Rhus verniciflua*)

long cluster

winged stalk

STAG'S-HORN SUMACH

Type	deciduous tree or shrub
Height	10m
Habitat	thickets
Flowering	May–July
Fruiting	September–October

TRUNK AND CROWN

Trunk	slender, often several and suckering
Bark	brown, with yellow warts
Crown	flattened, open dome; branches forking regularly
Twigs	curved, velvety when young

LEAVES

Buds	minute, lacking scales
Leaves	alternate, oval in outline, broadest at the middle, drooping, 11–29 stalkless leaflets, paired with one at the tip, each 5–12cm, very narrowly oval, pointed, coarsely toothed, softly hairy, rich orange and red in autumn; stalk hairy
Stipules	absent

FLOWERS AND FRUIT

Flowers	♂, more usually ♂ and ♀ on different trees in branched clusters 10–20cm; ♂ greenish, clusters open; ♀ dull red, clusters downy, spike-like
Petals	5, narrow, spreading; sepals 5, short, hairy
Stamens	5 in ♂ and ♀ flowers
Stigmas	3, on a single short style
Ovaries	1, in ♀ and ♂ flowers
Fruit	nut-like, c4mm, covered with crimson hairs, remaining on tree through winter
Seeds	1, not released

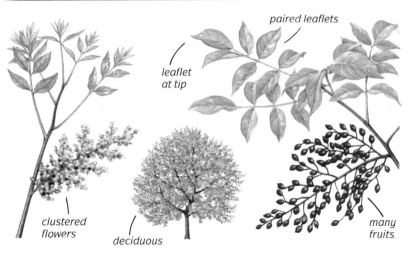

paired leaflets

leaflet at tip

clustered flowers

deciduous

many fruits

A common tree in dry, chalky scrubland. It has leathery leaves with 2–6 pairs of leaflets and a single leaflet at the tip. Dull flowers are followed by bright, coral red young fruits. *Status:* native to Mediterranean regions and south-western Asia. *Similar trees:* an Asian species cultivated in Mediterranean regions for its edible nuts, Pistachio has leaves with hairy stalks and usually only 3 leaflets. Mastic Tree, a native of dry parts of the Mediterranean, is usually an evergreen shrub; the leaves have 4 leaflets and end in a short spine.

1 Pistachio (*Pistacia vera*)
2 Mastic Tree (*Pistacia lentiscus*)

few leaflets

spine

edible fruit

1

2

	TURPENTINE TREE
Type	deciduous tree or shrub
Height	up to 10m
Habitat	scrub, light woodland, on dry chalky slopes
Flowering	March–April
Fruiting	September–October

TRUNK AND CROWN

Trunk	short, slightly sinuous, forking
Bark	grey, finely cracked into oblong plates
Crown	open, irregular; branches few, twisted
Twigs	reddish, becoming brown, stout, sticky with resin

LEAVES

Buds	3–9mm, dark-red, egg-shaped
Leaves	alternate, 3–9, stalked leaflets, each 2–8.5cm, oval, tipped with a small spine, leathery, smooth and shiny, dark green; stalks smooth, round in cross-section
Stipules	absent

FLOWERS AND FRUIT

Flowers	♂ and ♀ on different trees, many in long-branched clusters, greenish brown, appearing with the leaves
Petals	absent
Stamens	3–5 in ♂ flowers
Stigmas	3, on a single style
Ovaries	1 in ♀ flowers
Fruit	nut-like, 5–7mm, egg-shaped, tipped with slender point, coral-red, ripening brown
Seeds	1, not released

Pepper Tree *Schinus molle*

An evergreen tree with a crown of weeping foliage. The leaves are aromatic, smelling distinctly of pepper. It is most attractive in autumn, when the long clusters of pink fruits appear. Only flourishing in warm climates, it is widely planted in Mediterranean regions. *Status:* native to Central and South America, grown as an ornamental in southern Europe and naturalized in places. *Similar trees:* a less frequent South American species, Brazilian Pepper, has erect branches, broader leaflets and bright red fruits.

narrow leaflets

long cluster

evergreen

pink, berry-like

Brazilian Pepper (*Schinus terebinthifolia*)

winged

red

	PEPPER TREE			
Type	evergreen tree			smooth, aromatic; stalk flattened
Height	12m		**Stipules**	absent
Habitat	warm, dry areas			
Flowering	June–August			**FLOWERS AND FRUIT**
Fruiting	July–December		**Flowers**	♀, or ♂ and ♀ on different trees, many in loose, hanging clusters 25cm long, creamy-white
	TRUNK AND CROWN		**Petals**	5, *c*2mm, oval, widest above middle, blunt; sepals 5
Trunk	stout, straight, cylindrical		**Stamens**	10 in ♂ and ♀ flowers
Bark	grey-brown		**Stigmas**	3, on a single style
Crown	tall, domed; branches slender		**Ovaries**	1, in ♀ and ♂ flowers
Twigs	bluish, drooping		**Fruit**	berry-like, 6–7mm, globular, ripening shiny pink, remaining on tree throughout winter
	LEAVES		**Seeds**	1, not released
Buds	scaly, tiny			
Leaves	alternate, tipped with a leaflet or with a short spine, 7–13 pairs of leaflets, each 2–6cm, very narrow, spine-tipped, often toothed, hairy, becoming			

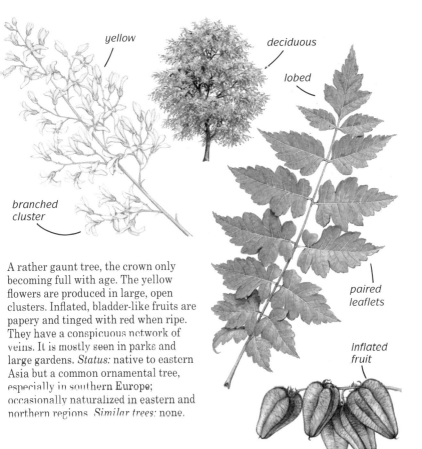

yellow

deciduous

lobed

branched cluster

paired leaflets

Inflated fruit

A rather gaunt tree, the crown only becoming full with age. The yellow flowers are produced in large, open clusters. Inflated, bladder-like fruits are papery and tinged with red when ripe. They have a conspicuous network of veins. It is mostly seen in parks and large gardens. *Status:* native to eastern Asia but a common ornamental tree, especially in southern Europe; occasionally naturalized in eastern and northern regions. *Similar trees:* none.

GOLDEN-RAIN-TREE

Type	deciduous tree
Height	9–18m
Habitat	parks and gardens, occasionally waste ground on rich soils
Flowering	July–August
Fruiting	September–October

TRUNK AND CROWN

Trunk	thick, sinuous
Bark	brown, showing orange in deep cracks
Crown	sparse when young, becoming full with age; branches angled upwards, twisted
Twigs	downy, becoming smooth

LEAVES

Buds	squat with curved tip
Leaves	alternate, 15–40cm; 9–15 paired

leaflets each 3–8cm, coarsely toothed, the lowest themselves sometimes divided into leaflets, smooth, dark green above, pale below; stalked

Stipules	absent

FLOWERS AND FRUIT

Flowers	☿, but often functionally either ♂ or ♀, in branched clusters up to 40cm at tips of shoots, 1cm across, yellow
Petals	4, narrow, pointed; 4 sepals short, hairy
Stamens	8, often less, hairy
Stigmas	1, style longer than stamens
Ovaries	1, 3-sided, 3-chambered, hairy
Fruit	pod-like, 5.5cm, conical and papery, red-tinged and veined, splitting into 3 when ripe
Seeds	3, black, released

Horse-chestnut *Aesculus hippocastanum*

A massive, spreading tree with large leaves divided like the fingers of a hand. Showy, upright clusters of flowers are visible from some distance away. Shiny seeds, called conkers, are enclosed in a thick, prickly case. Winter twigs have distinctive horseshoe-shaped leaf scars and very large, sticky buds. *Status:* originally a mountain species native to the Balkan Peninsula; widely planted in much of Europe for timber, ornament and shade; often naturalized. *Similar trees:* the widely planted Red Horse-chestnut is a hybrid between Horse-chestnut and an American species. It has red flowers and non-spiny fruits.

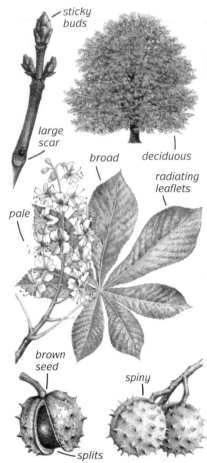

sticky buds

large scar

broad

deciduous

radiating leaflets

pale

brown seed

spiny

splits

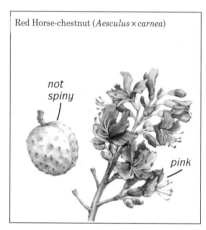

Red Horse-chestnut (*Aesculus* × *carnea*)

not spiny

pink

	HORSE-CHESTNUT	
Type	deciduous tree	
Height	up to 25m	
Habitat	thickets, hedges, woodland	
Flowering	May–June	
Fruiting	September	

TRUNK AND CROWN

Trunk	stout, broad-based, fluted
Bark	dark red- or grey-brown, scaly
Crown	huge, spreading dome; branches arching, tips upturned
Twigs	red-brown with pale lenticels; leaf-scars horseshoe-shaped

LEAVES

Buds	up to 3.5cm, shiny brown, sticky
Leaves	paired on stem; 5–7 radiating, stalkless leaflets, the largest up to 25cm, widest above middle, pointed, tapering at base, toothed, woolly below, becoming smooth; long-stalked
Stipules	absent

FLOWERS AND FRUIT

Flowers	♀ or ♂, in showy, erect, pyramidal spikes of 15–30cm at tips of shoots
Petals	5, or 4, *c*10mm, frilly, unequal, the lowest largest, white with yellow to pink spot at base; sepals 5, unequal, short, joined in a tube
Stamens	6–7, protruding, down-curved
Stigmas	1, on a long, curved style
Ovaries	1, 3-chambered
Fruit	spiny, 6cm, globular, ripening brown and splitting into 3
Seeds	1, sometimes 2–3, smooth, dark glossy brown with a round, pale scar, released when fruit splits

Very similar to Horse-chestnut, this Indian species differs in having stalked leaflets and fruits lacking prominent spines. The smaller spikes of flowers are white or pink, spotted with red and yellow. Winter buds are green, not brown like those of its more common relative. *Status:* native to the Himalayas; planted in parks and gardens for ornament. *Similar trees:* Yellow Buckeye, from south-eastern North America, has narrow yellow or sometimes pink flowers; it is frequently planted in parks.

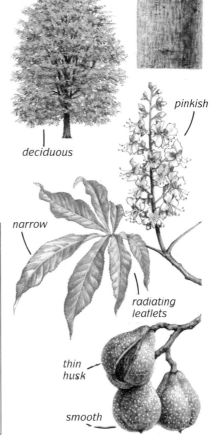

pinkish

deciduous

narrow

radiating
leaflets

thin
husk

smooth

Yellow Buckeye (*Aesculus flava*)

pale yellow

globular

narrow

	INDIAN HORSE-CHESTNUT	
Type	deciduous tree	
Height	19–30m	
Habitat	moist soils	
Flowering	June	
Fruiting	October	

TRUNK AND CROWN

Trunk	stout, straight, rather short	
Bark	greenish to reddish grey, smooth, cracking into rectangular plates	
Crown	tall, rounded; spreading branches arching upwards	
Twigs	grey-brown, with prominent horseshoe-shaped leaf scars	

LEAVES

Buds	*c*10mm, green, shiny, very sticky
Leaves	paired on stems; 5–9, but usually 7, radiating, short-stalked leaflets up to 8cm, narrowly oval, widest above middle, base tapered at both ends, finely toothed
Stipules	absent

FLOWERS AND FRUIT

Flowers	♂, in erect, pyramidal spikes of usually 10–15cm
Petals	5 or 4, white or pink, slightly unequal, the lowest largest, the upper spotted with red or yellow; 5 sepals small, joined in a tube
Stamens	5–8, long and protruding
Stigmas	1, on a long, protruding style
Ovaries	1, 3-chambered
Fruit	pear-shaped, ripening greenish brown with thin, rough-skinned husk splitting into 3 when ripe
Seeds	2–3, wrinkled, glossy brown, released when fruit splits

Sycamore *Acer pseudoplatanus*

Originally confined to mountain regions, Sycamore has been introduced to many parts of Europe and is now widely naturalized. The winged seeds help it to spread easily and rapidly. It makes a large, spreading tree, often wider than it is tall. *Status:* native to mountains of central and southern Europe, and western Asia; naturalized as far north as Sweden. *Similar trees:* with a similar distribution but reaching even further north, Norway Maple differs in its horizontally winged fruits. Italian Maple is also a mountain tree; its fruits have almost parallel-wings.

broad lobes

coarse teeth

branched clusters

paired

domed

cracks into plates

deciduous

angled apart

winged fruits

1 Norway Maple (*Acer platanoides*)
2 Italian Maple (*Acer opalus*)

slender teeth

almost parallel

opposite directions

1

2

	SYCAMORE		
Type	deciduous tree		
Height	up to 35m		
Habitat	woods, hedges, mountainous areas; often planted		
Flowering	April–May		
Fruiting	June–September		

TRUNK AND CROWN

Trunk stout, often developing buttresses

Bark smooth, grey, becoming pinkish brown, fissured and cracking into small irregular plates

Crown domed, spreading, dense; lower branches often stout

Twigs short, grey-green, smooth

LEAVES

Buds 0.8–1cm, oval, reddish green

Leaves opposite, 10–15cm, with 5 deep and broad spreading lobes, each pointed and coarsely toothed, dark green above, pale blue-green beneath; stalk up to 20cm, usually reddish

Stipules absent

FLOWERS AND FRUIT

Flowers ♂ and ♀ in separate clusters, many in branched, hanging clusters 6–12 cm long, with the leaves, greenish yellow, each *c*6mm

Petals 5; sepals 5

Stamens 8 in ♂; sterile in ♀

Stigmas 2, on short style

Ovaries 1, 2-chambered, hairy

Fruit paired, smooth, each with a grey-brown wing *c*2.5cm long; diverging at right-angles

Seeds 1 per fruit, not released

3-5 lobes · upright cluster · broad · deciduous · ridged · paired · toothed · spreading horizontally · often tinged red

A small, colourful tree with young leaves that are pink in spring and turn deep yellow in autumn. It is most common in northern Europe, where it often grows in hedges. The twigs become winged with thick, corky flanges, and the leaves have either 3 or 5 lobes. *Status:* native more or less throughout Europe and western Asia; planted for autumn colour. *Similar trees:* two species from southern and central Europe are distinguished by their parallel-winged fruits. Montpellier Maple has leaves with toothless lobes. The rarer Tartar Maple has undivided leaves and striped bark.

1 Montpellier Maple (*Acer monspessulanum*)
2 Tartar Maple (*Acer tataricum*)

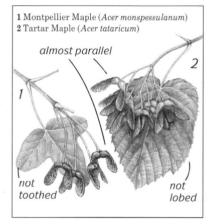

almost parallel · not toothed · not lobed

FIELD MAPLE		
Type	deciduous tree or shrub	
Height	up to 26m	
Habitat	hedgerows, open woods, usually on chalk or limestone soils	
Flowering	April–June	
Fruiting	May–September	
Trunk	sinuous, usually distinct	
TRUNK AND CROWN		
Bark	grey or light brown, finely ridged and fissured	
Crown	broadly domed; branches angled upwards at tips	
Twigs	dark brown and finely hairy, becoming paler and ribbed	
LEAVES		
Buds	3mm, red-brown, hairy at tip	
Leaves	opposite, 4–7cm, thick, deeply divided into 3 or 5 rounded lobes, opening pinkish, later dull green above, downy below, turning yellow in autumn; stalk c5cm	
Stipules	absent	
FLOWERS AND FRUIT		
Flowers	♂ and ♀, few in separate, upright, branched clusters, appearing with the leaves, each c6mm, yellow-green; stalkless	
Stamens	8 in ♂; sterile in ♀	
Stigmas	2, on single, short style	
Ovaries	1, 2-chambered	
Fruit	paired, each with a pale green wing, often tinged with crimson and hairy, spreading horizontally	
Seeds	1 per fruit, not released	

Box-elder   *Acer negundo*

A fast-growing North American tree that is readily distinguished from other maples by its leaves, which are mostly divided into 5 leaflets. The flowers open before the leaves, the crimson anthers of male trees being particularly noticeable. The fruits mature early and persist on the tree for a long time. The cultivar 'Variegatum' is planted for its yellow and green variegated leaves. *Status:* native to eastern North America; planted for ornament and shelter; naturalized mainly in central regions. *Similar trees:* the decorative Paper-bark Maple, from China, has reddish bark, which peels in broad, papery strips.

hanging clusters

red ♂

greenish ♀

deciduous

paired

3 or 5 leaflets

angled apart

Paper-bark Maple (*Acer griseum*)

papery strips

3 leaflets

	BOX-ELDER		
Type	deciduous tree		
Height	up to 20m		
Habitat	parks and gardens, street tree		
Flowering	March–April		
Fruiting	June–September		
	TRUNK AND CROWN		
Trunk	short, often sprouting numerous burrs		
Bark	smooth, grey, becoming darker and shallowly fissured		
Crown	irregularly domed, spreading		
Twigs	green, straight, smooth		
	LEAVES		
Buds	small, with 2 silky white scales		
Leaves	opposite, with 2 or 4 paired leaflets and a leaflet at tip, each oval, long-pointed, shallowly toothed; stalk 6–8cm		

Stipules	absent
	FLOWERS AND FRUIT
Flowers	♂ and ♀ on different trees, appearing before leaves
♂	in short, hanging clusters of 12–16, red
♀	6–12 in loose hanging clusters 5cm long, greenish
Petals	absent; sepals 5
Stamens	4–6 in ♂, red
Stigmas	2, spreading, styles very short
Ovaries	1, 2-chambered
Fruit	paired, *c*2cm, smooth, each with a brown wing and diverging at a narrow angle
Seeds	1 per fruit, not released

Valued in North America as a source of maple syrup, which is made from the sap, this tree is planted in Europe mainly for ornament. The leaves are silvery beneath and attractive in summer, before turning pale yellow or red later. *Status:* North American, native from Quebec to Florida; widely cultivated. *Similar trees:* a more important source of maple syrup, and the brightest autumn-coloured species, is Sugar Maple. Red Maple has dense red flower clusters, red fruits and red autumn leaves. Both are North American trees that are commonly planted in Europe.

small clusters

deciduous

deep lobes

paired

sharp teeth

silvery below

narrow angle

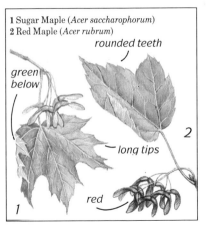

1 Sugar Maple (*Acer saccharophorum*)
2 Red Maple (*Acer rubrum*)

rounded teeth

green below

long tips

2

red

1

	SILVER MAPLE
Type	deciduous tree
Height	up to 36m
Habitat	roadsides, parks, gardens
Flowering	March
Fruiting	May–June

TRUNK AND CROWN

Trunk	short, stout, often with burrs
Bark	smooth, grey-brown, later flaking and becoming shaggy
Crown	tall, spreading above; branches numerous, slender, arching
Twigs	brown or purplish

LEAVES

Buds	*c*1cm, oval, angular, red
Leaves	opposite, 9–16 cm, deeply 5-lobed, lobes deeply and irregularly toothed, silvery-hairy beneath, pale yellow or occasionally brilliant red in autumn; stalk 8–13cm, pink
Stipules	absent

FLOWERS AND FRUIT

Flowers	♂ and ♀ in separate clusters of 4–5, appearing before the leaves, greenish or red
♂	short-stalked
♀	long-stalked
Petals	absent; sepals 5
Stamens	3–7 in ♂s
Stigmas	2, on short style
Ovaries	1, 2-chambered
Fruit	paired, 1 often fails to develop, 5–6 cm, stalked, with elliptical, twisted wing diverging at a narrow angle
Seeds	1 per fruit, not released

Père David's Maple *Acer davidii*

One of a group of decorative trees known as 'snake-bark' maples. The young olive-green bark is patterned with a network of white lines, resembling the skin of a reptile. The lines fade with age and the bark turns uniform dark brown. Several cultivars, all differing somewhat in overall shape, are planted. *Status:* native to China; cultivated for ornament. *Similar trees:* native to Japan, Snake-bark Maple has downy grey twigs and leaves with three triangular lobes. Hers's Maple, from China, has marbled bark and long spikes of flowers.

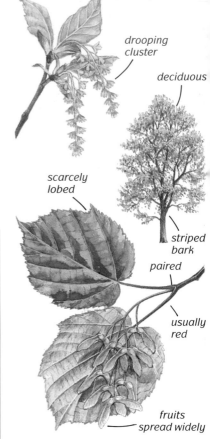

drooping cluster

deciduous

scarcely lobed

striped bark

paired

usually red

fruits spread widely

1 Snake-bark Maple (*Acer rufinerve*)
2 Hers's Maple (*Acer hersii*)

1

2

pink stripes

long cluster

3 triangular lobes

PÈRE DAVID'S MAPLE			
Type	deciduous tree		broadly oval, heart-shaped at the base, with a short slender tip, edges finely toothed, shiny green above, whitish green beneath; stalk 6cm, red
Height	up to 16m		
Habitat	parks and gardens		
Flowering	May		
Fruiting	July–August	**Stipules**	absent

TRUNK AND CROWN

Trunk short, stout

Bark smooth, greenish, with network of white stripes when young, becoming brown and fissured

Crown narrow; branches angled upwards

Twigs smooth, purple or red when young, white striped

LEAVES

Buds *c*1cm, narrowly conical, dark red with paler markings

Leaves opposite, up to 15 × 10 cm,

FLOWERS AND FRUIT

Flowers ♂ and ♀ in separate clusters, many in arching clusters 7–10 cm long, appearing with leaves, greenish yellow

Petals absent; sepals 5

Stamens 4–10 in ♂

Stigmas 2, spreading

Ovaries 1, 2-chambered

Fruit paired, each with a wing 2.5–3.7cm long, spreading nearly horizontally

Seeds 1 per fruit, not released

Various maples are cultivated for ornament and this species is particularly attractive, with many different forms. In the typical tree the leaves have narrow, pointed lobes and turn red or purple in autumn. In some cultivars they are finely divided and deep purple throughout the year. Others have bright red winter shoots. *Status:* native to China, Japan and Korea, and a common ornamental, especially in small gardens. *Similar trees:* Downy Japanese-maple, another ornamental species, has leaves with 7–11 short lobes. It too has fine-leaved cultivars.

5-7 lobes

deeply divided

broad, deciduous

sometimes finely cut

paired

spreading apart

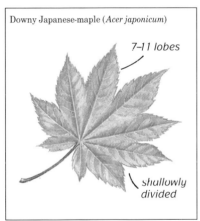

Downy Japanese-maple (*Acer japonicum*)

7–11 lobes

shallowly divided

SMOOTH JAPANESE-MAPLE

Type	deciduous tree or shrub
Height	up to 16m
Habitat	gardens and parks
Flowering	April–May
Fruiting	June–September

TRUNK AND CROWN

Trunk	usually very short, sinuously twisted and soon dividing
Bark	smooth and rich brown striped with pale yellow, becoming grey
Crown	domed and spreading
Twigs	slender, smooth, reddish above, green beneath

LEAVES

Buds	oval, 2–3mm, often red-tinged
Leaves	opposite, 7–9cm, deeply divided into 5–7 spreading, oval, pointed and sharply toothed lobes, bright green, turning yellow, red or crimson in autumn; stalks 3–5cm
Stipules	absent

FLOWERS AND FRUIT

Flowers	♀, in upright clusters of 12–15; each 6–8mm across, dark purple; stalks slender, *c*4cm long
Petals	absent; sepals 5
Stamens	4–10
Stigmas	2 on short style
Ovaries	1, 2-chambered
Fruit	paired, each with a pale green wing tinged with red, *c*1cm long and diverging at a wide angle
Seeds	1 per fruit, not released

Holly *Ilex aquifolium*

A stiff and prickly-leaved evergreen tree, often a shrub. When growing in deep shady woods it is often sterile. In more open sites it bears white flowers and, on female trees, bright red berries. *Status:* native to western and southern Europe and western Asia. *Similar trees:* Highclere Holly is a hybrid that is resistant to air pollution. It has broader, flatter leaves bearing short, forward-pointing spines. It is often planted in towns. Canary Holly, native to the Azores, Canaries and Madeira, has flat leaves with few, if any, fine spines and pale pink flowers.

wavy edge

white

evergreen

large spines

smooth, silvery

often variegated

red berries

1 Highclere Holly (*Ilex × altaclarensis*)
2 Canary Holly (*Ilex perado*)

forward-pointing spines

2

1

few, fine or no spines

	HOLLY		
Type	evergreen tree or shrub		oblong, 5–12cm, edges wavy and spiny, leathery and waxy, dark, shiny green above, pale and matt below; stalk 1cm, thick and grooved
Height	2–25m		
Habitat	woods, scrub, on moist soils		
Flowering	May–August		
Fruiting	September–March	**Stipules**	very small and inconspicuous

	TRUNK AND CROWN		**FLOWERS AND FRUIT**
Trunk	straight, cylindrical	**Flowers**	♂ and ♀ on different trees, in clusters in angles of leaves on old wood, white
Bark	silvery grey, smooth, warty or fissured when old		
Crown	narrow, conical to cylindrical; young branches curved upwards	**Petals**	4, *c*4mm, joined at base; sepals 4, joined
		Stamens	4 in ♂ flowers, rudimentary in ♀ flowers
Twigs	slightly hairy and bright green when young, becoming smooth and darker	**Stigmas**	1 in ♀
		Ovaries	1, green, barrel-shaped, rudimentary in ♂ flowers
	LEAVES	**Fruit**	berry-like, 8–10mm, globular, ripening scarlet, on ♀ trees only
Buds	2–3mm, egg-shaped		
Leaves	alternate, oval to roughly	**Seeds**	several, not released

A slender tree, often with several trunks, and small, inconspicuous flowers. In contrast the 4-lobed fruits are very obvious, ripening deep pink and splitting to reveal the fleshy, orange covering of the seeds. *Status:* native to all but the extreme north and south of Europe; several cultivars are used as ornamentals. *Similar trees:* a second European species, Broad-leaved Spindle, has flowers with 5 broad, pink petals. Japanese Spindle, from eastern Asia, has thick, blunt leaves and broad, yellowish petals. Several cultivars planted for their foliage are naturalized in southern Europe.

4 petals

deciduous

finely toothed

often several trunks

smooth

pink fruit

4-lobed

1 Broad-leaved Spindle (*Euonymus latifolius*)
2 Japanese Spindle (*Euonymus japonicus*)

pink   *evergreen*   *blunt*

broader

	SPINDLE		
Type	deciduous tree or shrub		
Height	2–6m		
Habitat	woodland and scrub on chalky soils		
Flowering	May–June		
Fruiting	September–October		

TRUNK AND CROWN

Trunk	slender, often several
Bark	fawn to grey-green, smooth, with fine vertical lines
Crown	bushy; numerous branches arching upwards
Twigs	green, 4-angled

LEAVES

Buds	5–6mm, greenish brown, slightly curved
Leaves	paired on stem, up to 10cm, narrowly oval to elliptical, pointed, base wedge-shaped, edges finely toothed, red in autumn; short-stalked
Stipules	absent

FLOWERS AND FRUIT

Flowers	☿, in clusters of 3–8 in angles of leaves, 8–10mm across, yellow with a green central disc
Petals	4, narrow, widely separated; sepals 4, 1–2mm, green
Stamens	4, alternating with petals
Stigmas	1, style short, straight
Ovaries	1, bright green
Fruit	10–15mm across, 4-lobed, pink and fleshy, splitting to release seeds
Seeds	4, each with a fleshy, bright orange covering

Box *Buxus sempervirens*

A neat, dense evergreen, often no more than a shrub. Slow-growing and small-leaved, it forms a dense bush when clipped. Tiny flowers form inconspicuous clusters. Fruits are tipped with distinctive, spreading and woody styles. The many cultivars are popular hedging and topiary plants. *Status:* native and scattered through parts of western Europe with chalky soils. *Similar trees:* the larger-leaved Balearic Box is a stiff tree with pinkish bark, confined to parts of Spain, the Balearic Islands and Sardinia.

clustered flowers

glossy

rounded

dense crown

evergreen

small fruit

notched tip

Balearic Box (*Buxus balearica*)

larger leaves

BOX			
Type	evergreen tree or shrub		
Height	2–5m, rarely as much as 11m		
Habitat	calcareous soils		
Flowering	April		
Fruiting	September		

TRUNK AND CROWN

Trunk cylindrical, often leaning
Bark brown, ageing grey, finely fissured
Crown dense, rounded
Twigs 4-angled, white-woolly, becoming smooth

LEAVES

Buds 5–7mm, narrow, bright green
Leaves paired on stem, 15–30mm, oval, oblong or elliptical, tip notched, edges slightly turned under, thick and leathery, glossy green above, pale below; stalk short
Stipules absent

FLOWERS AND FRUIT

Flowers ♂ and ♀, in clusters 5mm across in angles of leaves, each cluster with one stalked ♀ and several stalkless ♂ flowers
Petals absent; ♂ flowers with 4 small sepals; ♀ flowers with only a whorl of small bracts
Stamens 4 in ♂ flowers
Stigmas 3 in ♀ flowers, each 2-lobed on a thick, spreading style
Ovaries 1, 3-chambered, blue-green
Fruit nut-like, *c*7mm, oblong to egg-shaped, tipped with the horn-like styles, ripening brown, splitting into 3 parts
Seeds 6, 5–6mm, glossy black, released when fruit splits

A small, silvery, thorny tree. All parts of the plant, particularly the leaves and twigs, are covered with intricately shaped but minute silver scales. Growing in coastal sites, it is often only a shrub in more exposed habitats. *Status:* native to much of Europe, mainly coastal regions of the north-west, but also occurring inland; widely planted on sand dunes and often naturalized. *Similar trees:* Oleaster, from western Asia, and the North American Silver Berry are widely naturalized ornamentals. Both have fragrant flowers c1cm long. Oleaster has juicy berries; Silver Berry, dry berries.

1 Oleaster (*Elaeagnus angustifolia*)
2 Silver Berry (*Elaeagnus commutata*)

SEA-BUCKTHORN	
Type	deciduous tree or shrub
Height	up to 11m but often shorter
Habitat	dunes and sea-shores
Flowering	March–April
Fruiting	September–November
TRUNK AND CROWN	
Trunk	much-branched near the base, suckering
Bark	pale-brown, ridged
Crown	open, rounded
Twigs	thorny, covered with minute silvery scales
LEAVES	
Buds	3mm, squat with thick scales
Leaves	alternate or spiralled on stem, 1–6cm, very narrow, pointed, silvery green; stalks very short

Stipules	absent
FLOWERS AND FRUIT	
Flowers	♂ and ♀ on different trees, in short spikes appearing before leaves on previous year's growth; ♂ 4mm, stalkless, ♀ 1.5mm, stalked, greenish with rusty scales
Petals	absent; sepals 2, joined, short in ♂ flowers, long in ♀
Stamens	4 in ♂ flowers
Stigmas	1, thread-like on a long cylindrical style
Ovaries	1, sunk into base of ♀ flowers
Fruit	berry-like, 6–8mm, almost globular, ripening orange
Seeds	1, not released

Common Jujube *Ziziphus jujuba*

A small tree or tangled shrub, armed with very sharp, curved and straight spines. The long, slender twigs are markedly zigzag. Sweet and juicy, the fruits are edible. *Status:* native to Asia; widely grown in southern Europe for the edible fruits and often naturalized. *Similar trees:* Z. *lotus* is a shrub with deep yellow fruits, found in dry parts of Spain, Sicily and Greece. Christ's Thorn is a very spiny and tangled tree or shrub of Mediterranean regions. The distinctive, woody and winged fruit resembles a broad-brimmed hat.

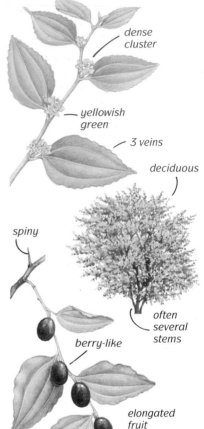

dense cluster

yellowish green

3 veins

deciduous

spiny

often several stems

berry-like

elongated fruit

1 *Ziziphus lotus*
2 Christ's Thorn (*Paliurus spina-christi*)

1

2

yellow

globular

winged fruit

	COMMON JUJUBE		
Type	deciduous tree or shrub		with tiny, gland-tipped teeth; stalk short
Height	up to 8m	**Stipules**	transformed into sharp, brown spines, 1 long and straight, 1 short and curved
Habitat	hedgerows near houses, orchards		
Flowering	April–May		**FLOWERS AND FRUIT**
Fruiting	September	**Flowers**	☿, in small, dense, stalked clusters in angles of leaves, yellowish green
	TRUNK AND CROWN		
Trunk	slender, sinuous, often several	**Petals**	5, 1.5mm, hooded, tapering at base; sepals 5, 2mm
Bark	dark grey-brown		
Crown	dense, rounded	**Stamens**	5, alternating with, and often concealed by, petals
Twigs	zigzag, smooth, green, non-flowering twigs often spiny		
		Stigmas	2, minute, styles joined at base
	LEAVES	**Ovaries**	1, sunk into 5-lobed disc in base of flower
Buds	pointed, hairy		
Leaves	alternate, 2–5.5cm, oval, blunt, with 3 conspicuous veins, bright, shiny green above, downy on veins below, edges	**Fruit**	berry-like, 1.5–3cm, egg-shaped, ripening red to black, sweet-tasting
		Seeds	1, 6–7mm, stony, not released

A regularly branched tree, its new twigs always growing out at right angles. The shoots are of two kinds, long and short; only short shoots bear flowers and fruits. *Status:* native to much of Europe but confined to chalky soils and absent from the Mediterranean region. *Similar trees:* Mediterranean Buckthorn is an evergreen shrub lacking spines, with yellow sepals. Alder Buckthorn has leaves with unbroken edges, ♀ flowers with 5 sepals and fruits ripening from yellow, through red to black. It grows in wet woods through most of Europe.

finely, toothed

4 petals

paired leaves

deciduous

paired buds

berry-like, black

short side shoots

spiny

1 Mediterranean Buckthorn (*Rhamnus alaternus*); 2 Alder Buckthorn (*Frangula alnus*)

evergreen

leaves not paired

2

1

few teeth

red, then black

no teeth

	BUCKTHORN		
Type	deciduous tree or shrub	**Leaves**	paired on twigs, crowded on short side shoots, 3–7cm, oval or elliptical, blunt or even notched at tip, edges finely toothed, 2–4 pairs of curving veins; stalk short
Height	4–6m		
Habitat	hedges and woodland on chalky soils		
Flowering	May–June		
Fruiting	September–October	**Stipules**	soft, soon falling
	TRUNK AND CROWN		**FLOWERS AND FRUIT**
Trunk	short, often several or forking near the ground	**Flowers**	♂ and ♀ on different trees, in clusters on short side shoots, 4mm across, greenish white, fragrant
Bark	black, flaking to reveal orange patches		
Crown	regular; branches spreading at right angles to trunk	**Petals**	4, rarely 5, triangular; sepals 4, very small
Twigs	smooth or hairy, grey, some ending in spines, many short side shoots	**Stamens**	4, rudimentary in ♀ flowers
		Stigmas	4 in ♀ flowers, on single style
	LEAVES	**Ovaries**	1 in ♀ flowers, globose
Buds	4mm, brown, pointed	**Fruit**	berry-like, 6–8mm, globose but slightly flattened, ripening black
		Seeds	2–4, stony, yellow

Tamarisk *Tamarix gallica*

Resistant to the drying effects of salt winds, this feathery tree or shrub is often seen near coasts, and thrives on sand-dunes. The pink flower-spikes normally appear in summer but may occur up to December in mild areas. *Status:* native to western Europe as far north as France; often planted and naturalized elsewhere. *Similar trees:* two other species widespread in western Europe can be distinguished by their flowers. African Tamarisk has larger, white flowers with petals 2–3mm long. It grows mainly in salt-marshes and along rivers. Canarian Tamarisk has pinkish petals, only 1.5mm or less, and is found on coastal sands.

very slender

5 stamens

usually pink

5 petals

deciduous

fruits

scale-like leaves

slender

1 African Tamarisk (*Tamarix africana*)
2 Canarian Tamarisk (*Tamarix canariensis*)

1

longer bract

smaller

larger, white *2*

	TAMARISK			
Type	deciduous shrub or small tree			stalkless
Height	up to 10m		**Stipules**	absent
Habitat	riversides, coastal areas, marshes			**FLOWERS AND FRUIT**
Flowering	April–September		**Flowers**	♀, in spike-like clusters to 3cm long on young shoots, each c2mm, pink or white
Fruiting	May–October			
	TRUNK AND CROWN		**Petals**	5, 1.5–2mm, elliptical; sepals 5, 0.75–1.25mm
Trunk	usually curved or twisted, slender		**Stamens**	5
Bark	dull brown to dark purple, rough and fibrous		**Stigmas**	3–4, styles very short
			Ovaries	1, bottle-shaped
Crown	much-branched with long slender branches		**Fruit**	hard brown capsule, splitting to release seeds
Twigs	willowy, very slender, reddish		**Seeds**	numerous, oval, brown, each with a long tuft of hairs
	LEAVES			
Buds	minute, green			
Leaves	alternate, c2mm, scale-like and clasping the stem, blue-green;			

A predominantly eastern
Mediterranean species that is more
often seen as a shrub than a tree. The
very slender twigs and tiny, scale-like,
clasping leaves give a delicate, wispy
effect. The flower spikes are also very
slim, being less than 5mm wide. The
pink or white petals usually number 4,
but sometimes there are 5. *Status:*
native to the Balkan Peninsula and
Aegean region; planted elsewhere for
ornament. *Similar trees:* two very
similar species are *T. tetrandra* and
T. dalmatica, also from south-eastern
Europe. Both have longer, broader
flower spikes and larger petals.
T. tetrandra has black bark.

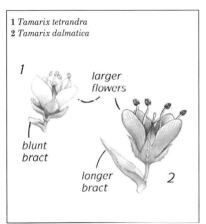

1 *Tamarix tetrandra*
2 *Tamarix dalmatica*

1

larger flowers

blunt bract

longer bract

2

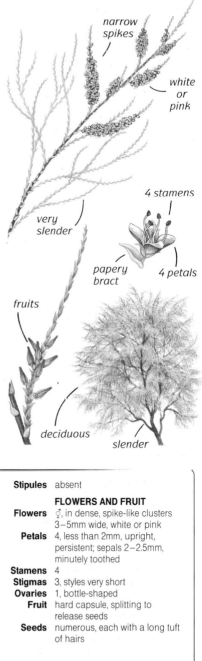

narrow spikes

white or pink

very slender

4 stamens

papery bract

4 petals

fruits

deciduous

slender

	SMALL-FLOWERED TAMARISK		Stipules	absent
Type	deciduous shrub or small tree			**FLOWERS AND FRUIT**
Height	2–3m		**Flowers**	♀, in dense, spike-like clusters
Habitat	hedges and river banks			3–5mm wide, white or pink
Flowering	March–June		**Petals**	4, less than 2mm, upright,
Fruiting	April–June			persistent; sepals 2–2.5mm,
				minutely toothed
	TRUNK AND CROWN		**Stamens**	4
Trunk	slender, often several or		**Stigmas**	3, styles very short
	branching low-down		**Ovaries**	1, bottle-shaped
Bark	brown to purple		**Fruit**	hard capsule, splitting to
Crown	low, rounded			release seeds
Twigs	very slender, drooping, red-		**Seeds**	numerous, each with a long tuft
	brown, black in winter			of hairs
	LEAVES			
Buds	minute, egg-shaped			
Leaves	alternate, 3–5mm, scale-like			
	and half clasping stem with tips			
	spreading, sharply pointed,			
	edges papery-edged; stalkless			

Large-leaved Lime   *Tilia platyphyllos*

This is the first of the limes to begin
flowering. A tall tree, it has upwardly
angled branches and large leaves. The
fragrant flowers hang in clusters
beneath a narrow, wing-like bract,
attracting large numbers of bees.
Status: native from central Europe to
Russia and western Asia; introduced
elsewhere and often planted. *Similar
trees:* Common Lime, a hybrid between
Large- and Small-leaved Limes, is
widely planted. In many areas it is more
common than the parent species. The
leaves have tufts of white hairs beneath
and drooping yellowish flowers.

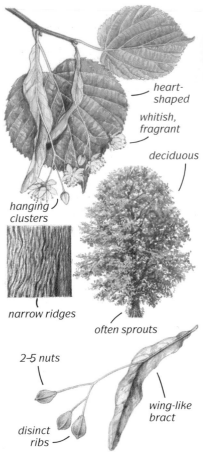

heart-
shaped

whitish,
fragrant

deciduous

hanging
clusters

narrow ridges

often sprouts

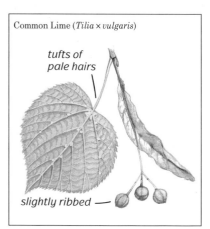

Common Lime (*Tilia × vulgaris*)

tufts of
pale hairs

slightly ribbed

2–5 nuts

disinct
ribs

wing-like
bract

	LARGE-LEAVED LIME	
Type	deciduous tree	
Height	up to 40m	
Habitat	woods, often on limestone	
Flowering	June–July	
Fruiting	July–October	

TRUNK AND CROWN

Trunk	occasionally with outgrowths of bushy stems from base
Bark	smooth, dark grey, developing narrow cracks and ridges
Crown	tall and narrowly domed; branches angled upwards
Twigs	dark reddish green, softly hairy

LEAVES

Buds	oval, dark red
Leaves	alternate, up to 12cm, heart-shaped, sharply pointed, sharply toothed, dark green, hairy above, paler, more densely hairy below; stalk 1.5–5cm, hairy
Stipules	small, acting as bud scales, falling early

FLOWERS AND FRUIT

Flowers	☿, yellowish white, fragrant, in clusters of 2–5 hanging beneath a whitish green, wing-like bract 5–12 cm
Petals	5, 5–8mm, spreading; sepals 5
Stamens	numerous
Stigmas	1, 5-lobed
Ovaries	1, 5-chambered
Fruit	cluster of hard, globular nuts, each 8–10mm, 3- to 5-ribbed, densely hairy; whole cluster and bract shed together
Seeds	1, not released

Growing on lime-rich soils, this tree has downward-arching branches and heart-shaped leaves. It is often planted as a street tree but aphids attack the leaves, dripping half-digested sap onto the pavements below, leaving them sticky and unpleasant. Fungi also attack and disfigure the leaves. Other, resistant, trees are now preferred. Bees are attracted by the nectar-rich flowers. *Status:* native to most of Europe and northern Asia; frequently planted. *Similar trees:* Caucasian Lime is a natural hybrid from the Crimea. It has rich yellow flowers and leaves with tufts of reddish brown hairs in the vein angles beneath.

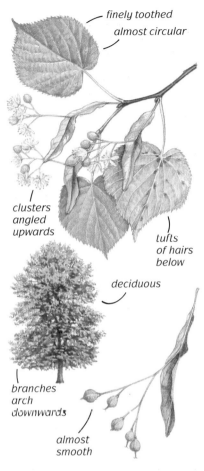

finely toothed

almost circular

clusters angled upwards

tufts of hairs below

deciduous

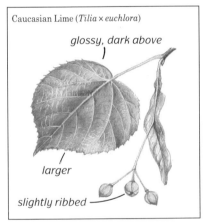

Caucasian Lime (*Tilia × euchlora*)

glossy, dark above

larger

slightly ribbed

branches arch downwards

almost smooth

	SMALL-LEAVED LIME		
Type	deciduous tree		shining green above, paler beneath, smooth except for reddish brown tuft of hair in vein angles; stalk 1.5–4cm
Height	up to 32m		
Habitat	woods, often on limestone		
Flowering	June–July	**Stipules**	small, scale-like, soon falling
Fruiting	July–September		
	TRUNK AND CROWN		**FLOWERS AND FRUIT**
Trunk	burred	**Flowers**	♂, greenish yellow, fragrant, in clusters of 4–15 held above leaf-like bract up to 8cm long
Bark	smooth, grey, becoming dark, fissured, cracked into plates		
Crown	irregularly domed; branches downwardly arching	**Petals**	5, 7–8mm, narrowly oval; sepals 5–6, 3mm, elliptical
Twigs	smooth, reddish above, greenish brown beneath	**Stamens**	c40
		Stigmas	1, 5-lobed
		Ovaries	1, 5-chambered
	LEAVES	**Fruit**	cluster of hard, globular nuts, each c6mm, smooth or shallow ribbed; whole cluster and bract shed together
Buds	dark red, smooth and shiny		
Leaves	alternate, 3–9cm, almost circular, finely pointed, notched at base, sharply toothed, dark		
		Seeds	1, not released

Silver-lime *Tila tomentosa*

A handsome tree with contrasting leaf surfaces, green above and silver below. Upwardly angled branches give a full, rounded crown. It is resistant to drought and frequently used as a street tree. The ground around these trees is often littered with drowsy and dying bees, drugged by the narcotic nectar from the flowers. *Status:* native from Hungary and the Balkans to western Asia; planted elsewhere for ornament. *Similar trees:* of unknown origin, and sometimes regarded as merely an odd form of Silver-lime, Weeping Silver-lime has branches that are angled upwards before drooping conspicuously towards the tips.

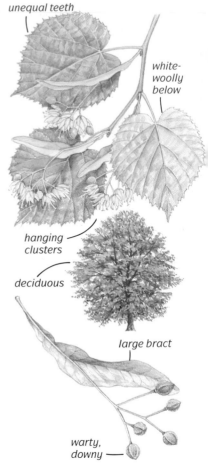

unequal teeth

white-woolly below

hanging clusters

deciduous

large bract

warty, downy

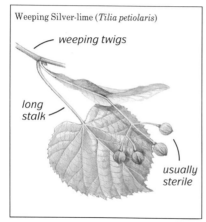

Weeping Silver-lime (*Tilia petiolaris*)

weeping twigs

long stalk

usually sterile

	SILVER-LIME	
Type	deciduous tree	
Height	up to 30m	
Habitat	woods; often planted	
Flowering	July–August	
Fruiting	July–September	

TRUNK AND CROWN

Trunk	stout, well-defined
Bark	dark grey-green or grey, networked with shallow ridges
Crown	broadly domed, compact; branches upwardly angled
Twigs	whitish hairy when young, becoming green, smooth

LEAVES

Buds	6–8mm, oval, green-brown
Leaves	alternate, 8–10cm, heart-shaped, finely pointed, lop-sided at base, sharply toothed, dark green above, white-woolly beneath, the hairs star-shaped; stalk c5cm
Stipules	small, acting as bud scales, falling early

FLOWERS AND FRUIT

Flowers	☿, dull white or pale yellow, fragrant, in clusters of 6–10 hanging beneath a yellowish green, leaf-like bract
Petals	5, 5–8mm; sepals 5
Stamens	numerous
Stigmas	1, 5-lobed
Ovaries	1, 5-chambered
Fruit	cluster of nuts, each 6–12 mm long, 5-sided, warty and downy; cluster and bract shed together
Seeds	1, not released

A spectacular tree when in full bloom, becoming completely covered with conspicuous, white flower-heads. The tree's real flowers are small and grouped into a globular, purplish head. This is enveloped by two large, triangular, handkerchief-like bracts – hence the common name. When the bracts unfold, they give the impression of a single large flower with white petals and a purple centre. Though the flower-heads are similar in structure to those of the dogwoods, Handkerchief-tree is usually placed within its own family. The most commonly planted form is var. *vilmoriniana*, which is distinguished by narrow, smooth and shiny leaves. *Status:* native to China; cultivated as an ornamental in parks and gardens. *Similar trees:* none.

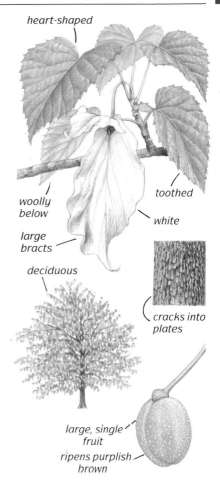

heart-shaped

woolly below

toothed

white

large bracts

deciduous

cracks into plates

large, single fruit

ripens purplish brown

	HANDKERCHIEF-TREE		
Type	deciduous tree		green above, white-woolly below, fragrant when unfolding; stalkless
Height	up to 18m		
Habitat	parks and gardens	**Stipules**	absent
Flowering	May		
Fruiting	October		**FLOWERS AND FRUIT**
		Flowers	♂ and ♀ in separate clusters, or ♀; flower cluster *c*2cm across, purplish, flanked by 2 very large, showy white bracts
	TRUNK AND CROWN		
Trunk	straight, well-defined		
Bark	grey-brown to purplish, cracking	**Perianth**	0 in ♂ flowers, many in ♀ and ♂ flowers
Crown	tall, domed; branches wide-spreading	**Stamens**	usually 5–6
		Stigmas	1, lobed, style curved
Twigs	brown, with lines of warty lenticels	**Ovaries**	1, 6–10-chambered, sunk into base of flower
		Fruit	single, berry-like, 4cm, egg-shaped, ridged, ripening purplish brown
	LEAVES		
Buds	9mm, dark, shiny red, pointed	**Seeds**	6–10, not released
Leaves	alternate, 3.5cm, broadly oval, pointed, base heart-shaped, edges sharply toothed, dull		

Black-gum *Nyssa sylvatica*

Growing in swampy areas, Black-gum forms a very tall tree, up to 100m, where it is native in eastern North America. In Europe, however, it is generally much smaller, reaching only 30m at the most. Producing inconspicuous flowers and rather dull fruits, it is planted for its brilliant autumn leaf colours, which are dominated by bright reds and orange. Black-gum only thrives in mild areas, so is little planted in northern regions. However, it is quite common from southern England southwards. *Status:* native to the swamps of eastern North America; grown in Europe mainly for ornament. *Similar trees:* relatives of the Black-gum are only rarely cultivated, in private gardens.

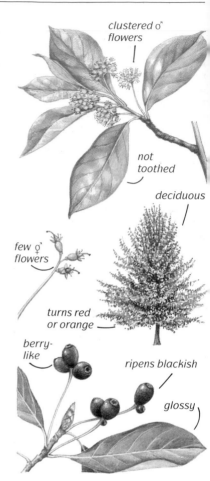

clustered ♂ flowers

not toothed

deciduous

few ♀ flowers

turns red or orange

berry-like

ripens blackish

glossy

	BLACK-GUM		
Type	deciduous tree		bright orange and red in autumn; stalkless
Height	up to 30m	**Stipules**	absent
Habitat	parks and gardens; wet soils		
Flowering	June		**FLOWERS AND FRUIT**
Fruiting	October	**Flowers**	♂ and ♀ on different trees; ♂ in rounded clusters 1cm across; ♀ single or paired
	TRUNK AND CROWN	**Petals**	5, free in ♂, in ♀ joined into a bell-shaped tube; sepals 5, tiny, tooth-like
Trunk	tapering		
Bark	grey or brown, deeply ridged and fissured	**Stamens**	8, longer than petals in ♂ flowers
Crown	cylindrical, flat-topped	**Stigmas**	1 in ♀ flowers, on a long, curved style
Twigs	grey-brown, smooth		
	LEAVES	**Ovaries**	1 in ♀ flowers, sunk into base of flower
Buds	small, red-brown, downy tips	**Fruit**	berry-like, 12mm, oval, widest above middle, ripening blue-black
Leaves	alternate, 4.5cm, oval, widest above middle, tapered at both ends, edge unbroken, slightly leathery, glossy green above, pale and matt below, turning		
		Seeds	1, stony

A very attractive tree in late winter, when bright yellow flowers appear. Dull green leaves which follow have strongly marked veins. The succulent fruits are often used in conserves. *Status:* native to central and south-eastern Europe; widely cultivated and naturalized elsewhere. *Similar trees:* Dogwood is a common summer-flowering shrub with clusters of small white flowers and black berries. Nuttall's Dogwood is a widely planted American species. The tight flower clusters are surrounded by 4–7 large pink or white bracts, the whole assembly resembling a single, large, flower.

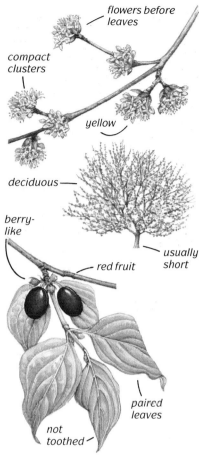

flowers before leaves

compact clusters

yellow

deciduous

berry-like

red fruit

usually short

paired leaves

not toothed

1 Nuttall's Dogwood (*Cornus nuttallii*)
2 Dogwood (*Cornus sanguinea*)

large bracts

white flowers

blackish fruit

1

2

	CORNELIAN CHERRY		
Type	deciduous tree or shrub	**Stipules**	pointed tip, base rounded, downy, dull green, 3–5 pairs of conspicuous curved veins; stalk 6mm
Height	up to 8m		
Habitat	scrub, thickets and woodland, especially on chalk		
			absent
Flowering	February–March		**FLOWERS AND FRUIT**
Fruiting	August–September	**Flowers**	♂, yellow, before leaves in paired, thick-stalked clusters of 10–25, 4 yellowish bracts at base of cluster soon falling
	TRUNK AND CROWN		
Trunk	short, often several		
Bark	grey-brown, scaly	**Petals**	4, 2–2.5mm, hooded; sepals very small
Crown	open; branches spreading or downswept		
		Stamens	4, alternating with petals
Twigs	greenish yellow, minutely downy	**Stigmas**	1–several, in base of flower-tube
	LEAVES		
Buds	7mm, paired, pointed, yellowish, lacking scales but with short, close-pressed hairs	**Ovaries**	1, sunk in base of flower
		Fruit	berry-like, 12–20mm, roughly cylindrical, drooping, ripening bright red
Leaves	paired on stem, 4–10cm, elliptical to oval, drawn out to a		
		Seeds	1, stony, not released

Orange-bark Myrtle *Myrtus apiculata*

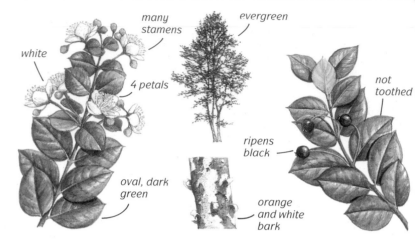

white · *many stamens* · *evergreen* · *4 petals* · *oval, dark green* · *not toothed* · *ripens black* · *orange and white bark*

Seldom more than a large shrub outside its South American home, this spicily aromatic plant has gland-dotted leaves, which release their scent when crushed. Attractive, cinnamon-coloured bark peels away from the base of the trunk, revealing the grey or creamy inner bark. *Status:* native to Chile; planted for ornament. *Similar trees:* Myrtle, from southern Europe, is very similar but always shrubby, and lacks colourful bark. Crape Myrtle, a deciduous shrub or small tree from China is grown in gardens and streets. Clusters of red, pink or white flowers, each up to 4cm across, have crinkled petals.

1 Myrtle (*Myrtus communis*)
2 Crape Myrtle (*Lagerstroemeria indica*)

crinkled petals · *pink* · *smaller narrower*

ORANGE-BARK MAPLE

Type	evergreen tree or shrub
Height	up to 13m
Habitat	parks, gardens
Flowering	August–October
Fruiting	October–November

TRUNK AND CROWN

Trunk	slender, often several
Bark	orange to cinnamon, peeling to leave areas of white; old trees with broad, tapering white streaks
Crown	loosely conical
Twigs	dark pink above, green to pale brown beneath, hairy

LEAVES

Buds	minute, globular, deep red, shiny
Leaves	opposite, 2.5 × 1.5cm, oval, finely and sharply pointed, dark green above, paler beneath and minutely hairy; almost stalkless
Stipules	absent

FLOWERS AND FRUIT

Flowers	⚥, 2cm across, white; stalks *c*1.5cm, pink
Petals	4, round, *c*1.3cm; sepals 4, bowl-shaped, persisting on fruit
Stamens	many, arranged in several rings
Stigmas	1, style long, straight
Ovaries	1
Fruit	berry, initially red, ripening to black
Seeds	3–6, not released

Large plantations of this gum are increasingly seen in hot European countries. It is one of the largest and fastest-growing trees, a source of timber, paper pulp and eucalyptus oil. Bark is shed annually and can be a fire-risk. Paired juvenile leaves are short and very blue, but adult leaves are alternate, long and dull green. *Status:* native to Tasmania and south-eastern Australia; planted on a massive scale in the Mediterranean region. *Similar trees:* common in gardens, Cider Gum has almost circular juvenile leaves and clusters of stalked flowers. The rarer Maiden's Gum has clusters of stalkless flowers.

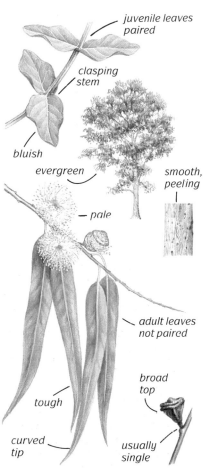

juvenile leaves paired

clasping stem

bluish

evergreen

pale

smooth, peeling

adult leaves not paired

broad top

tough

curved tip

usually single

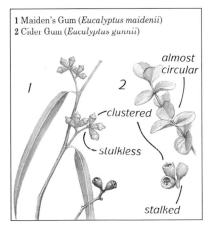

1 Maiden's Gum (*Eucalyptus maidenii*)
2 Cider Gum (*Eucalyptus gunnii*)

almost circular

clustered

stalkless

stalked

TASMANIAN BLUE-GUM

Type	evergreen tree
Height	up to 40m
Habitat	streets, plantations
Flowering	September–December
Fruiting	January–March

TRUNK AND CROWN

Trunk	tall, straight, cylindrical
Bark	smooth, grey-brown, peeling away in long strips
Crown	narrowly conical, very dense
Twigs	greenish brown, smooth

LEAVES

Buds	minute, concealed
Leaves	juvenile leaves opposite, to 16 × 9cm, oval, heart-shaped base clasps stem, blue-green, stalkless; adult leaves alternate, up to 30 × 4cm, narrowly oval to sickle-shaped, drawn out into a long slender tip, hanging downwards, dark green; shortly stalked
Stipules	absent

FLOWERS AND FRUIT

Flower buds	up to 30 × 20 mm, covered by a pale bluish, hemispherical, rough and waxy cap
Flowers	♂, single or clusters of 2–3; each c4cm, whitish; almost stalkless
Stamens	numerous
Stigmas	1, style short and straight
Ovaries	1, 2–8-chambered
Fruit	woody capsule, 10–25 × 15–25mm, top-shaped, strongly ribbed, with waxy white bloom
Seeds	numerous, hard, wedge-shaped, black

Red Mahogany *Eucalyptus resinifer*

One of the 'stringybark' group of gums, the rough, reddish bark of this large tree is very fibrous. The narrow adult leaves are similar to the juvenile leaves, but darker in colour. The flowers have a pointed, orange lid. Red Mahogany favours sandy soils in sheltered places and is grown mainly for timber. *Status:* native to Queensland and New South Wales; planted from Portugal to Italy, mainly in coastal areas. *Similar trees:* Swamp Mahogany has pink-lidded fruits and prefers wet ground. It has larger fruits with a rim raised above the short teeth.

pale

orange, beaked cap

evergreen

rough, fibrous

stringy bark

juvenile leaves often paired

projecting teeth

narrow

clusters of 5–10

stalked

Swamp Mahogany (*Eucalyptus robustus*)

broad juvenile leaves

rim

almost stalkless

	RED MAHOGANY		
Type	evergreen tree		
Height	up to 40m		
Habitat	plantations		
Flowering	September – February		
Fruiting	December – March		

TRUNK AND CROWN

Trunk	tall, straight, cylindrical
Bark	reddish, fibrous, rough
Crown	small, narrowly domed and open
Twigs	green, smooth

LEAVES

Buds	minute, concealed
Leaves	juvenile leaves opposite, to 6 × 2cm, lance-shaped, pale green, stalked; adult leaves alternate, up to 16 × 3cm, lance-shaped to narrowly oval, dark, glossy green above; stalked
Stipules	absent

FLOWERS AND FRUIT

Flower buds	up to 17mm, with an orange, conical or beak-like cap
Flowers	⚲, in clusters of 5–10, white; stalks of clusters up to 2cm, flattened
Stamens	numerous
Stigmas	1; style short
Ovaries	1, 2–8-chambered
Fruit	woody capsule, 5–18 × 5–18mm, hemispherical, stalked, opening by 3–4 teeth
Seeds	numerous

A large, pallid tree with thin outer bark, which shreds and hangs from the trunk and branches in long ribbons, revealing the white inner bark. Both juvenile and adult leaves are pale green. Red flowers have rounded, woody lids. Ribbon Gum provides timber but is mainly used for shade and shelter in towns. *Status:* native to southern and eastern Australia and Tasmania; planted in Spain, Portugal and Italy. *Similar trees:* Snow Gum has peeling grey outer bark over white inner bark, and leaves which age from orange-brown to grey-green. It grows at high altitudes in the wild and is planted as a cold-tolerant ornamental.

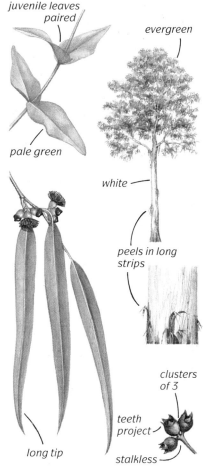

juvenile leaves paired

evergreen

pale green

white

peels in long strips

clusters of 3

teeth project

stalkless

long tip

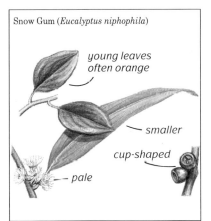

Snow Gum (*Eucalyptus niphophila*)

young leaves often orange

smaller

cup-shaped

pale

	RIBBON GUM
Type	evergreen tree
Height	up to 50m
Habitat	plantations
Flowering	December–June
Fruiting	January–July
	TRUNK AND CROWN
Trunk	tapering from base
Bark	smooth, white, falling away in long ribbon-like strips
Crown	drooping branches festooned with ribbons of bark
Twigs	greenish brown, smooth
	LEAVES
Buds	minute, concealed
Leaves	variable, pale green, juvenile leaves opposite, up to 10 × 3cm, oval, stalkless, surrounding the stem at their base; adult leaves alternate, up to 18 × 2cm, narrowly oval, drawn out into a long slender tip; stalked
Stipules	absent
	FLOWERS AND FRUIT
Flower buds	7mm, covered by a scarlet, hemispherical to conical cap
Flowers	♀, in shortly stalked clusters of 3, 1.5cm across
Stamens	numerous
Stigmas	1; style short
Ovaries	1, 2–8-chambered
Fruit	woody capsule, 5–8 × 7–9mm, more or less spherical, slightly tapering to the base, opening by 3–4 valves; stalkless
Seeds	numerous

Red Gum · *Eucalyptus camaldulensis*

Cultivated for its timber, this tree is widely planted on a world scale. Large and spreading, it shows considerable natural variation. The white bark is mottled with pink and grey and is shed in plates. It has red flowers with conical, woody lids, and fruit with projecting teeth. *Status:* native to much of Australia; planted in the Mediterranean region, especially Spain. *Similar trees:* Lemon-scented Spotted Gum, from Queensland, is a slender tree with strongly lemon-scented leaves. The flowers have domed lids and the fruits have inward-pointing teeth. It is grown as an ornamental in Spain, Portugal and Italy.

red

conical cap

juvenile leaves bluish

dull / green

projecting teeth

evergreen

smooth

falls in plates

Lemon-scented Spotted Gum (*Eucalyptus citriodora*)

domed cap

lemon-scented

inward-pointing teeth

	RED GUM		
Type	evergreen tree		green; shortly stalked
Height	up to 20m	**Stipules**	absent
Habitat	plantations		
Flowering	December – February		**FLOWERS AND FRUIT**
Fruiting	May	**Flower buds**	up to 10 × 5mm, cap brownish, conical or beak-like
	TRUNK AND CROWN	**Flowers**	♀, in clusters of 5–10, white; stalk of cluster up to 2.5cm, slender
Trunk	short, stout, soon forking		
Bark	smooth, white, pink and grey, falling away on plates	**Stamens**	numerous
Crown	open; irregularly branched	**Stigmas**	1; style short
Twigs	green, strongly ribbed	**Ovaries**	1, 2–8-chambered
		Fruit	woody capsule, 7–8 × 5–6mm, hemispherical with a broad raised rim, opening by 4 teeth
	LEAVES		
Buds	minute, concealed	**Seeds**	numerous
Leaves	young leaves opposite, up to 9 × 4cm, oval, bluish green; adult leaves alternate, up to 25 × 2cm, narrowly oval, drawn out into a long slender tip, dull		

Striking scarlet flowers tip the shoots of this small tree. White-flowered forms of Pomegranate also occur but are much rarer. Both petals and sepals are variable in number; the petals are noticeably crumpled until fully expanded. The branches are sometimes unarmed, but more usually bear spines. Pomegranate's large, globular fruit has a leathery, rather hard rind and a tubular crown formed by the persistent sepals; the pulp contains numerous seeds. Although at first acid-tasting, the fruit usually becomes sweet. *Status:* introduced from western Asia in ancient times for its fruit; cultivated and widely naturalized in Mediterranean regions. *Similar trees:* none.

red petals

joined, thick sepals

not toothed

paired

deciduous

short

leathery outside

ripens reddish

sepals remain

	POMEGRANATE		
Type	deciduous tree	**Stipules**	absent
Height	up to 8m		**FLOWERS AND FRUIT**
Habitat	scrub, field margins, orchards	**Flowers**	♀, single or paired at tips of shoots, 2.5–4cm across, red, occasionally white
Flowering	June–October		
Fruiting	July onwards	**Petals**	5–7, crumpled before opening fully; sepals 5–7 hooded, leathery, red, joined into a long tube, persisting on fruit
	TRUNK AND CROWN		
Trunk	slender, branching from near ground		
Bark	pale brown, finely grooved	**Stamens**	numerous, in whorls in throat of flower
Crown	irregular; branches slender, angled upwards		
		Stigmas	1, globular on a long style
Twigs	4-angled, smooth, often spiny	**Ovaries**	1, sunk into base of flower
	LEAVES	**Fruit**	berry-like, 5–8cm, globular, leathery skin surrounding translucent purple or yellowish pulp, ripening reddish or yellow
Buds	small, pyramidal, tinged red		
Leaves	paired on stem, 2–8cm, oblong to narrowly oval and widest above middle, smooth and shiny; stalk very short		
		Seeds	numerous, embedded in pulp, not released

Date-plum *Diospyros lotus*

Persimmons, the group to which this tree belongs, produce edible fruit, but that of Date-plum is small, only c1.5cm across, and rather insipid. It may be either yellow or blue-black when ripe. The tree is cultivated in the south as a fruit tree but in the north only as an ornamental. *Status:* native to Asia; cultivated and sometimes naturalized in Europe. *Similar trees:* Common Persimmon, from eastern and central North America, has tart fruit. Chinese Persimmon, from Asia, has much larger fruit, up to 7.5cm, which is very sour until overripe.

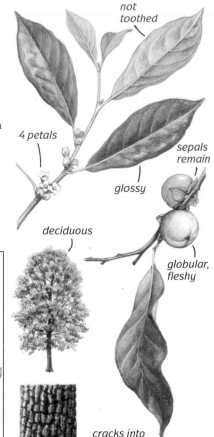

not toothed

4 petals

sepals remain

glossy

deciduous

globular, fleshy

1 Chinese Persimmon (*Diospyros kaki*)
2 Common Persimmon (*Diospyros virginiana*)

1

large

broad

2

cracks into plates

	DATE-PLUM			
Type	deciduous tree			smooth; stalk hairy
Height	up to 14m		**Stipules**	absent
Habitat	gardens, parks, orchards			
Flowering	July			**FLOWERS AND FRUIT**
Fruiting	July–October		**Flowers**	♂ and ♀ on different trees, stalkless, reddish or greenish white, petals forming an urn-shaped tube with 4 fringed, curved-back lobes, sepals forming a 4-lobed cup
	TRUNK AND CROWN			
Trunk	well-defined			
Bark	grey, tinged pink, cracking into small plates			
Crown	tall and narrowly domed		♂	in clusters of 2–3, each c5mm
Twigs	downy when young		♀	single, each 8–10mm
			Stamens	4 in ♂; reduced and sterile in ♀
	LEAVES		**Stigmas**	4 in ♀
Buds	4–5mm, sharp-pointed		**Ovaries**	1, several chambers
Leaves	alternate, elliptical to oblong with wavy edges, base rounded, somewhat leathery, dark green above, bluish below, hairy on both sides but becoming almost		**Fruit**	1.5cm, globular, fleshy and ripening yellow or nearly black with a glistening bloom
			Seeds	3–4, large, not released

A small tree in which all the parts, including the drooping white flowers and grey fruits, are covered with star-shaped hairs. It is one of the very few plants native to the climatically similar Mediterranean region and California. Storax yields an aromatic gum, also called storax, collected from cuts made in the trunk and branches, and used for incense. *Status:* native from Italy eastwards; naturalized in parts of France. *Similar trees:* Snowbell-tree, from the Far East, reaches 11m and flowers prolifically. Snowdrop-tree is a North American species with flowers opening mostly before the leaves, and 4-winged fruits up to 5cm long.

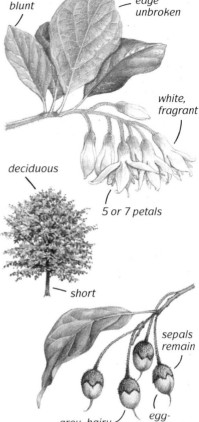

blunt

edge unbroken

white, fragrant

deciduous

5 or 7 petals

short

sepals remain

grey, hairy

egg-shaped

1 Snowbell-tree (*Styrax japonica*)
2 Snowdrop-tree (*Halesia monticola*)

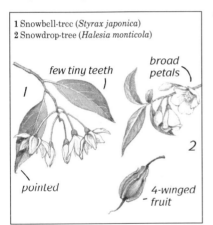

few tiny teeth

broad petals

1

2

pointed

4-winged fruit

STORAX	**FLOWERS AND FRUIT**
Type deciduous shrub or small tree	**Flowers** ♀, in short, drooping clusters of 3–6, each 2cm long, bell-shaped, white, fragrant
Height 2–7m	
Habitat thickets, woods, stream-sides	
Flowering April–May	**Petals** 5 or 7, overlapping at the edges above, joined into a short tube at the base; sepals joined for most of their length, cup-shaped, hairy
Fruiting July–September	
TRUNK AND CROWN	
Trunk short, slender	
Bark brown, shredding slightly	
Crown irrgularly branched	**Stamens** 10, fused to base of the petal-tube
Twigs white-woolly	
	Stigmas 1, style long, slender
LEAVES	**Ovaries** 1, 3-chambered
Buds small, ellipsoid, white-woolly	**Fruit** egg-shaped, dry, leathery, grey and densely hairy, cupped by persistent white-woolly sepals
Leaves alternate, 3–7cm, oval, blunt-tipped, base rounded, edge unbroken, green above, white-hairy, especially beneath; stalked	
	Seeds 1 or 2, large, hard
Stipules absent	

Manna Ash *Fraxinus ornus*

Unlike most European ashes, this species has scented flowers with petals, forming large showy heads after the leaves appear. In winter it can be distinguished by its very smooth bark and pale brown buds. It is a commercial source of manna, not the biblical food but an edible sugary gum, which seeps from cuts in the trunk and dries into flakes on contact with air. *Status:* native to central Europe and the Mediterranean region; planted for ornament. *Similar trees:* two North American species are planted, mainly for timber. Red Ash has sharp-toothed leaves, hairy below. White Ash has bluntly toothed, smooth leaves.

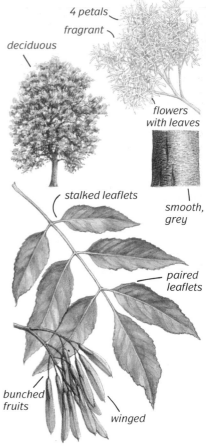

4 petals
fragrant
deciduous
flowers with leaves
stalked leaflets
smooth, grey
paired leaflets
bunched fruits
winged

1 Red Ash (*Fraxinus pennsylvanica*)
2 White Ash (*Fraxinus americana*)

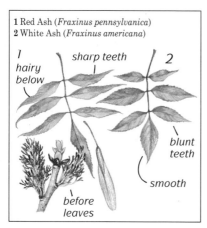

1
hairy below
sharp teeth
2
blunt teeth
smooth
before leaves

	MANNA ASH		
Type	deciduous tree		toothed, unequal at base, pale and hairy on the veins beneath; stalks up to 1.5cm
Height	up to 24m, often smaller		
Habitat	open woods, thickets, rocky places; often planted	**Stipules**	absent
			FLOWERS AND FRUIT
Flowering	April–June	**Flowers**	⚥, many in pyramidal clusters to 20cm long, white, fragrant
Fruiting	May–September		
	TRUNK AND CROWN	**Petals**	4, 5–6mm, narrow, strap-shaped; sepals 4, joined near base
Trunk	cylindrical		
Bark	smooth, dark grey, or black	**Stamens**	2, on long stalks
Crown	hemispherical, fairly dense	**Stigmas**	2
Twigs	grey to yellowish, smooth	**Ovaries**	1, 2-chambered
		Fruit	hanging in dense bunches, 1.5–2.5cm, on wiry stalks 3–10mm long, with slender wing 1.5–2.5cm, sometimes notched at tip, green becoming brown
	LEAVES		
Buds	pyramidal, blunt, grey or brown		
Leaves	opposite, up to 30cm, with 4–8 paired, stalked leaflets and a leaflet at the tip, each 3–10cm long, oblong-oval, abruptly and sharply pointed, shallowly		
		Seeds	1 per fruit, not released

A common tree, readily distinguished by its divided leaves in pairs on the stem and by its distinctive, winged fruits. In winter it is recognized by the prominent, paired, black buds. Growing mainly on lime-rich soils, it is sometimes planted for its tough timber. The cultivar 'Pendula' is a weeping form, often grafted onto the trunk of the common form and grown as an ornamental. *Status:* native throughout Europe, western Asia and North Africa. *Similar trees:* Narrow-leaved Ash is similar but has very narrow leaflets. It has a more southern distribution.

black bud — no petals

before leaves

paired leaflets

leaflets stalkless

toothed

winged

becomes fissured

deciduous

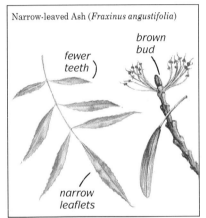

Narrow-leaved Ash (*Fraxinus angustifolia*)

fewer teeth

brown bud

narrow leaflets

	ASH
Type	deciduous tree
Height	up to 40m
Habitat	hedgerows, open woods, roadsides, often on limestone
Flowering	April–May
Fruiting	July–November

TRUNK AND CROWN

Trunk	suckering; many pollarded
Bark	smooth, grey, becoming rough and shallowly fissured
Crown	domed; branches well-spaced
Twigs	flattened at nodes, greenish grey, smooth

LEAVES

Buds	pyramidal, hard, black
Leaves	opposite, up to 35cm, with usually 6–12 paired leaflets and a leaflet at tip, each 3–12cm, oblong-oval, with long slender tip, shallowly toothed, dark green above, hairy at the base and on the midrib beneath; stalked
Stipules	absent

FLOWERS AND FRUIT

Flowers	♀, or ♂ and ♀ in separate rounded clusters before leaves, purplish, dark red, then yellow
Petals	absent; sepals absent
Stamens	2
Stigmas	2
Ovaries	1, 2-chambered
Fruit	2.5–5cm, with twisted wing notched and spiny at tip, green ripening dull brown, in hanging clusters
Seeds	1 per fruit, not released

Olive *Olea europaea*

Long-lived, this evergreen tree has a distinctive silvery grey bark. Old trees have gnarled trunks pitted with holes. Ripe fruits are black; green olives are simply unripe fruits. Widely cultivated since classical times, olives crop heavily and are the basis for the important olive and olive-oil industries. Wild Olives (var. *sylvestris*) are bushy, spiny trees of dry woodlands, with smaller leaves and fruits. *Status:* native throughout the Mediterranean region. *Similar trees:* Phillyrea is a dense, rounded tree with shallowly toothed leaves and round, purplish black fruits. It grows in evergreen woods and is planted for ornament.

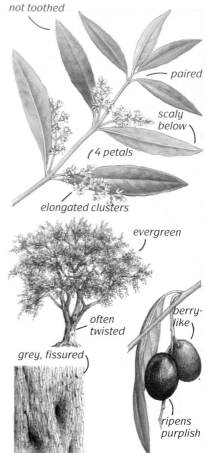

not toothed

paired

scaly below

4 petals

elongated clusters

evergreen

often twisted

grey, fissured

berry-like

ripens purplish

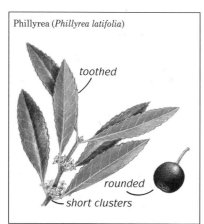

Phillyrea (*Phillyrea latifolia*)

toothed

rounded

short clusters

	OLIVE		
Type	evergreen tree or shrub		smooth above, greyish or brownish white and hairy beneath; almost stalkless
Height	up to 15m		
Habitat	dry rocky places, woods and scrub; planted in large groves	**Stipules**	absent
Flowering	May–June		**FLOWERS AND FRUIT**
Fruiting	September–November	**Flowers**	mostly ♂, many in branched or unbranched clusters from angles of leaves, each *c*1cm across, yellowish white
	TRUNK AND CROWN		
Trunk	thick, becoming gnarled and twisted, developing holes		
Bark	silvery grey, shallowly fissured	**Petals**	4, joined for most of their length, spreading at the top; sepals 4, short, joined
Crown	broad; irregularly branching		
Twigs	slender, greyish, covered with small, scurfy scales	**Stamens**	2
		Stigmas	1, style short
	LEAVES	**Ovaries**	1, 2-chambered
Buds	very small, greyish	**Fruit**	berry-like, 1–3.5cm, oval, somewhat fleshy with a tough outer skin, green ripening blackish purple
Leaves	opposite, 2–10cm, lance-shaped, with a sharp tip, leathery, dark grey-green and		
		Seeds	1, stony, brown

Highly glossed leaves and clusters of fragrant white flowers produced late in the year, when few other trees are flowering, make this an attractive ornamental tree. It is often seen in towns and cities. *Status:* native to China; planted for ornament, mainly in southern Europe. *Similar trees:* Wild Privet is a native species that is widespread on chalky soils. Always a shrub, it is semi-evergreen, sometimes losing its leaves late in the year. Garden Privet is the commonly seen hedge plant. Also semi-evergreen, it tolerates poor soil but sheds leaves in polluted air and cold weather. It originates in Japan.

4 petals

branched head

fragrant

glossy

paired leaflets

pointed

rounded

small berries

evergreen

short

1 Wild Privet (*Ligustrum vulgare*)
2 Garden Privet (*Ligustrum ovalifolium*)

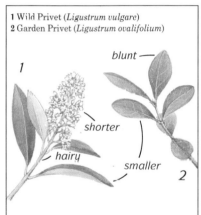

blunt

shorter

hairy

smaller

1

2

	GLOSSY PRIVET		
Type	evergreen tree		
Height	up to 15m		
Habitat	gardens, especially as a hedge, streets, parks		
Flowering	August–September		
Fruiting	October–November, often not produced		

TRUNK AND CROWN

Trunk short, often several
Bark grey with brown streaks, smooth or finely cracked
Crown domed
Twigs grey with white lenticels

LEAVES

Buds globular to egg-shaped, tiny
Leaves opposite, 8–12cm, oval, tip drawn out to a long point, edge unbroken, thick and leathery, reddish when young, later very glossy dark green above, pale and matt below; stalked
Stipules absent

FLOWERS AND FRUIT

Flowers ♀, many in branched, conical clusters 12–20cm long, at shoot-tip; each white, fragrant
Petals 4, joined in a long tube with spreading lobes; sepals 4, forming bell-shaped, short-toothed tube
Stamens 2, attached to petal-tube
Stigmas 1, style short
Ovaries 1, 2-chambered
Fruit rather egg-shaped berry, c1cm long, ripening black with conspicuous white bloom
Seeds 1, not released

Strawberry-tree *Arbutus unedo*

Taking a full year to mature, the fruits on this tree ripen as the next year's flowers open. The fruits barely resemble strawberries, being round and covered with soft pimples; they are edible though insipid. Attractive bell-shaped flowers hang in large clusters. *Status:* native to Mediterranean region and Atlantic Europe north to Ireland; planted for ornament. *Similar trees:* Eastern Strawberry-tree, from the Aegean region, has orange-red bark, and flowers in spring. Fruits are nearly smooth. This and Strawberry-tree are the parents of Hybrid Strawberry-tree, which has bright bark, and flowers in spring or autumn.

forward-pointing teeth

branched cluster

bell-shaped

evergreen

5 joined petals

1 Eastern Strawberry-tree (*Arbutus andrachne*)
2 Hybrid Strawberry-tree (*Arbutus × andrachnoides*)

often not toothed

flowers in spring

nearly smooth

small teeth

very short

scaling in strips

globular berry

ripens red

tiny bumps

STRABERRY-TREE

Type	evergreen tree or shrub
Height	tree up to 10m, or shrub
Habitat	dry rocky slopes, bushy places
Flowering	October–November
Fruiting	October of following year

TRUNK AND CROWN

Trunk	very short, soon forking
Bark	dull reddish brown, rough, scaling away in thin strips
Crown	dense, rounded; branches numerous and ascending
Twigs	red above and hairy when young, green beneath

LEAVES

Buds	1–2mm, conical, purplish red
Leaves	alternate, 4–10 × 1.5–5cm, oblong-oval, leathery, with forward-pointing teeth towards tip, dark glossy green above, paler beneath; stalks 5–10mm, pinkish red, hairy
Stipules	absent

FLOWERS AND FRUIT

Flowers	♀, many in drooping, branched clusters 4–5cm long, pinkish white, each urn-shaped, 0.5–1cm
Petals	5, joined for most of length, tips bent back; sepals 5, *c*1.5mm, forming circular lobes
Stamens	10
Stigmas	1
Ovaries	1, 5-chambered
Fruit	fleshy, globular berry, 1.5–2cm across, covered with pimples, yellow, ripening to orange and finally bright red
Seeds	numerous, tiny, pear-shaped, brown, not released

An attractive, rounded tree with very smooth, dark green leaves and pale green twigs. It is usually a small tree but is very variable in size and may form only a shrub. The flowers have petals spotted with purple and bearing a beard of curled, white hairs on the inner face. Used mainly to provide shelter, it is sometimes planted as an ornamental tree in streets and squares. *Status:* native to eastern Australia and New Caledonia; planted in Spain, Portugal and the Balearic Islands. *Similar trees: M. tetrandrum* is a shrub that has toothed leaves; it is planted along the coasts of Portugal.

narrow

white spotted purple

evergreen

5 petals

sharp tip

short

few or no teeth

berry-like

ripens blackish purple

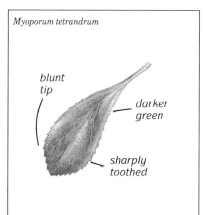

Myoporum tetrandrum

blunt tip

darker green

sharply toothed

BOOBIALLA		**FLOWERS AND FRUIT**	
Type	evergreen tree or shrub	**Flowers**	☿, usually in dense clusters in angles of leaves, each 10–12mm across, white, spotted with purple and with curly white hairs on inner surface, fragrant; stalks up to 12mm
Height	up to 8m		
Habitat	planted for shelter		
Flowering	January–April		
Fruiting	March–June		
	TRUNK AND CROWN	**Petals**	5, joined at the base into a short tube, spreading above; sepals 2–3mm, joined at the base for about half their length
Trunk	short, rather sinuous		
Bark	brownish grey, finely fissured		
Crown	rounded or domed	**Stamens**	4
Twigs	greenish, smooth	**Stigmas**	1, style slender with short bristles
	LEAVES	**Ovaries**	1
Buds	dark, very small	**Fruit**	berry-like but only slightly fleshy, 7–9mm, oval, ripening blackish purple
Leaves	alternate, 4.5–10cm, narrowly oval, pointed, base sharply tapered, bright green and glossy above, dotted with pale, shiny glands; stalk 5–10mm		
		Seeds	1, stony
Stipules	absent		

Foxglove-tree *Paulownia tomentosa*

The branches of this deciduous tree are clothed with very large leaves. They are heart-shaped with unbroken edges but in young trees may have up to 3 short, tapering lobes on each side. The tubular flowers, violet to bluish on the outside and flushed yellow within, form large and very showy heads before the leaves appear. *Status:* native to China; common as an ornamental and, in southern Europe, a street tree. *Similar trees:* Jacaranda, an especially attractive ornamental tree from Argentina, has leaves twice-divided into small leaflets, and clusters of drooping, blue, trumpet-like flowers.

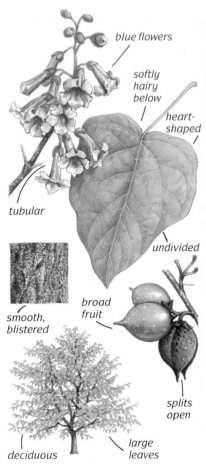

blue flowers

softly hairy below

heart-shaped

tubular

undivided

broad fruit

smooth, blistered

splits open

deciduous

large leaves

Jacaranda (*Jacaranda mimosifolia*)

many leaflets

FOXGLOVE-TREE			10–15cm, pink-yellow, densely hairy
Type	deciduous tree	**Stipules**	absent
Height	up to 15m		
Habitat	roadsides, parks and gardens	**FLOWERS AND FRUIT**	
Flowering	April–May	**Flowers**	♀, in large upright clusters 20–30 cm long, opening before the leaves, each 5–6 cm long, violet-blue, yellow within
Fruiting	July		
TRUNK AND CROWN		**Petals**	bell-shaped tube with 5 spreading lobes; sepals 5, joined below
Trunk	slightly sinuous		
Bark	greyish, smooth, marked with orange blisters	**Stamens**	4, inside petal-tube
		Stigmas	2-lobed, style long
Crown	domed; branches stout, spreading	**Ovaries**	1, 2-chambered
Twigs	pale pink-brown	**Fruit**	3–5cm long, oval, beaked, green, ripening brown and splitting to release seeds, sticky; stalk 1.5cm, stout, hairy
LEAVES			
Buds	minute, purplish, hairy		
Leaves	opposite, to 30cm long, oval to heart-shaped with 3 to 5 lobes, tip long and slender, pale green above, softly hairy below; stalk	**Seeds**	numerous, winged, released when fruit splits

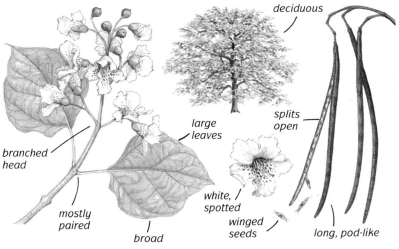

deciduous

large leaves

splits open

branched head

mostly paired

broad

white, spotted

winged seeds

long, pod-like

Conspicuous in winter, when the very long, slender pods hang in numbers from the bare branches, this showy tree is a common sight in parks and gardens. The leaves are light, matt green and heart-shaped. The large flowers have spreading, frilled lobes and are borne in branched, conical heads. *Status:* native to south-eastern North America; widely planted in all but northern parts of Europe. *Similar trees:* Yellow Catalpa, from China, has roughly 5-sided leaves and smaller, yellow flowers. Hybrid Catalpa has 5-sided leaves, up to 60cm, and large heads of white flowers. Both are planted for ornament.

1 Hybrid Catalpa (*Catalpa × erubescens*)
2 Yellow Catalpa (*Catalpa ovata*)

yellowish

angled

red

large

1

2

	INDIAN BEAN-TREE		
Type	deciduous tree		above, hairy beneath; stalk 10–18cm
Height	up to 15m, occasionally taller	**Stipules**	absent
Habitat	streets, parks and gardens		
Flowering	June–August		**FLOWERS AND FRUIT**
Fruiting	July–October but persisting on tree all winter	**Flowers**	⚲, in branched, pyramidal heads, each to 5cm across, bell-shaped, white, spotted with yellow and purple, fragrant
	TRUNK AND CROWN	**Petals**	5, unequal, upper 2 smaller, crinkly-edged, joined for most of their length; sepals 5, joined
Trunk	short, stout		
Bark	dull pink- or grey-brown, fissured or scaling	**Stamens**	2, curved
Crown	domed; branches wide-arching	**Stigmas**	2-lobed, style long, slender
Twigs	stout, grey-brown, smooth, with prominent oval leaf scars	**Ovaries**	1, 2-chambered
		Fruit	pod-like, slender, 15–40cm, hanging, dark brown,
	LEAVES	**Seeds**	many, 2.5cm, white, flat, with a tuft of long hairs at each end and papery wing, released in spring
Buds	minute, orange-brown		
Leaves	opposite or in 3s, up to 25 × 22cm, heart-shaped with slender tip, pale green, smooth		

Elder *Sambucus nigra*

Large, plate-like heads of white flowers decorate this common tree in summer. They are followed by heavy clusters of berries, which droop as the fruit ripens. The flowers have a sweet, slightly cloying scent, in contrast to the leaves, which smell unpleasant when bruised. Both flowers and fruit are used to make wines; the fruit is also used in pies and preserves, and Elder is often planted near houses for this reason. *Status:* native throughout Europe, western Asia, North Africa; often cultivated in southern Europe. *Similar trees:* Red-berried Elder, also native to Europe, is a shrub to only 4m, with egg-shaped clusters of flowers and scarlet fruit.

5 petals

broad head

toothed

paired leaflets

paired

deeply grooved

deciduous

often several

berry-like

broad head

ripening black

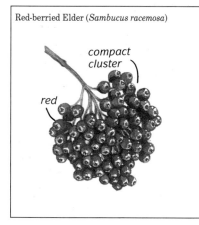

Red-berried Elder (*Sambucus racemosa*)

compact cluster

red

	ELDER		
Type	deciduous tree, often shrubby	**Leaves**	paired on stem; 2–4 pairs of leaflets, leaflet at tip, 3–12cm, oval to elliptical, pointed, sharply toothed, sparsely hairy below, dull green; stalkless
Height	up to 10m		
Habitat	damp woods, hedgerows, on rich, disturbed soils		
Flowering	June–July	**Stipules**	very small or absent
Fruiting	August–September		
			FLOWERS AND FRUIT
	TRUNK AND CROWN	**Flowers**	♂, many in large, circular, branched heads, each 5mm, white, rarely pink
Trunk	often crooked, vigorous straight shoots grow from base		
Bark	deeply grooved, brownish grey, becoming thick and corky	**Petals**	5, equal, spreading; sepals 5, small joined into a tube
Crown	irregularly rounded; branches arching downwards	**Stamens**	5, yellowish white
		Stigmas	3–5, very short
Twigs	thick, fawn, warty, filled with white pith	**Ovaries**	1
		Fruit	berry-like, globular, 6–8mm, ripening black
	LEAVES		
Buds	lacking scales, tight-furled young leaves purplish	**Seeds**	3, leathery, not released

Distinctive flower-heads readily identify this attractive small tree. The small, fertile inner flowers are surrounded by much larger, showy, but sterile blossoms. *Status:* native to most of Europe except for much of the Mediterranean region. *Similar trees:* from similar areas, Wayfaring-tree has oval, lobeless leaves white-felted below, lacks sterile flowers and has fruit eventually ripening black. It favours chalky soils. Laurustinus is a winter-flowering evergreen with glossy, oval leaves, equal-sized, pink-tinged flowers and metallic blue fruit. Native to southern Europe, it is often planted as an ornamental elsewhere.

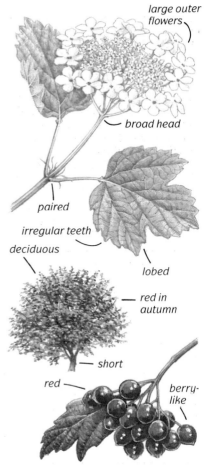

large outer flowers

broad head

paired

irregular teeth

deciduous

lobed

red in autumn

short

red

berry-like

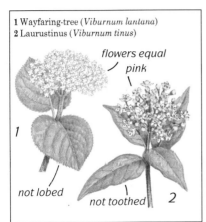

1 Wayfaring-tree (*Viburnum lantana*)
2 Laurustinus (*Viburnum tinus*)

flowers equal

pink

1

not lobed

not toothed 2

GUELDER ROSE

Type	deciduous tree or shrub
Height	1–4m
Habitat	damp woods, hedges, riversides
Flowering	May–June
Fruiting	September–October

TRUNK AND CROWN

Trunk	short, slender
Bark	greyish brown
Crown	spreading; branches few
Twigs	angled, smooth

LEAVES

Buds	5mm, green, edges purple
Leaves	paired on stem, 5–8cm, with 3–5 radiating, pointed, irregularly toothed lobes, sparsely hairy below, becoming smooth, dull red in autumn; stalk 1–2.5cm

Stipules	very narrow, thread-like

FLOWERS AND FRUIT

Flowers	☿, many in broad, circular clusters, stalk of flower-head 1–4cm; funnel- or bell-shaped, inner flowers 6mm, fertile; outer flowers 15–20mm, sterile, both types white
Petals	5, equal; sepals 5, very small
Stamens	5, as long as petals
Stigmas	3, short
Ovaries	1
Fruit	berry-like, *c*8mm, almost globular, ripening red, drooping and persisting on stems after leaves fall
Seeds	1, stony, not released

Cabbage Palm *Cordyline australis*

This palm-like tree often has several trunks, which fork after flowering. The 2m-long flower-head emerges from the centre of the crown. A hardy tree, often planted as an unusual ornamental. *Status:* native to New Zealand; often planted in mild, coastal areas of western and central Europe. *Similar trees:* two related species, both native to south-eastern North America, are commonly planted in parks and gardens. Spanish Bayonet is a much-branched tree up to 10m. Adam's Needle has a very short, thick, unbranched trunk topped with a single, dense rosette of leaves. Both species have large, white flowers, tinged with purple.

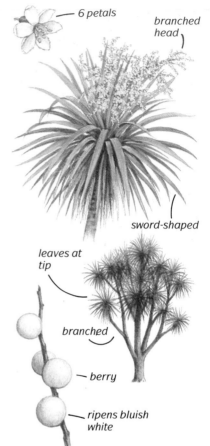

6 petals

branched head

sword-shaped

leaves at tip

branched

berry

ripens bluish white

1 Spanish Bayonet (*Yucca aloifolia*)
2 Adam's Needle (*Yucca gloriosa*)

larger flowers

1

much branched

not branched

2

	CABBAGE PALM		FLOWERS AND FRUIT	
Type	evergreen tree	**Flowers**	♀, many in very large, upright, branched head from centre of crown, each c10mm, creamy-white, fragrant	
Height	up to 13m			
Habitat	dry soils in mild coastal areas			
Flowering	June–July			
Fruiting	September–October	**Perianth**	3 inner and 3 outer segments, all petal-like, joined at base	
	TRUNK AND CROWN	**Stamens**	6	
Trunk	cylindrical, often forked after flowering, suckering from base	**Stigmas**	1, slender	
		Ovaries	1	
Bark	pale grey-brown	**Fruit**	berry, 6mm, globose, ripening bluish white	
Crown	dense tuft of leaves	**Seeds**	several, black, not released	
	LEAVES			
Buds	1, large, hidden by leaves			
Leaves	in a single, domed cluster at tip of trunk, mostly upright but lowermost drooping, 30–90cm, sword-shaped, veins all parallel, dark green; stalkless			

A very slow-growing tree capable of attaining a great age – one specimen, destroyed in a hurricane in 1867, was said to be over 6000 years old. The tree forms a very thick trunk and short, stubby branches with a dense, umbrella-shaped crown of spiky leaves. It can survive in areas of low rainfall; moisture condensing on the leaves runs down the trunk to the roots. The Dragon Tree is very rare in the wild, but often planted for ornament. A bright red resin obtained from this tree, and known as dragon's blood, has been used medicinally since the Middle Ages. *Status:* native to the Canary Islands and Madeira; commonly planted in Mediterranean areas in streets, gardens and parks. *Similar trees:* none.

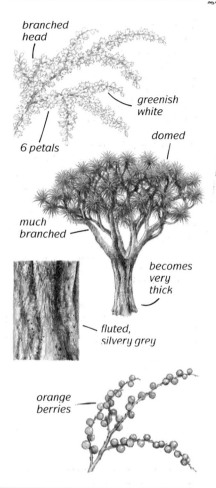

branched head

greenish white

domed

6 petals

much branched

becomes very thick

fluted, silvery grey

orange berries

	DRAGON TREE		FLOWERS AND FRUIT	
Type	evergreen tree	**Flowers**	☿, in spreading, much-branched heads from centre of leaf tufts, greenish white
Height	2–6m		
Habitat	dry, rocky slopes often near the sea; street tree	**Perianth**	3 inner and 3 outer segments, all petal-like and united towards base
Flowering	August–September		
Fruiting	February–April	**Stamens**	6
	TRUNK AND CROWN	**Stigmas**	1, style slender
Trunk	massive, cylindrical, becoming fluted	**Ovaries**	1
		Fruit	berry, c1.5cm, globular, ripening deep orange
Bark	silvery		
Crown	broad, shallow-domed; branches thick, short, regularly forked	**Seeds**	1, not released
	LEAVES		
Buds	1, large, hidden by leaves		
Leaves	in dense tufts at tips of branches, 30–50cm, sword-shaped, bluish green; stalkless		

European Fan-palm *Chamaerops humilis*

Usually forming clumps of several well-developed trunks, this Fan-palm may have only one trunk. Wild trees often produce no trunk at all, the crown of leaves growing directly from the ground. A thick covering of fibres from old leaves protects the stem from fire damage. It is the only common native European palm. *Status:* native to coastal areas of the Mediterranean region; often planted for ornament. *Similar trees:* Australian Fan-palm is native to eastern Australia. It is a tall tree with golden-green leaf-segments, which droop at the tips, and is often planted as a street tree.

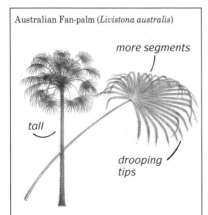

radiating segments

evergreen

branched clusters

with old leaf-bases

Australian Fan-palm (*Livistona australis*)

more segments

tall

drooping tips

not branched

often very short

ripening yellow to brown

berry-like

	EUROPEAN FAN-PALM	green, greyish or bluish; stalk very long and spiny
Type	evergreen tree, often bushy	
Height	rarely more than 2m	**FLOWERS AND FRUIT**
Habitat	sandy soils near the sea	**Flowers** ♂ and ♀ on separate trees, many crowded in large branched spikes initially sheathed by 2 large bracts and hidden among leaves, yellow
Flowering	March–June	
Fruiting	September–October	

TRUNK AND CROWN

Trunk short, thick, sometimes absent, covered with white or grey fibres and bases of old leaves

Bark grey, concealed by fibres

Crown single, large tuft of leaves

LEAVES

Buds 1, large, hidden by leaves

Leaves up to 1m across, stiff, fan-shaped blade deeply divided into spreading segments; segments many, sword-shaped,

Perianth 6, inner 3 spreading

Stamens 6; in ♂ flowers bases joined into fleshy disc; in ♀ flowers sterile, forming cup-shaped base

Stigmas 3, styles short

Ovaries 1, 3-chambered

Fruit berry-like, 4.5cm, globular to oblong, ripening yellow or brown

Seeds 3, grooved on one side, not released

Trachycarpus fortunei **Chinese Windmill-palm**

A frost-resistant, compact tree and the only palm widely grown in northern regions. Very stiff leaves form a spreading crown. As they die, they hang downwards, together with the old leaf bases, hiding the upper part of the trunk. *Status:* native to China; widely grown, mainly as a street and park tree. *Similar trees:* Petticoat Palm has the upper part of the trunk hidden by a 'petticoat' of numerous dead leaves. The fan-shaped leaves have many long threads attached to the segments, giving a frayed appearance.

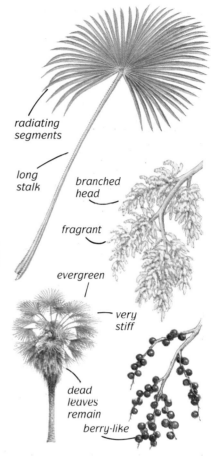

radiating segments

long stalk

branched head

fragrant

evergreen

very stiff

dead leaves remain

berry-like

Petticoat Palm (*Washingtonia filifera*)

long threads on leaves

more dead leaves

	CHINESE WINDMILL-PALM		
Type	evergreen tree		
Height	up to 14m		
Habitat	gardens, streets, sea-fronts		
Flowering	March–June		
Fruiting	September–October		

TRUNK AND CROWN

Trunk slender, straight, at least upper part covered with old, shaggy, brown leaf-bases

Bark brown, with irregular rings

Crown spreading, open tuft of leaves

LEAVES

Buds 1, large, hidden by leaves

Leaves stiff blades up to 1m, divided almost to base into radiating segments; segments many, narrow, pleated, bluish above, dark green below; stalk 50– 100cm, toothed, with long, brown fibres at base

FLOWERS AND FRUIT

Flowers ♂, many in large, much-branched spike 70–80cm long sheathed by large bract when young, bright yellow, fragrant

Perianth 6, inner 3 large, touching near tips

Stamens 6, small and sterile in ♀

Stigmas 1, tiny, style short

Ovaries 3, only 2 developing; all small and sterile in ♂

Fruit berry-like, *c*2cm, 3-lobed, ripening purplish black with bluish white bloom

Seeds 1, grooved

Chilean Wine-palm *Jubaea chilensis*

A very slow-growing tree, producing a dense crown and the thickest trunk of any palm. The leaden-grey bark is distinctive. Native to Chile, where it is cut for its sugary sap, it grows well in mild climates and is a common ornamental palm, especially in southern France. *Status:* native to central Chile; widely grown in Mediterranean regions. *Similar trees:* two other South American palms are also grown as street trees in the Mediterranean region. Queen Palm is a slender tree with a distinctly ringed trunk and leaves 5m long. Royal Palm has a smooth trunk, bulging in the middle, and leaves that are only 3m long.

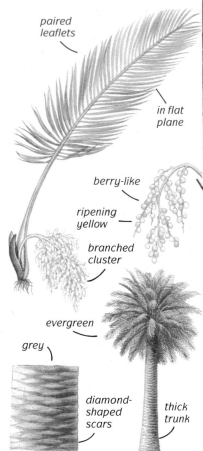

paired leaflets

in flat plane

berry-like

ripening yellow

branched cluster

evergreen

grey

diamond-shaped scars

thick trunk

1 Royal Palm (*Roystonea regia*)
2 Queen Palm (*Arecastrum romanzoffianum*)

bulge

1

2

slender

	CHILEAN WINE-PALM		FLOWERS AND FRUIT
Type	evergreen tree	**Flowers**	♂ and ♀ on the same tree, purplish; many upright, dense, branched clusters 1.5m long in angles of lower leaves and initially sheathed by large woody bracts
Height	up to 30m		
Habitat	parks and streets near coasts		
Flowering	July–September		
Fruiting	November–January		
	TRUNK AND CROWN	**Perianth**	6; in ♂ 3 outer narrow, joined at base, 3 inner longer, thick, pointed; in ♀ 3 outer broad, 3 inner overlapping
Trunk	straight, up to 2m thick		
Bark	grey, smooth, patterned with diamond-shaped leaf-scars		
Crown	dense tuft of upright to spreading leaves arranged in almost vertical rows	**Stamens**	c30; in ♀ sterile, joined in a membranous cup
		Stigmas	3; minute and sterile in ♂
	LEAVES	**Ovaries**	3-chambered in ♀
Buds	1, large, hidden by leaves	**Fruit**	berry-like, in large, drooping clusters, roughly globose to egg-shaped, ripening yellow
Leaves	feathery, up to 4m; numerous paired leaflets up to 70cm, split at tip; stalkless		
		Seeds	1, with 3 vertical lines alternating with 3 black pores

Large and spreading, this is the most common ornamental palm in Europe. The thick trunk is covered with old leaf-bases. These leave diamond-shaped scars when they fall away. The fruits are rather dry and inedible. *Status:* native to the Canary Islands; common as an ornamental in streets and parks around the Mediterranean region. *Similar trees:* Date-palm is a taller, more slender tree with larger, succulent fruits, and is planted for ornament and as a fruit tree in southern Mediterranean areas. *Phoenix theophrasti* is a very small, slender tree with blackish, fibrous fruits, and is restricted to Crete.

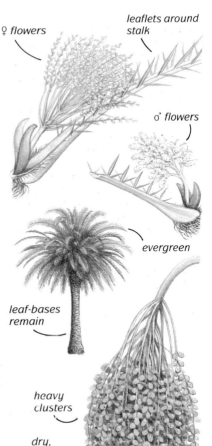

♀ flowers

leaflets around stalk

♂ flowers

evergreen

leaf-bases remain

heavy clusters

dry, inedible

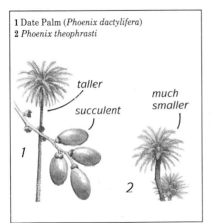

1 Date Palm (*Phoenix dactylifera*)
2 *Phoenix theophrasti*

taller

succulent

much smaller

1

2

	CANARY ISLAND DATE-PALM		
Type	evergreen tree		longitudinally, light green; stalk stout, very spiny
Height	up to 20m		
Habitat	dry places; also streets, coastal roads		**FLOWERS AND FRUIT**
Flowering	March–May	**Flowers**	many in upright, branched clusters up to 2m hanging from angles of lower leaves, ♂ and ♀ on separate trees, creamy yellow
Fruiting	September–October		
	TRUNK AND CROWN		
Trunk	stout, straight, patterned with old leaf scars	**Perianth**	6; in ♂ outer fused into a small cup, 3 inner longer, edges touching; in ♀ 3 outer form 3-lobed cup, 3 inner overlapping
Bark	brown, with old leaf bases		
Crown	large, spreading tuft of up to 200 leaves		
		Stamens	usually 6, very small in ♀
	LEAVES	**Stigmas**	3, style short, curved
Buds	1, large, hidden by leaves	**Ovaries**	3 in ♀, only 1 developing
Leaves	feathery, 5–6m; 150–200 pairs of leaflets radiating from stalk at different angles, narrow, pointed, folded upwards	**Fruit**	nut-like, in heavy, hanging clusters, 3cm, egg-shaped, ripening orange
		Seeds	1, cylindrical, with a deep longitudinal groove

Index

Index

Index

Index

Index

Index

Societies and Useful Addresses

Botanical Society of the British Isles
c/o British Museum (Natural History),
Cromwell Road,
London, SW7 5BD.

Men of the Trees
Crawley Down, Crawley
Sussex, RH10 4HL

English Nature
Headquarters for Great Britain and for England
Northminster House,
Northminster Road,
Peterborough,
Cambridgeshire, PE1 1UA.

Scottish Heritage
12 Hope Terrace,
Edinburgh, EH9 2AS.

Countryside Council for Wales
Plas Penrhos, Penrhos Road,
Bangor, Gwynedd, LL57 2LQ.

Royal Society for Nature Conservation
The Green, Nettleham,
Lincolnshire, LN2 2NR.

Woodland Trust
Autumn Park, Dysart Road,
Grantham
Lincolnshire, NG31 6LL
